D0777895

South Carolina

Henry Leifermann
Photography by Eric Horan

COMPASS AMERICAN GUIDES
An Imprint of Fodor's Travel Publications, Inc.

South Carolina

LIBRARY OF CONGRESS CATALOGING-IN-PUBLICATION DATA
  Leifermann, Henry P.
  South Carolina /by Henry Leifermann: photography by Eric Horan.
  p. cm. —(Compass American Guides)
  Includes bibliographical references and index
  ISBN 1-878867-66-0 (paper): $16.95
  1. South Carolina—Guidebooks. I. Title II. Series: Compass American Guides (Series)
  F 267.3.L45 1994   94-16974
  917.5704'43—dc20   CIP

Editors: Kit Duane, Barry Parr, Jessica Fisher   Designers: Christopher Burt,
Managing Editor: Kit Duane   Candace Compton-Pappas
Photo Editor: Christopher Burt   Map Design: Mark Stroud

Compass American Guides, 6051 Margarido Drive, Oakland, CA 94618
Production House: Tulip, Berkeley, CA., Twin Age Ltd., Hong Kong   Printed in China
10 9 8 7 6 5 4 3 2 1

The Publisher gratefully acknowledges the following institutions and individuals for the use of their photographs and/or illustrations on the following pages:
  Tony Arruza, pp. 53, 183 (top); Robert C. Clark, pp. 190, 205, 231, 245, 258, 262; David Crosby, pp. 234, 235; Lyle Lawson, pp. 80, 88, 144, 145, 241; Greenville County Museum of Art, pp. 22, 27, 30-31, 96, 253; South Carolina Historical Society, pp. 25, 29, 37, 78, 92, 101, 105, 113, 131, 147, 151, 156, 215, 219; South Caroliñiana Library, Univ. of S.C., pp. 14, 15, 17, 23, 52, 83, 84, 114, 117, 121, 125, 194, 199, 201, 238, 251; Penn School Collection, p. 70. The Publisher is especially grateful to the following people for their generosity in contributing their valuable experience and scholarship to this guide: Mr. Pat Hash at the South Carolina Historical Society; Martha Severens at Greenville County Museum of Art; Ms. Eleanor Richardson and Dan Boice at the South Caroliniana Library, Univ. of S.C.; Aïda Rogers at Sandlapper magazine; Sara Bethell for proofreading; Sara Deseran, Debi Dunn, and Michael Chavez for research. The Author wishes to thank Mr. Dan Turpin of the South Carolina State Parks System; Frances Leifermann; Margaret Penix; and a special thank you to Jane.

For the fine people of South Carolina.

C O N T E N T S

Sidebars and Timelines

Literary Extracts

Maps

MAP INDEX

FACTS ABOUT SOUTH CAROLINA

The Palmetto State

Carolina wren

CAPITAL: Columbia
STATE FLOWER: Carolina (yellow) jessamine
STATE BIRD: Carolina wren
STATE TREE: Palmetto
ENTERED UNION: May 23, 1788

Carolina (yellow) jessamine

FIVE LARGEST CITIES:

Charleston/N. Charleston	150,632
Columbia	98,052
Greenville	58,282
Spartanburg	43,467
Rock Hill	41,643

POPULATION: 3,559,618 (1991)

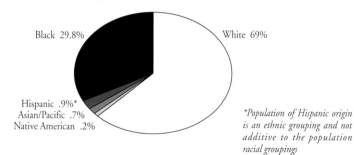

Black 29.8%

White 69%

Hispanic .9%*
Asian/Pacific .7%
Native American .2%

Population of Hispanic origin is an ethnic grouping and not additive to the population racial groupings

*P*almetto

ECONOMY:

Principal industries:
tourism, agriculture, manufacturing

Principal manufactured goods:
textiles, chemicals, fabricated metal products

Principal crops:
tobacco, soybeans, cotton, corn, peaches, hay

Per capita income:
$11,897 (38th highest)

GEOGRAPHY:

Size: 32,007 sq. miles (91,859 sq. km) 40th largest
Highest point: 3,560 feet (1,079 meters) Sassafras Mountain
Lowest point: sea level (Atlantic Ocean)

CLIMATE:

Wettest Place	Driest Place	Lowest Temp.	Highest Temp.
Caesar's Head	Columbia	Caesar's Head	Camden
81.16"	41.95"	-19°	111°
per annum	per annum	1/21/85	6/28/54

FAMOUS SOUTH CAROLINIANS:

Charles Bolden ❖ James Francis Byrnes ❖ John C. Calhoun
Chubby Checker ❖ Andrew Jackson ❖ Jesse Jackson
Francis "Swamp Fox" Marion ❖ Jasper Johns

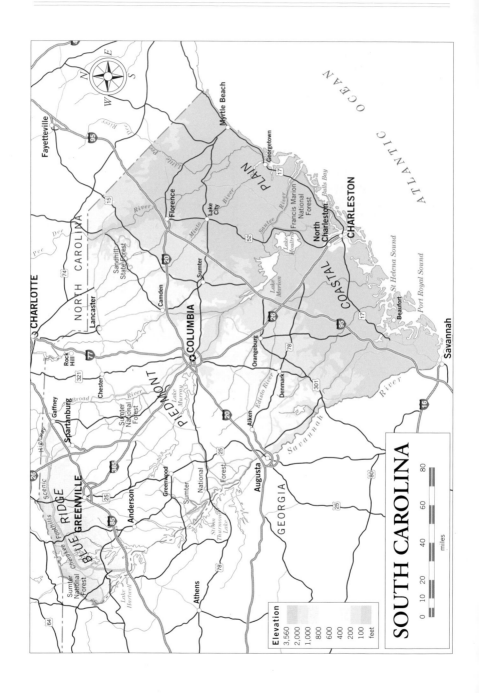

SOUTH CAROLINA

Elevation
3,560
2,000
1,000
800
600
400
200
100
feet

0   10   20   40   60   80
miles

HISTORY AND CULTURE

ONE COULD (AND MANY DO) write gothic romance novels and film gauzy, escapist movies based on true stories from the remarkable history of South Carolina. It's a rich and gamy tale. Perhaps the most curious aspect of the history of this small state, a history which changed the course of this nation, is that to South Carolinians those stories, the true ones and the false ones, aren't history at all. To South Carolinians, most of whom *still* are born, live, and die right here, it all happened yesterday, is happening again today, and will happen again tomorrow. To them, history is almost a religion, whose cathedral is the historic port city of Charleston. To be *of* South Carolina, or even simply to be *in* South Carolina, it is imperative to understand how this unique history (and the culture it fosters) influences even the latest high-tech manufacturing plants springing up along the Interstate 85 industrial corridor.

■ GEOLOGY

South Carolina's destiny was determined not so much by its geography as by its geology. While the surface soil in the northwestern third of the state is formed by the erosion of some of Earth's oldest rocks, nowhere within the 31,000 square miles of the state (40th in land area among the 50 states) are there geologic deposits from the Upper Silurian or Carboniferous ages—meaning there are no significant mineral deposits, no iron ore, and no coal. That in turn meant that until South Carolina harnessed its rivers and waterfalls to power its first textile mills, the state was destined to have the virtues and shortcomings of an agricultural economy. That economy came to rest upon one crop—first rice, later cotton—which in turn depended upon the labor of slaves, and therein lies the tale.

The broad belts both of South Carolina's geologic formations and its historical development run parallel with the shoreline of the Atlantic Ocean, from southwest to northeast. The four natural regions, or physiographic provinces, are the coastal plain, the red hills and sand hills of the fall line (where the land drops and rivers form rapids and waterfalls), the Piedmont, and the Blue Ridge.

The back-and-forth fluctuations of the rising and falling ocean waters over millions of years created the coastal plain that comprises two-thirds of the state. The

An engraving by Jacques Le Moyne depicts the French expedition under René de Laudonnière entering Port Royal Sound in 1564. (South Caroliniana Library, Univ. of S.C.)

edge of the plain runs roughly parallel to the routes of Interstate 20 and US 1, from Augusta, Georgia, through Columbia, Camden, and Cheraw to North Carolina. The three major river systems traversing these plains, the Savannah, the Santee, and the Pee Dee, all flow from headwaters arising above the Piedmont, and are unnavigable beyond the limits of the coastal plain, where they are blocked by the rapids and waterfalls of the fall line.

From the region's earliest days as a British colony, the fall line has split South Carolina into two distinct economic, political, and social provinces: the Up Country and the Low Country. The Up Country was settled by small farmers and tradesmen in the valleys and rolling hills above the fall line. In the Low Country —along the Atlantic coast, on the Sea Islands, and up the river deltas, from Georgetown through Charleston to Beaufort—plantations spread, and planters and seaport financiers and merchants amassed great wealth, taking total political control of the colony, and then the state, and cultivating an assumed social superiority. An old saying alive today among natives of Charleston illustrates the continuing social schism: "I'd rather be dead in Charleston than alive in Columbia or rich in Greenville."

■ COLONIAL ERA

The Spanish were the first European adventurers to reach South Carolina. A caravel from Santo Domingo in what is now the Dominican Republic entered St. Helena Sound between Edisto Island and Beaufort on August 18, 1520. Two more Spanish caravels from Santo Domingo explored Winyah Bay at Georgetown the following summer, both times taking slaves from the welcoming Native American tribes, then returning to Santo Domingo. In July 1526, the Spanish don, Lucas Vásquez de Ayllón of Toledo, led 500 settlers back to Winyah Bay and established San Miguel. This was the first European settlement in the state, predating the English settlement at Jamestown, Virginia, by 81 years.

A severe winter, disease, and the vengeful attacks of the Indians forced the Spanish to abandon San Miguel after a year, withdrawing only 150 survivors. In 1540, Hernando de Soto, the "Kilroy Was Here" of that century, marched up from Spanish

"The Indians till the soil very diligently, using a kind of hoe made from fishbone fitted to wooden handles," wrote engraver Jacques Le Moyne during the Laudonnière expedition of 1564. (South Caroliniana Library, Univ. of S.C.)

Florida and into the interior of South Carolina, crossing the Savannah River near Aiken at Silver Bluff. De Soto took more slaves from the natives, stole their pearls, failed to find any silver or gold yet again, then headed west for El Dorado.

The French came next. A group of Huguenots fleeing religious persecution from their Catholic king, and led by Jean Ribaut, sailed up Port Royal Sound between Beaufort and Hilton Head Island and landed near what today is the Parris Island Recruit Training Depot of the United States Marine Corps. That was in 1562, and four years later, from their base in St. Augustine, Florida, the Spanish came back. As the historians put it, "the brilliant, ruthless conquistador," Pedro Menéndez de Avilés, routed the French from their Charles Fort settlement, then built Fort San Felipe (under excavation today just south of the parade fields at Parris Island). Twenty years later, when Sir Francis Drake led English forces attacking St. Augustine, the Spanish withdrew from Fort San Felipe.

Finally, during the 1670s, the English made a go of it after King Charles II, up to his ermine collar in financial and political debts, granted "Carolina," from Virginia to Cape Canaveral in Spanish Florida, to eight of his backers, the Lords Proprietors.

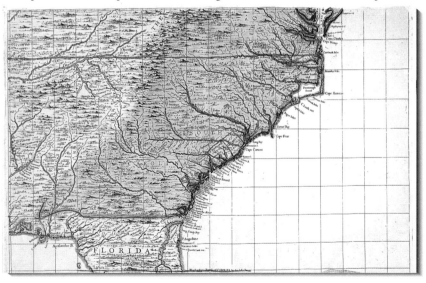

This map illustrates the spheres of influence of the British (red), the Spanish (yellow), and the French (green) in 1733 and shows the disputed southern border between the English Carolina Grant of 1665, demarcated at the 31st parallel, and that granted two years later by King Charles II, extending south to the 29th parallel.

A fanciful rendition of the Yemassee Indian massacre of 100 settlers near Port Royal in April of 1715. (South Caroliniana Library, Univ. of S.C.)

The lords recruited tough, savvy, often unsavory, and often wealthy sugar cane and tobacco planters from the English colony at Barbados in the West Indies. The first of them arrived in 1670 at Albemarle Point on the Ashley River, and during the next decade they and other settlers moved across the river to build Charles Town, today's Charleston. The Barbadian English planters and their successors would create England's wealthiest American colony, a crown jewel of the British Empire.

By 1700, plantations spread through the Low Country and Sea Islands: along the Ashley, Cooper, Combahee, Pee Dee, Santee, Black, and Waccamaw rivers, and along St. Helena and Port Royal sounds near Beaufort. Settlers battled and cheated the native Yemassee tribe, the Westoes, and the Cherokee Nation, and fought off Spanish expeditions from Florida and pirate attacks from Blackbeard. In 1719, they threw out the assembly appointed by the Lords Proprietors to make laws and elected their own. A select few of the settlers could lay claim to finer instincts and valiant deeds; most were part of a small social set, a few hundred men of the rich and powerful plantation aristocracy.

The small Seewee tribe near Charles Town thought those swells were a bit too smooth on fur and skin trading prices. Noticing all ships leaving the port sailed due east (the ships went east 50 to 75 miles to catch the Gulf Stream circling north to England), the Seewees figured the markets must be just over the eastern horizon. In hopes of cutting out the middleman, the tribe secretly built a fleet of large canoes with sails of woven grass and reed, loaded the fleet with all their furs and skins, and with every able-bodied male in the tribe, then set sail. No one ever heard from them again.

By the 1730s, there were settlements along the fall line at New Windsor (North Augusta), Fredericksburg (Camden), Saxe-Gotha (Lexington), and soon after, the Up Country towns of York, Lancaster, and Chester were founded. Their citizens included Welsh Baptists from Pennsylvania and Swiss, Irish, Scottish, and German immigrants arriving via overland routes from northern colonies. These pioneer Up Country settlers, by inclination and background, differed from the planter class, and the families soon learned not to trust the Low Country landed aristocracy. The planters froze the newcomers out of the colony's government, denying them even their own courts and law officers, which led to vigilante law during the 1760s by Up Country posses calling themselves "regulators."

During those same three decades from 1730 to 1760 in the Low Country, a wild orgy of land grabbing and slave importation by the Barbadian planters and the English gentry who followed them set in motion forces which would rip apart the nation a century later. By the 1740s, the 22,000 slaves in the colony, most of them natives of what today are the west African nations of Senegal and Sierra Leone, outnumbered the colony's white population three to one. Almost all of the slaves worked Low Country plantations.

The Africans cleared swamps and built dikes and canals on plantations along the Low Country rivers, and then planted a crop they had cultivated in Africa—rice. It was rice, not cotton, that created an extraordinary concentration of wealth and a cultured gentry on river plantations near Beaufort, Charleston, and especially Georgetown. In 1754, the colony's rice crop was almost 100,000 barrels weighing about 600 pounds each, and millions of English pounds poured into the accounts of a few hundred plantation owners, Charleston merchants, and seaport shippers. No other group anywhere in the American colonies had such wealth.

A decorative map made for the Huguenots in 1555 to aid them in their colonization efforts of 1562–64. If the Seewee Indians had been aware of this map, it might have forestalled their efforts to trade directly with Europe by sailing there in canoes.

▪ HISTORY TIMELINE ▪

1400s   Fifteen thousand to 20,000 indigenous people reside in the Carolinas.

1521   Spaniards from Santo Domingo visit South Carolina.

1665   Seven Lords Proprietors receive a charter from King Charles II to establish the colony of Carolina.

1670   First permanent European (English) settlement is established on the west bank of the Ashley River at Albemarle Point.

1670s   British planters from Barbados arrive in Carolinas with African slaves.

1680   First English settlement moves to location of present-day Charleston.

1680s   Scots and French Huguenots settle in the Carolinas.

1708   Colony's population includes 3,960 free white men, women, and children, and 4,100 African slaves.

1715   Yemassee Indians attack colonial settlements.

1720   European population reaches 19,000.

1729   Colony divides into northern and southern provinces.

1730s   Germans move into Midlands; Welsh along Big Pee Dee River.

1731   Georgia is carved out of the southern part of the original grant.

1739   Slaves burn plantations along Stono River and kill whites before they are stopped by the local militia.

1750s   Scotch-Irish move into Piedmont area through the 1760s.

1770   College of Charleston is founded; chartered in 1785.

1776   South Carolina sends four delegates to the Continental Congress in Philadelphia. They sign the Declaration of Independence.

During the Revolutionary War, 137 battles are fought in South Carolina.

1780   British troops occupy Charles Town.

1786   Capital moves from Charleston to Columbia.

1788   South Carolina ratifies the U.S. Constitution and becomes the eighth state in the Union.

1800s   Close to one-third of the slaves who arrive in the U.S. come through Sullivan's Island.

1801   University of South Carolina is chartered; opens in 1805.

1822   Denmark Vesey, a free black carpenter, leads a slave revolt and is betrayed.

1860   South Carolina secedes from the Union. Ten states follow to form the Confederate States of America in February 1861.

1861   First engagement of the American Civil War begins on April 12, when Confederate troops attack (Union) Fort Sumter in Charleston Harbor.

1863   Union assault and siege of Fort Wagner begins. After 58 days fort falls.

1865   The Union's General Sherman invades South Carolina. Confederate Gen. Robert E. Lee surrenders at Appomattox.

1867   Reconstruction Period: During the next 10 years, under the Union's military and political supervision, the state re-establishes its government.

1877   Old guard (planters and merchants) establish "Bourbon Rule."

1880s Textile mills are built in the Piedmont.

1890   Benjamin R. Tillman, leader of the farmers' movement, is voted into the State House and later the U.S. Senate, ending the domination of the old guard.

1918   During World War I, more than 70,000 men from South Carolina join the armed services.

1923   Revenue from manufactured goods exceeds that of agricultural products for the first time.

1928   Julia Peterkin (born in Calhoun County) is awarded the Pulitzer prize for her novel *Scarlet Sister Mary.*

1941   Military training centers are established at Fort Jackson, Camp Croft, and Shaw Field; 173,642 people from South Carolina serve in World War II.

1953   Savannah River Site begins producing H-bomb tritium.

1960   Civil rights demonstrations begin.

1961   Desegregation is extended to city buses, railway, and bus station facilities.

1975   James Edwards becomes first Republican governor in 100 years.

1990s South Carolina population reaches 3.5 million.

       The Spoleto Festival in Charleston closes its second decade.

       Myrtle Beach becomes known as the country music capital of the East Coast.

■ AMERICAN REVOLUTION

South Carolina's history of slavery, its antebellum Old South image, and its instigation of the Civil War eclipse the often overlooked role the state's people played in the Revolutionary War. More battles and skirmishes (137) were fought here than in any other state.

One month after the Battle of Bunker Hill in Massachusetts, South Carolina rebels seized the first British military installation taken by force in the war—Fort Charlotte, in McCormick County—on July 12, 1775. As historian David Duncan Wallace put it, from 1778 through 1780, South Carolina experienced "three years of war of a constancy and severity unparalleled in the North."

The Low Country planters, always a rebellious bunch of sahibs, and more than a little concerned about British grumblings over slavery, took up the revolutionary cause with fervor. During the summer of 1775 in Charleston, Tory loyalists to the British crown were tarred, feathered, and paraded through the streets. Francis Marion, scion of French Huguenots, left his plantation on the Cooper River above Charleston to become a general known as "the Swamp Fox," raiding the British near

Marion Crossing the Pee Dee *on his way to raid British forces at Georgetown, as depicted by artist William Tylee Ranney. (Greenville County Museum of Art)*

Francis Marion, Swamp Fox

Born of French Huguenot heritage in Winyah, near Georgetown, in 1732, young Francis Marion grew up amongst the swamps and thickets of the wild South Carolina backcountry. At the age of 29, he joined the army to fight in the Up Country Cherokee wars, where he studied the art of guerilla warfare. He proved an attentive student.

Commissioned as an officer during the Revolutionary War, Marion served at Fort Moultrie in the defense of Charleston. When the city fell to the British in 1780, he took to the countryside to organize motley bands of South Carolina partisans against the British.

Before long, Marion's "armies" were attacking British wagon convoys and soldiers, inflicting sharp losses, and disappearing into the swamps, where pursuit was hopeless. From bases hidden on islands and pathways known barely even to locals, Marion sent spies, who kept him well posted on British plans and movements. Even with meager supplies and small numbers of fighting men, he successfully mired British operations, tying up soldiers and supplies in skirmishes for two years, without losing a battle.

When British Gen. Banastre Tarleton was sent to capture him near Kingstree, Marion fought his last battle of the war before disappearing into Ox Swamp. Whipped and retreating, the English general supposedly gnarled that the Devil himself couldn't catch that "old Swamp Fox."
The name stuck.

In later years, Marion served in the state senate. Though he died in 1795, the Swamp Fox lives on in fiction, film, and history, and not least in William Cullen Bryant's poem, the "Song of Marion's Men."

Francis "the Swamp Fox" Marion. (South Caroliniana Library, Univ. of S.C.)

Georgetown and on the Pee Dee River, then hiding his forces in Low Country swamps. When the young Marquis de Lafayette sailed from France to join the cause, it was South Carolina, near Georgetown, where he chose to land. Low Country rebels built a log fort of palmettos (now the state tree and emblem of the state flag) at Fort Moultrie on Sullivan's Island near the mouth of Charleston Harbor, then withstood shelling by nine British warships and blocked the land advance of 2,000 British troops. The victory delayed the British occupation of Charleston for four years, until 1780.

If in 1776 Low Country planters sent four delegates to sign the Declaration of Independence in Philadelphia, Up Country settlers remained Tory Loyalists. These small farmers and merchants were unaffected by and indifferent to rising British taxes on imports and exports and considered their enemy to be the Low Country planter, not the British. In November 1775, it was these Tories who laid siege to a Patriot fort at the Piedmont town of Ninety Six, and there was not a British officer on the field of battle.

Lord Cornwallis established his British headquarters at Camden, winning—or at least not losing—14 battles in the vicinity, and taking Charleston in 1780. Not until later that year, when British forces massacred a surrendering force of the Continental Army near Lancaster, did the Up Country colonials join forces in anger with the Low Country rebels. Cornwallis's strategy had been to join his regulars with the Up Country Tories and march north to defeat George Washington in Virginia. Cornwallis had marched as far as North Carolina when the angry Up Country rebels attacked and defeated British troops in the Battle of Kings Mountain near the Piedmont town of Gaffney. Many historians consider that battle the turning point of the Revolution, since Cornwallis was forced to split his forces, returning half to South Carolina, leaving him too weak to defeat Washington, and leading to his surrender at Yorktown.

■ ANTEBELLUM ERA AND CIVIL WAR

Eli Whitney's invention of the cotton gin in 1793 (on a plantation just across the state line near Savannah) changed everything. As with some other technological breakthroughs in history, the society using the new tool became more its servant than its master.

Cotton meant almost nothing to the rice barons of the Low Country until after the Revolutionary War. During the 1790s, cotton seed from Bermuda, the Bahamas, and the Caribbean was planted extensively on Sea Islands such as Edisto and St. Helena. The long, silky fibers of this Sea Island cotton were prized for laces and fine muslins, but rice remained the fortune-maker until Whitney's new gin went into production. The machine separated seeds from fibers in the cotton boll, or flower, freeing slaves from that job to work clearing, planting, and tilling new cotton fields. Whitney's gin made profitable the bulk production of shorter-fibered, cheaper cotton, as long as free labor worked the fields.

By 1811, South Carolina's cotton crop totaled 40 million pounds, 26 times the total just two decades earlier. By 1834, the state's crop reached 65.5 million pounds. By the outbreak of the Civil War in 1861, cotton accounted for 57 percent of the entire nation's exports. No other crop in the history of the United States has been so influential, and to see a cotton field in bloom today, usually by late August or mid-September, is to see a historic battlefield, of a sort.

Coastal plain, fall line, and Up Country farmers and merchants wanted in on the cotton boom, and Charleston's cotton shippers and bankers, who simply wanted more of everything, built canals to spread cotton and slavery through the interior. The second important shipping canal built in the nation, after New York's

Erie Canal, was the Santee, linking Charleston's Cooper River to the inland Santee River system by 1800. That 22-mile-long canal was followed by another, 67 miles long, linking the Catawba and Wateree river in the Up Country near Lancaster, and other canals soon opened river routes for cotton barges all across the fall line.

In 1833, the South Carolina Canal & Railroad Company, owned by Charleston investors, began running the nation's first railroad—its first engine was named "The Best Friend of Charleston"— on a route from the port city inland

Cotton gins at work.
(South Carolina Historical Society, Charleston)

to Aiken and west to the Savannah River. By the 1840s, the canals were virtually forgotten as railroads extended from Charleston to Columbia, Camden and beyond into the Up Country.

By then, Georgia and Alabama, where land was cheaper, had surpassed South Carolina in cotton production, and many Charleston cotton merchants and bankers, as well as Low Country cotton planters, were on the brink of ruin brought about by overexpansion. Despite that, and perhaps in part because of it, South Carolina led and almost controlled Southern politics in these antebellum decades, and South Carolina's politics were controlled by the Low Country planters and Charleston financiers.

Their spokesman, who became the South's central political figure, was John C. Calhoun, an Up Country congressman from Abbeville, who married a Low Country plantation heiress. As David Duncan Wallace, a South Carolinian himself, wrote, "Calhoun's career is one of the saddest tragedies of American history— a great mind and character caught up in a mistaken cause without being great enough to perceive and conquer the error."

The economy of Calhoun's home state and the fortunes of his planter backers rested upon cotton and slavery. He devoted his life to the preservation of both, resigning as President Andrew Jackson's vice president in 1832 to enter the U.S. Senate and lead the fight against federal export taxes on cotton. South Carolina threatened to secede from the Union over the tariff issue that same year. "From 1832 to 1860, South Carolina was in effect not so much a part of the country as a dissatisfied ally, for the last 13 years of the period only awaiting a favorable opportunity to dissolve the alliance," Wallace wrote.

Calhoun died penniless and in debt in 1850, but South Carolina pressed the battle, trying and failing through the 1850s to draw other Southern states into secession with it. By 1860, the Low Country planters and Charleston financiers felt the only way to force other Southern states to join was with an irrevocable act. On December 20 of that year, a secession convention at St. Andrews Hall in Charleston voted to secede. Commissioners were dispatched to other Southern states seeking a confederacy, and the South Carolina militia occupied without resistance the lightly guarded Union forts of Castle Pinckney at the mouth of the Cooper River, and Fort Moultrie on Sullivan's Island at the entrance to Charleston Harbor and overlooking the island of Fort Sumter. Still, no other slave state joined

Portrait of John C. Calhoun by George P. A. Healy. (Greenville County Museum of Art)

WHY SOUTH CAROLINA WILL SECEDE

Abraham Lincoln's election in 1860 was won without the electoral vote of a single state south of the Mason-Dixon line. Most Southerners felt that with the election of a Republican President would come the end of any Southern influence over the policies of the national government and the end of the Southern way of life. Resisting the warnings of moderates, South Carolina became the first state to secede from the Union on December 20, 1860. It was soon followed by six other Southern states. The South Carolina "Declaration" states the causes which induced its secession.

On the 4th of March next this party will take possession of the government. It has announced that the South shall be excluded from the common territory, that the judicial tribunal shall be made sectional, and that a war must be waged against slavery until it shall cease throughout the United States.

The guarantees of the Constitution will then no longer exist; the equal rights of the states will be lost. The slaveholding states will no longer have the power of self-government or self-protection, and the federal government will have become their enemy.

Sectional interest and animosity will deepen the irritation; and all hope of remedy is rendered vain by the fact that the public opinion at the North has invested a great political error with the sanctions of more erroneous religious belief.

We, therefore, the people of South Carolina, by our delegates in convention assembled, appealing to the Supreme Judge of the world for the rectitude of our intentions, have solemnly declared that the Union heretofore existing between this state and the other states of North America is dissolved; and that the state of South Carolina has resumed her position among the nations of the world, as [a] separate and independent state, with full power to levy war, conclude peace, contract alliances, establish commerce, and to do all other acts and things which independent states may of right do.

the secession. Finally, on April 15, 1861, state troops bombarded the Union's Fort Sumter. After 34 hours of shelling, the fort surrendered. President Lincoln declared war, and by May, the 11 Confederate States of America had followed South Carolina's Low Country planters and Charleston cotton financiers into the Civil War they wanted.

To hear the many chapters of the Sons or Daughters of the Confederacy tell the story today, or to get it from South Carolina's roadside historical markers, one might think the state was a major battleground during the military campaigns of the Civil War. In fact, only one other major battle took place on South Carolina soil, and it was minor in terms of battles fought in Virginia, Tennessee, Mississippi, and Georgia. It was the Battle of Rivers Bridge in February 1865, two months before Lee surrendered at Appomattox.

The bombardment of Charleston by Union forces in 1863 resulted in the destruction of the city's Catholic cathedral. (South Carolina Historical Society, Charleston)

That battle of about 1,000 Confederates against 8,000 Federals lasted two days and occurred on the banks of the Salkehatchie River between Allendale and Ehrhardt. The river crossing was on General Sherman's route from Savannah north through South Carolina; Rivers Bridge was the only major resistance Sherman's army encountered on its destructive march through what he called "the hellhole of secession."

Blockade-running by Confederate and black-market ships was of far greater military significance than Rivers Bridge. However, of greater historical curiosity than the blockade or the battle was the Union occupation of Beaufort, St. Helena, and Hilton Head islands and the surrounding coastal plantations on November 7,

Artist John Ross Key's painting The Bombardment of Fort Sumter. *It depicts the attack by Rebel forces April 15, 1861. (Greenville County Museum of Art)*

1861, seven months after Fort Sumter. The Union held that area throughout the war. In 1863, it began giving small tracts of Sea Island and mainland plantations to freed slaves. On January 16, 1865, from his headquarters in Savannah, General Sherman's Special Field Order Number 15 granted "the islands from Charleston south, the abandoned rice fields along the rivers for 30 miles back from the sea, and the country bordering the St. Johns River, Florida," to freed slaves. Nearly 40,000 freedmen took title to 485,000 acres of land, usually in 40-acre tracts, in that swath of Sea Island and tidewater plantation land during 1865. At the end of 1866, President Andrew Johnson reversed the order and returned most of the tracts to their former white owners.

SOLDIERS AND PATRIOTS

CONFEDERATE MONUMENT

Let the Stranger,
Who May in Future Times
Read This Inscription,
Recognize That These Were Men
Whom Power Could not Corrupt,
Whom Death Could not Terrify,
Whom Defeat Could not Dishonor,
And Let Their Virtues Plead
For Just Judgment
Of the Cause in Which They Perished.
Let the South Carolinians
Of Another Generation
Remember
That the State Taught Them
How to Live and How to Die.

—Inscription on the Monument to the Confederate Dead,
north of the State House in Columbia.

■ POST–CIVIL WAR ERA

Officially, Congress removed federal troops from all the Confederate states in 1877, ending the occupation of the South and Reconstruction. In reality, after the Civil War, as historian David Duncan Wallace wrote, "It appeared as if [South Carolina] had sunk into a lethargy which it did not shake off until after World War II." When the Great Depression of the 1930s occurred, few in South Carolina could tell the difference. What had been one of the nation's wealthiest states in 1860 became and remains today one of its poorest.

The collapse of slavery and of the plantation system (which could not exist without slaves) was only the beginning. By 1890, the state's cotton production was

JAMES PETIGRU

*U*nawed by Opinion,
Unseduced by Flattery:
Undismayed by Disaster,
He confronted Life with antique Courage:
And Death with Christian Hope:
In the Great Civil War
He withstood his People for his Country:
But his People did homage to the Man
Who held his Conscience higher than their Praise:
And his Country
Heaped her Honours upon the Grave of the Patriot,
To whom, living,
His own righteous Self-Respect sufficed
like for Motive and Reward.

—Epithet for James Louis Petigru, South Carolina's leading Unionist at the time of secession and the state's finest lawyer in his day. His epithet was read by President Woodrow Wilson (who spent part of his youth in South Carolina) at the Peace Conference in France following World War I.

twice its 1860 crop. But South Carolina, like most other Southern states, vainly sought income by planting more and more cotton, driving the market price lower and lower.

Cotton mills spread throughout the Up Country during the 1890s, but mill villages and towns often served only to enrich their owners and enslave to ignorance and poverty their all-white labor force. In 1900, the State Board of Health termed mill villages "pest holes for the corruption of the whole state." In the Piedmont mill town of Union, mill hands backed by the owners physically fought public health officials trying to inoculate them against smallpox, which then became epidemic in Union and spread to other Piedmont mill towns.

During the first decade of the twentieth century, there were only 13 public high schools in the state (mill owners and farmers opposed compulsory school attendance, wanting children to work for them instead), and none of the state's colleges or universities got even regional accreditation until the 1920s. As an article in the *New York Times* in 1930 said, "More than any other state of the Confederacy, South Carolina has seemed to the rushing industrial regions of the United States 'a land of monuments and memories.'" When World War II brought the military draft, illiteracy and/or poor health resulted in the rejection of 56 percent of black and 34 percent of white South Carolina draftees, among the nation's worst rates.

Hundreds of thousands of slaves on cotton farms and plantations across South Carolina became free after the Civil War, but they and their descendants for generations had no place of their own to go. Thousands of them moved to industrial jobs in northern cities during World War I and continued the migration during the Depression. By 1940, whites were the majority race in South Carolina for the first time since 1700.

The often empty and fallow Sea Island plantations succumbed to an infestation of the boll weevil in 1922 and Sea Island cotton never recovered from it. What was left of the rice plantations along rivers upstream from Georgetown was devastated by a fierce hurricane in 1911, ending commercial rice production in South Carolina. The famous financier, Bernard Baruch, a native of Camden, bought two rice plantations for use as hunting preserves and winter retreats. During a three-week period in 1925, more than one million acres of Low Country real estate changed hands, and by 1940, wealthy northerners owned more than half the 38 major, former rice plantations in Georgetown County. Throughout the Low Country, they owned 159 old plantations by then, using them as retreats and hunting preserves.

■ POLITICS

In his classic history of the state, David Duncan Wallace lamented, "Politics since the early colonial days have been the South Carolina bull ring. The passions profitlessly expended in it, if turned into other energies, might have produced a great literature or a triumphant industrial civilization . . ."

An abandoned country home illustrates the flight of many rural Carolinians to the new opportunities of city life.

Politics is a blood sport in South Carolina and, like the rest of the state's history, is unique. As Wallace noted, "Issues between Whig and Tory, coast aristocrat and Up Country farmer, slave owner and abolitionist, on which the life of the state seemed to depend, developed an intolerance making difference of opinion seem treason to class or country or race; and the desperation thus bred gave factional politics the spirit of the vendetta."

The most vindictive of South Carolina's many political feuds pitted (and sometimes still pits) the Low Country and Charleston against the Up Country. It is a class conflict born in colonial and antebellum days, and it has nurtured some of the state's most bizarre political figures. One such, "Pitchfork" Ben Tillman of Edgefield County, was elected governor in 1890 and to the U.S. Senate in 1894 by fanning class antagonism. Tillman rallied small Up Country farmers by calling himself a "clodhopper" and calling Charleston "greedy," its Citadel state military college a "dude factory," and Low Country planters the "broken-down, Bourbon aristocracy." Another colorful character, Cole Blease of Newberry, was elected governor in 1910 by the "cracker proletariat"—white mill hands in the Up Country who were recruited to the mill villages from farms and were scorned as "lint heads" and "poor white trash" by many in the Low Country.

The most enduring legacy of South Carolina's political wars, however, is the "legislative state." It makes little difference who is governor, since members of the state legislature hold the real power over everything from state finances to the election of judges and members of various powerful state boards which control colleges, highways, and local sewer, water, and fire districts. In 1993, the legislature relaxed its grip on state government by consolidating some agencies and changing how some boards are filled, but the reform was mostly marginal, in effect putting the government into the twentieth century just in time for the start of the twenty-first.

Even that slight reform would not have occurred were it not for a series of scandals which rocked state government during the late 1980s and early '90s. The worst of these, in 1989, was "Operation Lost Trust," a sting in which a former lobbyist working undercover for the FBI offered bribes for supporting legalized betting on horses. In all, 27 persons were convicted or pleaded guilty to various charges, including 17 members of the legislature who offered to sell their votes for money. Charles W. Dunn, a political science professor at Clemson University, says, "On a scale of democratic institutions, South Carolina is perhaps the least democratic state in the nation." Alex M. Sanders, former legislator and appellate court judge now president of the College of Charleston, believes the scandals were "the darkest days for the spirit of South Carolina since the Civil War. For the whole term of its existence, South Carolina has demonstrated that it can endure guilt, but it can't endure shame, and shame is where we are today."

■ RACE

For almost all of its history, the same single social issue in South Carolina—race—has been the state's main political issue. Up Country and Low Country political leaders fought each other, but both sides fought to exclude African Americans from the political, social, and economic life of the state. For a century following the Civil War and Emancipation Proclamation, they succeeded.

African-American citizens of the state actively voted, usually for Republicans associated with the party of Abraham Lincoln, during the 1870s and '80s. "Pitchfork" Ben Tillman put an end to that in 1895, rewriting the state constitution to

A rare pre–Civil War photo depicts a black church near Charleston with slaves worshipping under the leadership of a white minister. (South Carolina Historical Society, Charleston)

exclude their votes. This bit of tyranny went unchallenged for a half century, until the mid-1940s when Supreme Court decisions began reversing it. The essence of what Tillman had done in 1895 was to make the Democratic Party primary the only election which counted in the state. Fearing federal court decisions might admit black voters to that primary, the state legislature in 1944 passed a record 147 pieces of legislation in six days and made their state Democratic Party a private club. In retrospect, it seems incredible that white legislators thought this sham would work.

The illegal scheme was foiled in 1948 by a completely unexpected person, J. Waites Waring, son of a prominent, old, white Charleston family and the federal district court judge for the Low Country. Waring ruled the white-only Democratic primary unconstitutional. His decision was upheld on appeal, but Waring and his wife were ostracized and shunned by Charleston society and white South Carolina until their deaths.

It was another 20 years, however, after the 1965 Voting Rights Act was passed by Congress, before African Americans in South Carolina began to vote in large numbers. The 1968 state Democratic Party convention desegregated for the first time. In 1970, the first African Americans elected to the legislature since 1900 took office. By 1994, there were 25 black state legislators, and across the state another 322 held local offices from small-town mayors to members of the school board.

In 1896, one year after Tillman disenfranchised African Americans in South Carolina, the Supreme Court made "separate but equal" public accommodations and schools the law of the land in its infamous *Plessy v. Ferguson* decision. "Jim Crow" laws flew through Southern state legislatures, and in South Carolina "white" and "colored" signs were posted over drinking fountains, in theaters, at railroad passenger stations, and lunch counters. Not until the late 1950s was any of this apartheid challenged, and then it was black college students who led the protest, with lunch-counter sit-ins in Orangeburg and Rock Hill.

"Separate but equal" public education had turned out to be not only separate but also wholly unequal. In 1948, about 62 percent of adult African Americans in South Carolina were totally or functionally illiterate. In 1950, African-American parents in the small farm town of Summerton filed suit in federal court, contending that "separate" never would mean "equal." Two years later, in yet another of its grand but empty gestures, the legislature voted to take the state out of the public school business entirely if federal courts ordered South Carolina to desegregate its

Police Chief Fred Brown of Summerton.

schools. Meanwhile, with Thurgood Marshall as their attorney, the Summerton parents' suit became part of a similar suit—*Brown v. Board of Education*—and in 1954, the Supreme Court outlawed segregated public schools.

Desegregating the school system clearly would mean desegregating much of the daily life of ordinary white and black citizens of the state. During the decade following the Brown decision, many other states of the old Confederacy which South Carolina hounded into the Civil War resisted desegregation with Ku Klux Klan-led beatings and murders. South Carolina did not.

Another old saying about South Carolina—that it's "the last good feudal system left"—is slightly exaggerated today. But in January 1963, when its first white school enrolled its first black student, that joke was no joke. In what was its last hurrah and perhaps its only act of nobility, the barons of legislature, a few influential Low Country planters, a few Up Country textile lords, and their counterparts in the state's major banks and utilities, in short, the tiny group of white men who controlled almost everything in the state, put out the word. There would be no violence. Nobody in South Carolina, least of all the cowards of the KKK, dared challenge the police, courts, regulatory agencies, employment opportunities, loan money, and social status those men controlled. Harvey Gantt began classes at Clemson College that January of 1963 on a campus which includes the old home of John C. Calhoun. Later accounts of why there was no violence as schools slowly desegregated across South Carolina during the 1960s and 1970s credit two motives.

The feudal lords who ran things then feared that "another Ole Miss" or "another Birmingham" would chase away the manufacturing industry they were just beginning to charm, induce, and persuade to build new plants in South Carolina. The second motive, in its own way just as compelling to the lords, was a matter of style. This is South Carolina, where "one does not rouse rabble," where we prefer to believe "Pitchfork" Ben Tillman and Cole Blease were exceptions.

The only major aberrations in the state's nonviolent, although prolonged, desegregation of its schools and public accommodations occurred on February 8, 1968 in Orangeburg. Students from South Carolina State University demonstrated outside a segregated bowling alley near the campus. White highway patrolmen, overreacting to a thrown wooden banister which came out of the crowd of students, opened fire with shotguns, killing three and wounding 27 others. One person went to jail after the attack, and it was one of the demonstrators, Cleveland

Sellers. Although Sellers was born and raised 20 miles from the campus in the farm town of Denmark, he was branded an "outside agitator" and spent seven months in state prison on a riot charge which stemmed from another incident two days before the shooting.

Sellers went on to earn a master's degree from Harvard, a doctorate from the University of North Carolina, worked 18 years with the city and housing authority in Greensboro, North Carolina, then returned to his home state. He teaches sociology today, is a member of the state Board of Education, and in the summer of 1993 was granted a pardon of the riot charge. Like the best of South Carolinians, with manners and nobility, Sellers accepted the state's apology.

Cleveland Sellers was one of 6.5 million African Americans who fled South Carolina and other Southern states between 1910 and 1970. It was one of the greatest emigrations in American history. Just as Sellers returned to his home state eventually, so have others much like him. The Census Bureau first noticed the quiet reverse migration during the 1980s, when the proportion of African Americans living in the South increased, from 52 percent in 1980 to 56 percent in 1988. Urban decay and violence in major Northern and Midwestern cities accounts for some of the change, as does the shifting industrial base which once drew Southerners of both races to those cities. The poet and author Maya Angelou wrote of another reason why she returned to the South a decade ago: It's home, and, "When I walk in, they may like me or dislike me, but everybody knows I'm here."

■ SO, WHO ARE THESE PEOPLE?

As is true with most of the world, the first generalization one makes about South Carolinians today is also likely to be the first mistake one makes in speaking of them. They are a unique group, and include all kinds. On the other hand, there are some basic qualities which make South Carolinians who they are.

Most South Carolinians eat grits, which is coarsely ground corn of scant nutritional value, but with a little butter, salt, and pepper, or especially with red-eye gravy, usually made from the pan drippings of fried country ham with a little black coffee stirred in, can be one of those warm filling breakfast foods that are emotionally good for you.

They eat more rice (white) than potatoes, actually do fry green tomatoes, and okra, and boil collards and turnip greens, drink Royal Crown colas (or RC,

pronounced "ar-uh-c") and eat Moon Pies, a chocolate-coated, marshmallow gooey-ness. They also make she-crab soup so delicate and subtle that smokers and drinkers should consider abstinence for a month before enjoying.

According to a report by the federal Center for Disease Control and Prevention, South Carolinians also have the most sedentary lifestyle in the nation, almost 70 percent saying they spend less than three 20-minute sessions of leisure time weekly in any form of physical activity. The infant death rate was the third worst in the nation in 1990, and 16 percent of the population lives below the federal poverty line of about $14,000 for a family of four or $7,000 for a single person. Among the 22 states utilizing the Scholastic Aptitude Test (SAT) for college admission, South Carolina ranks last.

South Carolina has the highest incarceration rate in the nation—484 prison inmates per 100,000 residents in fiscal 1991–92—which means it locks up more of its citizens per capita than anywhere else in the world. New prisons are a growth industry in the state's poorest, rural regions such as Edgefield and Hampton counties. Its highway troopers, by the way, are the best dressed in the nation, winning the

Some of the faces of South Carolina today include Sis Wilder and Walter Senn, both of the Clarendon County town of Summerton.

1993 award from the National Association of Uniform Manufacturers and Distributors for a uniform of banker's gray trousers and jacket, navy blue tie, silver gray shirt, and graphite gray, wide-brimmed hat.

There's a sign in the parking lot of the public library in Aiken which says, "Lot Prone to Flooding," as opposed to "subject to" or "may." There are baby girls such as Carlie Marie Condrey, from the community of Eureka in Aiken County, who by the age of one had won the beauty pageant titles of Aiken County Infant Miss Angel of Beauty, Aiken County Baby Miss, Queen of Queens Infant Miss Valentines, and the statewide Infant Miss Angel of Beauty Pageant. Kimberly Aiken of Columbia was the first African-American woman to win the Miss South Carolina contest, in 1993, and went on to become Miss America.

Until after World War II, the Fourth of July holiday was observed in South Carolina mostly by African Americans, not whites. Not until 1984 was the national legal holiday Memorial Day observed as a legal state holiday in South Carolina, where it was considered a memorial day for the Grand Army of the Republic, the Union army of the Civil War. All along, however, the state did and still does recognize legal holidays for the birthdays of Gen. Robert E. Lee (January 19) and Confederate president Jefferson Davis (June 3) and for Confederate Memorial Day (May 10).

There is rarely a week which passes without one local chapter or another of the Daughters or the Sons of the Confederacy holding some kind of ceremony to revive their myths of what antebellum South Carolina and the Civil War were all about. Memorial stones are continually laid on the graves of Confederate veterans. One Sunday afternoon in September of 1993, the General Wade Hampton Camp Number 273, Sons of Confederate Veterans, awarded the

A monument to the women of the Confederacy unveiled in South Carolina during the 1930s. (Underwood Photo Archives)

Confederate Medal of Honor to Hampton's descendants—on the steps of the State House, where the Confederate "stars and bars" battle flag still flies atop the cupola just under the "stars and stripes."

Most white South Carolinians probably wish this embarrassing kind of display were at least limited to private property, especially those who remember what General Hampton himself said in the dark days of Reconstruction after the Civil War: "The only way to bring about prosperity in this state is to bring the two races in friendly relations together." As for black citizens of the state, patience regarding the Confederate flag is wearing thin, and the "stars and bars" will likely come down before too long.

Prosperity remains somewhat distant for most South Carolinians of either race, but in pockets of economic development throughout the state, that has been changing. In 1961, the state opened its first technical education center, in Greenville, to train students and re-train workers for any specific industry which would build a new plant in South Carolina. The innovative system, since copied by other states and in other nations, brought scores of new industries to the state. South Carolina's stretch of I-85 between Anderson, Greenville, Spartanburg, and Gaffney in the Up Country is lined with new factories. Many of them are owned by European corporations, so many that the state has the third-highest per capita foreign investment in the nation. A new BMW automobile assembly plant near Spartanburg, the latest coup, has been designed to roll out two-seater sports cars.

Textiles remain the state's biggest industry, but since the late 1960s, tourism has boomed, and it is now the second largest source of income in the state. Four out of five tourism dollars spent in South Carolina are spent along its Low Country Atlantic coast. The Grand Strand resorts around Myrtle Beach, historic Charleston, and Beaufort County, heart of the Sea Island resorts such as Hilton Head, lead the dollar list in that order. As is often the case for popular travel destinations, visitors return to retire, and the growth rate of retirees settling in South Carolina is now higher than that of Florida.

Because it is a small state with a good highway system, the new pockets of development, whether Up Country industries, Low Country resorts, or other centers of jobs in between, are easily reached by most of the state's population. About 75 percent of South Carolina's workers commute to their jobs from nearby small towns, by themselves, in their own cars. On average, it's a 20-minute drive, one way.

In a nation of transients, South Carolina remains an anomaly. In only two of its 46 counties are there more residents who were born in another state than in South Carolina, one being Aiken, where the federal Savannah River Site nuclear weapons fuel reactors have employed tens of thousands of newcomers since the 1950s; the other Beaufort County, where resorts, retirees, and two Marine Corps bases skew the figures. Statewide, 70 percent of South Carolina's residents were born here.

That small fact of sociology accounts for much of the state's soothingly slow pace, and the sometimes frustratingly slow pace of change. It also accounts for an underlying xenophobia. Lisa Steward Potter moved from the northeast to Edisto Beach, where she writes for the local newspaper, *Islander,* and lives with what she terms "geographical racism."

"The ironic part of geographical racism is that the South is known for its laid-back lifestyle and friendly people. This is true in every sense, until the word Yankee or Northerner is brought up," she wrote in an editorial.

Her complaint echoes what Colorado natives sometimes say about visiting Texans, Wyoming residents say about Colorado natives, Mainers say about New Yorkers, and native Floridians about anyone who isn't. The difference in South Carolina, however, is all that history is personal, living, full of the loss in "The War," full of (white) guilt, (black) anger at slavery, full of antebellum Old South myths subscribed to even by descendants of white families which never owned a camellia bush, much less a slave, never fought at Bull Run, never danced in Charleston. It is a somewhat schizophrenic state of mind to the usual newcomer.

Agriculture remains an important factor in the state's economy, but tobacco, peaches, and soybeans, as well as pulpwood pine farms, bring in far more money now than cotton. In 1945, the state had more than a million acres planted in cotton. By 1980, only 97,000 acres grew cotton, and by that same year, only two percent of the state population lived and worked on farms. Small farm market towns across South Carolina either lured a new industrial plant, usually an apparel manufacturer, or became ghost towns.

As might be expected in a place so captured by its past, the memory of farming, if not the economy of agriculture, continues to figure in the collective South Carolina consciousness. Everyone who can, from banker to state bureaucrat to factory foreman, owns a small piece of land in the country, often for no reason other than to go look at it from time to time. More than 16 percent of all occupied housing in the state are mobile homes—the highest percentage in the nation—and 80 percent of those trailers rest not in a trailer park but on a small piece of rural land from which the occupants commute to school, shopping, and work.

It is a state and state of mind of small towns, smaller towns, and towns so small the VCR movie rental rack at the crossroads gas station is the best marriage counselor and cop in town.

It is a state where the residents wave to passing cars of friends or strangers, expecting a wave back, a ritual which has nothing to do with "Southern hospitality," but with manners, a pure South Carolinian example of style becoming substance.

A bucolic scene from Edisto Island.

SEA ISLANDS

NO OTHER STRETCH of the nation's three saltwater coasts, the Atlantic, Pacific, and Gulf of Mexico, has developed in the manner and with the results of South Carolina's Sea Islands. Half the state's 190-mile ocean shoreline is on these islands, which reach south from Charleston to the Savannah River. Some, such as Hilton Head Island, are now world famous resorts.

■ LANDSCAPE

This is a gentle coast, with no cliff-and-boulder seascapes, no outer capes meeting surf whipped by storms. Its appeal is subtler: a place of low islands and saltwater marshes stretching languidly out to a horizon where earth and air blend softly into an indefinite line. Narrow country roads meander through tunnels of massive, old, and gnarled live oaks dripping tendrils of gray Spanish moss. One of the most beautiful of these drives is the route between Hilton Head and Beaufort on 170 off 278; most roads on Edisto Island and many on St. Helena Island are equally beautiful.

The Sea Islands range from small, transitory outcroppings of wave-washed, wind-blown sand to large forested islands. Deep-water sounds such as St. Helena and Port Royal near the small, historic town of Beaufort, and wide estuaries at the mouths of rivers once lined by rice and cotton plantations spawn and support shrimp, shad, sturgeon, and scores more species.

The islands themselves were formed by rising sea levels. During the past 15,000 years, water from melting polar ice caps has caused the ocean to rise more than 400 feet. Although the rate at which the sea level has risen slowed drastically about 5,000 years ago, sea levels continue to rise about one foot per century on average. Since 1920, the sea level at Charleston Harbor has risen 14 inches. Thousands of years ago the seashore dune line was breached by this rising tide, flooding the coast behind the dunes and creating the Sea Islands between ocean and mainland or marsh.

■ HISTORY

Until the eighteenth century, small tribes of Native Americans inhabited the Sea Islands, fishing the sounds and estuaries, leaving behind huge middens and rings of oyster shells visible today. They also left behind their names—Edisto, Kiawah, Stono, Combahee, Ashepoo— adopted by European settlers to identify the rivers and islands of this maritime province. Warlike and more powerful tribes, such as the Yemassee and Westo, raided and weakened the Sea Island tribes, and European colonization drove them finally into assimilation or extinction.

From the 1780s to the Civil War, the Sea Islands became the domain of planters, their African slaves, and vast, prosperous plantations producing first "Carolina gold" rice, then the silky, prized fibers of Sea Island cotton. (See "COASTAL PLANTATIONS" for a detailed account.) The Civil War, a fierce hurricane, infestation by the cotton-loving boll weevil, low cotton prices, and especially the end of slavery all doomed the plantation era of the Sea Islands. For almost a century, the islands were backwaters, home to vegetable farms, shrimp boats, oyster factories, heavily logged pine and pulpwood forests, and

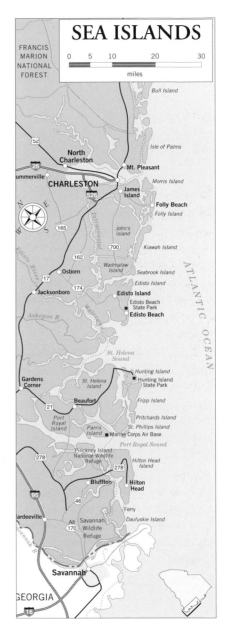

isolated communities of the descendants of former slaves whose unique Gullah culture is the only living survivor of the plantation system. Beginning in the 1960s, all of that changed, and the Sea Islands were transformed again, as thoroughly as the Civil War itself had changed them.

■ DEVELOPMENT

The islands' remoteness, even their inaccessibility—at that time few were connected by bridge to the mainland—became their major attraction. Developers of resort, second home, and retirement communities from Daufuskie Island south of Hilton Head to Kiawah Island near Charleston sought a well-to-do clientele, luring it with exclusive, private, guarded developments of luxurious homes with marinas, private docks, and especially golf courses.

In part this was made possible by federal funds, extended in the 1960s and '70s to cover the cost of flood (and hurricane) insurance on the nation's coasts. Thousands of new homes were built in areas subject to hurricanes and/or close to the high tide line. Increasingly, these developments were protected by jetties and seawalls, which themselves cause beach erosion, in many cases causing sand to disappear.

In January of 1987, a violent northeaster stormed along the Sea Island beaches and up the South Carolina coast, wrecking homes, washing away beaches, and accomplishing what no amount of political lobbying had been able to in previous years. The next year, South Carolina adopted its Beachfront Management Act, widely regarded as a model for the nation. The law mandates a retreat from the beach, requiring any structure of more than 5,000 square feet to be built behind a "setback" line. It also bans construction of new seawalls and other beachfront "armor" that protect buildings but erode beaches.

Hurricane Hugo, in 1989, was the deadliest and most destructive to hit South Carolina in a century, and it, like the northeaster of 1987, chilled many insurers from underwriting Sea Island development. Still, the federal flood plain insurance laws which led to Hilton Head's boom remain in effect, a national subsidy anesthetizing owners of real estate to the dangers which come with the natural beauty of South Carolina's Sea Islands.

■ PROTECTING THE ISLANDS

Throughout the Sea Islands, environmental and conservation groups and government agencies regularly negotiate with developers, or take them to court, to preserve the salt marshes or the endangered sea turtles who dig nests in the dunes and lay eggs in the late spring and early summer. Development is so intense, and the demand for water so great, that saltwater now intrudes into the underground aquifer. The **Savannah National Wildlife Refuge** on the river opposite Savannah's seaport facilities and industrial plants, is dying from pollution and saltwater intrusion into its vast marsh. The state of South Carolina in 1993 gave the town of Hilton Head Island two years to cut by almost half the amount of water it draws from the aquifer. More expensive sources of fresh water must be used, and stringent water conservation measures employed.

■ COMMERCIAL OYSTERING AND SHRIMPING

There was a time when all through the Sea Islands and on the state's northern, Grand Strand coast, thousands of oystermen rowed weathered, wooden bateaux along the tidal creeks and rivers like the May near Bluffton, while thousands of other workers shucked and canned that fresh catch. In 1908, South Carolina's **commercial oyster production** was 2.2 million bushels. By 1992, that had dwindled to 107,000 bushels, three shucking houses, 238 licensed oyster pickers, and not one packing plant.

The last oyster-shucking house on Daufuskie Island closed in 1959, its source of supply polluted by the port, factories, and sewage of Savannah. It was an almost fatal blow to the old-time self-supporting black Gullah community on Daufuskie. Today, smoked oysters are still sold under the "Daufuski" brand and label, but they are imported oysters from Korea. Almost a third of the oyster beds along 60 miles of coastline from the Savannah River to Edisto Island are closed because of water pollution.

Still, the Bluffton Oyster Company pulls its unpolluted crop from the May River, and even on Hilton Head, some restaurants pull their fresh oysters from the island's Broad Creek beds.

Oystermen at work among the marshes of Beaufort County.
(South Caroliniana Library, Univ. of S.C.)

Just as oystering was once a commercial mainstay of the Sea Islands, so was **commercial shrimping.** Nearly every Sea Island village had its own small fleet of trawlers. In the early 1980s, the state still licensed about 1,100 shrimp trawlers. By the early 1990s, the fleet was estimated to number about 400.

Imported "pond shrimp," mostly from shrimp farms in Ecuador, Thailand, and China, drove down prices and dominated the U.S. market during the 1980s; they now account for almost 75 percent of all shrimp eaten in the nation. The only share of the market left to Sea Island trawlers is for large shrimp, which are not cost-effective to grow in ponds. The busiest harvest is in the fall, but to make a living, most commercial shrimpers work the entire harvesting season, usually set by state and federal agencies to last from May or June through December or January.

In the past several years, about a dozen commercial shrimp-pond farms began operations in South Carolina, as well as about three dozen small crawfish farms. Several of these are in the Sea Islands, but so far the largest aquaculture operation

FISHING FOLKLORE

Along the coast, where fishing was once a major source of livelihood, fishermen practiced certain rituals in hopes of improving their odds. Some fishermen believed it was good luck to talk to a young girl before casting off. Dogs were not allowed to accompany the fishermen, nor was food to be eaten while fishing was underway. Some fishermen spit on their bait to ensure that fish would bite. Finally, according to one proverb,

> If the wind comes from the north
> Fish bite like a horse;
> If the wind comes from the south
> They bite like a louse;
> If the wind comes from the east
> They will bite the least;
> If the wind comes from the west
> They will bite the best.

A rope is tied to a shackle on board a commercial shrimp trawler.
(Photo by Tony Arruza)

offering a new source of income for the islands is a growing clam-farm industry. **Atlantic Littleneck Clam Farms** of **James Island** near Charleston has thousands of commercial clam pens in the Kiawah and Folly rivers. The company's Family Farmers program helps islanders with $25,000 to invest into raising clams in their own tidal waters and will buy their crop. The company, which claims to be the largest of its kind in the world, is expanding its operations to tidal waters around St. Helena Island, where it is building a second packing plant.

■ RECREATIONAL CRABBING AND SHRIMPING

For residents of the Sea Islands, recreational crabbing and shrimping is one of the delights of the estuarine cornucopia. It also is so easy, any newcomer can catch their own fresh crab and shrimp.

To get your own crabs, get string, weight, dip net, and chicken parts. Let the parts get hot and stinky. Find a bridge, tidal creek, or channel shallow enough to wade. Low tide is the best time, but almost anytime is good. Tie a one-ounce lead weight and a chicken part to one end of twine and toss it into the water. If wading, keep the twine short enough to let the chicken part almost but not quite drag on the bottom, and walk slowly. When you feel a gentle tug on the string, slowly pull it up. The crab will hold on as long as it's in the water, so dip the net under the crab just before pulling the chicken bait out of the water.

Recreational crabbing requires no license. If the crab you catch is at least five inches across the back, and has no yellow roe (eggs) on the underside, toss it into the ice chest—not into a bucket of water—until cooking. Crabs with roe are female, and keeping them is illegal.

You can catch shrimp anywhere there is salt or brackish water, just as with crabs, but the equipment is a cast net and a bucket of salt water to keep them in until cooking. A cast net is round, with weights on the circumference which sink in the open position when the net is cast. Then a draw line is pulled, trapping whatever is inside the net. It takes an hour or so of practice to learn this simple, durable skill from ancient times. Most variety stores, convenience stores, and bait shops sell cast nets, and many marinas rent small outboards for reaching backwater creeks. Locals find the many causeway bridges just fine for cast-net shrimping.

■ MARITIME ENVIRONMENT

The mountains of the Blue Ridge in northwestern South Carolina often block or weaken winter cold fronts dropping southeasterly on the state, and the warm waters of the Gulf Stream (68 degrees F. and above) moderate winters on the Sea Islands even more, flowing north only 55 miles from the South Carolina coast.

Warm weather and natural beauty make for wonderful beachcombing and bird-watching. The surf is placid, the sea and landscape merging together in subtle, muted blues, greens, and yellows, and a dozen variations on the color white. The southern ends of the islands tend to have silky white-sand beaches, the northern ends more pebbles; on the estuarian shores (where rivers enter), if muddy, are the distinctive poignant footprints of wildlife struggling to keep a foothold in an ever-diminishing space.

Wandering the shoreline you should see at least one marine snail, hermit crab, starfish, Atlantic blue crab, or sand dollar. In the dunes grow morning glories, pennywort, wild bamboo, and sea oats. (Sea oats are protected by law and if locals see you trampling them, they may turn you in.) Behind the dunes grows the maritime forest, extending into the marshes behind the islands. Here you'll see the

SOUTHERN MOON

. . . *T*he new gold of moon astonishing and ascendant, the depleted gold of sunset extinguishing itself in the long westward slide, it was the old dance of days in the Carolina marshes, the breathtaking death of days before the eyes of children, until the sun vanished, its final signature a ribbon of bullion strung across the tops of water oaks. The moon then rose quickly, rose like a bird from the water, from the trees, from the islands, and climbed straight up–gold, then yellow, then pale yellow, pale silver, silver-bright, then something miraculous, immaculate, and beyond silver, a color native only to southern nights.

—Pat Conroy, *The Prince of Tides,* 1986

(following pages) Moonrise over tidewater marshes on Hilton Head Island.

wide-spreading live oak, with its dark green leaves; palmettos with their fan-shaped fronds bending in the breeze; and 50-foot-high red cedar trees.

Saltwater marshes (comprising about 25 percent of those remaining on the East Coast) curve around most Sea Islands and estuaries. The spartina, or cord grass, of the marsh captures mainland river silt behind the islands, slowing erosion. The matted growth absorbs in-rushing tides, protecting the mainland. Four times more productive than the most intensely cultivated Iowa corn field, the grass grows 10 tons to the acre. It dies, decays, and re-seeds itself twice a year, pouring its nutrients into the estuarine nursery, feeding plankton, oysters, shrimp, clams, crabs, and small fish which in turn support larger fish, birds, reptiles, and mammals.

In some offshore marshes, you'll see small islands called hammocks. These miniature refuges support live oak, red cedar, bayberry, and palmettos. Cedar waxwings, white ibis, and least flycatchers flutter about the hammocks, and animals capable of crossing over the marsh to them, such as raccoons and deer, often give birth here.

As the Sea Islands are an important stopover on the Atlantic flyway and during the October migration south and the March and April migration north, a tremendous variety of birds can be seen in this region. (Florida's wood stork, threatened by pollution and overdevelopment, is even moving its rookery up into South Carolina, especially into the old rice plantations.)

Those interested in a close experience with the ecology and beauty of the salt marsh and the Sea Islands' maritime environment should be sure to visit the state parks at Hunting Island and Edisto Beach, both blessedly protected from the development found on Hilton Head.

■ HILTON HEAD HISTORY

Hilton Head, named for the English sea captain William Hilton who claimed it for England in 1663, was settled by Sea Island cotton planters around 1800. Among its 15 large plantations was the Stoney-Baynard Plantation at the island's southern tip in what today is Sea Pines, the original golf course development on the island. By the outbreak of the Civil War, Confederate forces had hastily built two earthwork forts to guard the entrance to Port Royal Sound and the rice and cotton plantations of the Low Country. One, Fort Walker, was on the northern tip of Hilton Head at what today is the Hilton Head Plantation development. The other, Fort Beauregard, was on St. Phillips Island on the northern side of the sound, still today an uninhabited sea island.

On November 7, 1861, six months after South Carolina launched the Civil War up the coast by bombarding the Union's Fort Sumter in Charleston Harbor, a massive Union flotilla sailed into the mouth of Port Royal Sound. Eighteen Union warships led by Adm. Samuel Francis du Pont's flagship, the steam frigate *Wabash,* launched salvos from their 11-inch cannons. Fort Beauregard and the palmetto forest behind it were leveled in minutes. Fort Walker held out for four hours, then the Rebels retreated. From 55 support craft in the Union fleet, a force of 13,000 troops then made an amphibious landing on Hilton Head. A landing of that size was not attempted again until World War II.

FIRST SOUTH CAROLINA VOLUNTEERS, 1863

*T*he services began at half past eleven o'clock, with prayer by our chaplain . . . Then the President's Proclamation was read by Dr. W. H. Brisbane, a thing infinitely appropriate, a South Carolinian addressing South Carolinians; for he was reared among these very islands, and here long since emancipated his own slaves. Then followed an incident so simple, so touching, so utterly unexpected and startling that I can scarcely believe it on recalling, though it gave a key-note to the whole day. The very moment the speaker had ceased, and just as I took and waved the flag, which for the first time meant anything to these poor people, there suddenly arose, close beside the platform, a strong male voice (but rather cracked and elderly), into which two women's voices instantly blended, singing, as if by an impulse that could no more be repressed than the morning note of the song-sparrow.—

"My Country, 't is of thee,
Sweet land of liberty,
Of thee I sing!"

People looked at each other, then at us on the platform…firmly and irrepressibly the quavering voices sang on, verse after verse; others of the colored people joined in. I never saw anything so electric; it made all other words cheap; it seemed the choked voice of a race at last unloosed.

—*Col. Thomas Higginson, recalling religious services held January 1, 1863 for his regiment, the First South Carolina Volunteers, which consisted primarily of runaway*

Hilton Head became the headquarters and supply base for the Union's naval blockade of the Confederacy's Atlantic coast, as crucial an element in the war as any land campaign. Fort Walker, rebuilt and renamed Fort Mitchell, led to the creation of nearby Mitchelville, where some of the thousands of slaves, suddenly freed as the white planters fled the Sea Islands, soon found jobs in the garrison town.

Within weeks, the town of Beaufort was occupied by the Union, and within months, the abandoned Sea Island plantations were being carved into small plots and sold (for a nominal price) to their former slaves. During Reconstruction, many of the deeds held by the former slaves were invalidated when the previous owners returned and wanted the land. On the other hand, many more deeds remained in the hands of the newer black owners. Known as the Port Royal Experiment, this established the Gullah communities still found today on Daufuskie, Hilton Head, St. Helena, Edisto, Wadmalaw, and Johns islands.

Today, Hilton Head is a mecca for golf, tennis, and restaurant and nightclub prowling, with scores of boutiques, several outlet malls, and one of the Eastern Seaboard's best wide beaches. Its upscale, slightly swift, often crowded milieu attracts hundreds of thousands of visitors a year. There used to be an off-season at

Oceanfront homes and development (above) are at the heart of controversy surrounding attempts to maintain Hilton Head's pristine areas. The Pinckney Island National Wildlife Preserve (right) is one such area.

Hilton Head between November and March, but no more; Hilton Head is always busy.

The island's first development, **Sea Pines Plantation,** won national and international acclaim on environmental, architectural, and social grounds. During the late '60s and '70s, more faux "plantation" developments patterned after Sea Pines spread over the island: Port Royal, Shipyard, Wexford—by the 1990s a continuous sprawl of 12 major, gate-guarded, private residential developments.

None of the "plantations" on Hilton Head permit through streets to connect their private preserves, and as a result, all traffic coagulates on a single thoroughfare, **US 278, the William Hilton Parkway,** winding 25 miles over the 42-square-mile island. If you drive onto Hilton Head at 8 A.M. or off the island at 4 P.M., you will crawl in stop-and-go traffic with about 10,000 service and construction commuters who work on the island but cannot afford to live there. The town, meant to be idyllic, is now planning to build an elevated, four-lane expressway over its salt marshes and creeks. Another four-lane expressway is already planned to connect the island to Interstate 95 at Hardeeville, some 15 miles inland.

With the "plantations" also came aesthetically jolting shopping malls, outlet malls, boutique malls, massive time-share condo complexes, budget motels, and fast-food outlets. Much of the island now lives behind or nearby a mall or a shopping center, while the spirit of the Home Shopping Network struggles with the soul of *Architectural Digest.*

Still, Hilton Head has one of South Carolina's best Atlantic beaches, and even the average nature lover can enjoy hours exploring the Hilton Head shores.

■ ENJOYING HILTON HEAD

Hilton Head beaches are beautiful and diverse; some are broad and flat, with long tidepools, perfect for hours of browsing and poking about. There are also wild beaches, muddy clamming beaches, birding beaches, dolphin-watching beaches, and the inevitable, packed sunbathing beaches.

Dolphin Head, the island's northern shore, is located in Hilton Head Plantation. The bluffs overlook Point Royal Sound, home of the bottlenosed dolphin, and have eroded dramatically (the land has lost 250 feet since 1860). Heading northeast, hikers will find the red cliffs of Hilton Head, in the stretch between Dolphin Head and Fish Haul Creek. These are craggy headland bluffs facing Port

Royal Sound, and are high compared to Hilton Head's usual gently sloping shore-line. The bluffs are eroding three feet a year due to storm surf, tidal currents, and a rising sea level.

Hilton Head Beach is the island's eastern "heel," the curving bit of beach and mud bordering Port Royal Sound and the Atlantic. This is where Capt. William Hilton guided his ships inshore, in 1663. The beach is located within Port Royal Plantation, and the best beachwalking is next to the "Steam Cannon," where Fort Walker Drive ends. There are views here of Port Royal Sound's headwaters and neighboring islands.

North Forest Beach (*south* of Hilton Head Beach) is submerged under 10 feet of water at high tide and suffers from extreme erosion (10 feet a year). Residents here have constructed seawalls to protect their homes, and the seawall rocks are home to some odd creatures (such as sea roaches: long-tailed, brown cockroach doubles).

At the toe end of Hilton Head Island is **South Beach.** Here, a southbound longshore current bringing squeaky-fine sand eroded from North Forest Beach, hits Calibogue Sound's rip tide outflow. The two currents neutralize each other and sand is dumped at the mouth of the sound. This is Hilton Head's widest beach, and it is actually getting bigger. (In 1979, Hurricane David left a "big berm" of sand five feet high, 50 feet wide, and 600 yards long at the high-water line.) The sound and beach are a feeding ground for gamefish, pelicans, osprey, and dolphin.

As so much of Hilton Head is privately owned and gated with access limited, those who hope to enjoy it should probably make plans to rent a place to stay for a week or so. (For ideas, look under Hilton Head in the "Accommodations" section of the "PRACTICAL INFORMATION" chapter at the end of this book.) When you inquire at a rental agency, ask for specifics as to the access afforded by particular condos or vacation homes.

■ INLAND FROM HILTON HEAD

The massive resort development of Hilton Head Island has not, yet, been imitated on any other South Carolina Sea Island, but a new, mega-retirement town is under construction 15 miles west of Hilton Head on the mainland coast. This is the Del Webb Corporation's **Sun City East.** The billion-dollar development, restricted to residents 55 or older, boosts South Carolina's reputation as a retirement destination.

The historic village of **Bluffton** (population 750) nestles on a high bluff along the **May River** just down US 278 from Sun City East, on the busy, 40-mile route from Hilton Head to Savannah on SC Highway 46. Settled in 1825 as a summer haven for rice and cotton planters, Bluffton has yet to create any attractions to visit. Its residents merely maintain Bluffton, and in doing so provide an unselfconscious, unchanging glimpse of how life goes on.

Shady streets, plankboard homes, and serenity typify a community that in time may become as endangered or extinct as many Sea Island Gullah communities are. Ask directions to the small public dock by the Episcopal Church of the Cross on the May River. From the dock, there is a spectacular view of the river, saltwater marshes, and old homes along the bluff. The weathered little cypress-plank church was built in 1854 for a congregation of planters founded in 1767. Its cool interior and grounds shaded by cedars and live oaks offer a peaceful respite.

South of Bluffton and Hilton Head Island lies **Daufuskie Island** which now beckons wealthy retirees and vacationers to three new golf course developments. Daufuskie is reached only by a small **passenger ferry** and private boat (check locally at Harbortown marina for ferry schedules). Its developers promise buyers

Bass-fishing guide Erwin Wright cruises an inlet of Lake Marion.

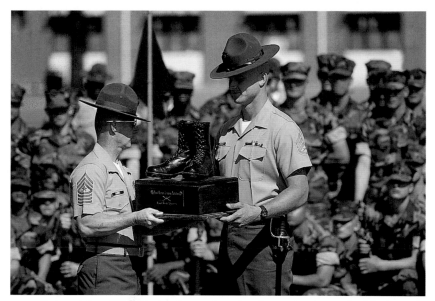

Basic training of U.S. Marine Corps cadets takes place at their Parris Island facility.

the island will never be another Hilton Head. A genuinely unique and quaint place to visit, it was the setting for Pat Conroy's novel *The Water Is Wide*.

■ PARRIS ISLAND

Anyone who knows *Semper Fidelis* (Always Faithful), the motto of the U.S. Marine Corps, knows Parris Island, located north of Hilton Head Island across Port Royal Sound on SC 802. The 40-mile drive from Hilton Head to the Parris Island and Beaufort area, via US 278 and SC 170, passes under canopies of live oaks and across broad expanses of salt marsh. It is one of the most scenic drives in the Sea Islands.

Former members of the Corps were the first significant retiree population here, and learned of the area through service at the Corps' recruit training depot 10 miles south of the town of Beaufort, or at the **Marine Corps Air Base** for jet fighters five miles north of Beaufort.

Unlike some military bases, Parris Island encourages visits by the public. It's possible to drive past recruits in training, tour old navy yards, see Marine Corps and island history in the **Parris Island Museum,** and visit archaeological excavation in progress. The island is open every day, and events such as parades and graduation ceremonies are open to the public. The guards at the base gate will provide directions to the Douglas Visitors Center, where maps and brochures are available. Call 525-3650.

What today is the seventh fairway of the (private) base golf course, right behind the course clubhouse, was from 1566 to 1587 the site of Santa Elena, Spain's northern outpost in America, settled one year after St. Augustine. Santa Elena succumbed to disease, privation, and attacks by Native American tribes the Spanish tried to enslave, but for two decades, about 500 colonists clung to the New World settlement. Its governor, Diego de Velasco, ate from Ming Dynasty porcelain and slept on scarlet satin sheets. Those artifacts, plus remnants of three forts and the

French Huguenots constructed a fort on Parris Island sometime during the 1560s named Charles Fort. It was later abandoned.

oldest European-style pottery kiln yet found in North America, are among the Santa Elena discoveries so far.

■ BEAUFORT

On Port Royal Island, Beaufort (pronounced "Bweu-fort") is South Carolina's second oldest town, after Charleston. Established in 1711, it is the county seat of Beaufort County, and movie fans around the world already know something about it. One of Beaufort's scores of antebellum mansions and homes, **Tidalholm,** was that quintessential, Baby-Boomer-Yuppie dream house in the film *The Big Chill.*

Beaufort (population 12,000) is one of those rare towns where residents and visitors alike find one of the most rewarding aspects of life is strolling the quiet, shady streets of the large national historic district downtown, called **Old Point.** From US 21, take Bay Street into the historic district.

More than 170 public and private buildings of historic interest are in the district, which includes the town's Beaufort River public marina, waterfront park, and rejuvenated business district of art and craft galleries and restaurants. A first stop might be the visitor information center, where visitors can pick up town maps and information about house tours and other annual events.

The Union victory over the Confederacy in the Battle of Port Royal Sound was so swift and complete that Beaufort was abandoned to the Federals without serious resistance. Since it was held by the Union for the rest of the Civil War, the town's historic buildings were not destroyed when Sherman's Union army advanced through South Carolina. For example, the **George Parsons Elliot House Museum,** at 1001 Bay Street (across from the chamber of commerce) served as a Union hospital during the Civil War. It is open February through December for a small fee (call 524-8450 for information).

Self-guided walking tours and horse-drawn carriage tours begin from the chamber of commerce office at the marina. Among the stops are the "movie" mansions, early-eighteenth-century homes, antebellum mansions, the 1724 **St. Helena Episcopal Church,** and the national cemetery established during the Civil War by President Lincoln. While many private houses in Old Point are not usually open to the public, some may be during the annual **Fall House Tour,** in mid-October, and **Spring Tour of Homes and Gardens,** in April or May.

■ ST. HELENA ISLAND AND BEYOND

The winding road is deeply rutted in sand and crosses numerous
tidal rivulets. In summer the wild phlox spreads a varicolored carpet
over uncultivated fields, and the aroma of sweet myrtle is brought in
by the ocean breezes.

—*South Carolina, the* WPA *Guide to the Palmetto State,* 1941

The largest of Beaufort County's 65 islands, St. Helena is pronounced "S'int Hel-
lena." Native Indians in the area were subdued between 1715 and 1718. Planters
grew wealthy here in the following years, first trying indigo as a crop, then replac-
ing that with the more successful long-fibered Sea Island cotton.

These planters were dismayed in 1815 to hear that Napoleon was to be exiled
to St. Helena Island. They wrote protests to the English government, which informed them that there was more than one St. Helena.

The crop of cotton here was so fine that French mills often bought the crop
before it was planted, making St. Helena Island planters quite wealthy and allowing them to purchase large numbers of slaves. In fact, slaves outnumbered whites
by a large margin, and when their owners fled Union ships in 1861, the slaves remained, living on their former owners' properties.

A view out to sea over the marshes of St. Helena Island.

GULLAH CULTURE

The word Gullah refers to the African-American descendants of plantation slaves who lived in virtual isolation for generations in the Sea Islands of South Carolina and Georgia, speaking a hybrid dialect of English and African words, passing on herbal medicines and religious ceremonies, existing by harvesting oysters, fish, vegetables, and pulpwood.

Today they are threatened in two ways. One is from within, as more opportunities open up for blacks and their children leave; secondly, the land that is integral to their culture and way of life is increasingly priced beyond their means.

Following are a few Gullah proverbs and phrases:

Ef yo' play wid puppy, ee lick yo' face.	Familiarity breeds contempt.
Cut finguh f'aid ax.	Once burnt, twice shy.
Ef yo' ent hab hoss to ride, ride cow.	Half a loaf is better than no bread.
Po' buckra an' dog walk one pat'.	The poor man and dog walk the same path.
Mos' kill bud don't make soup.	Most killed bird don't make soup.
clean gone	having left earlier
crack'e'teet'	speak
curly flower	cauliflower
muffledice	hermaphrodite

As Marine Corps veterans know Parris Island, so do veterans and students of African-American history from the Civil War through the civil rights movement of the 1960s know St. Helena Island's **Penn Center.**

Every January, for about a decade, the late Dr. Martin Luther King Jr. and his Southern Christian Leadership Conference met privately for a week or more in the cottages and dormitories of Penn Center to plan their next civil rights campaigns, from Selma and Birmingham to Chicago and Cicero, from Memphis and Mississippi to the Poor People's March on Washington.

Penn Center's 49 acres and 16 buildings along Land's End Road are a National Historic District themselves, not because of King and the SCLC but because of

Netting and basket weaving were once popular folk arts among the Gullah people of St. Helena Island. (Penn School Collection, St. Helena Island)

■ AFRICAN-AMERICAN HISTORY ■

1670   Five of colony's 148 original settlers are black. Importation of slaves from Africa begins; especially valued are farmers from the rice-producing region of Ghana, as well as Ibo, Shanan, and Angolans.

1730s   Two-thirds of population in bondage; other third fears revolt.

1739   Slaves burn plantations along the Stono River.

1800s   Thirty percent of slaves come to U.S. through Sullivan's Island.

1818   Emanuel African Methodist Episcopal Church opens in Charleston.

1820   Manumission is outlawed in South Carolina.

1822   Denmark Vesey, a free black carpenter, plots slave revolt. Participants executed.

1860   South Carolina secedes from Union; Civil War begins.

1862   Escaped slaves form first black regiment in the U.S. Army, the First South Carolina Volunteers, and begin to fight for the Union.

    Robert Smalls and other black crewmen pilot a Confederate gunship out of Charleston Harbor and deliver it to the Union.

    Penn School is established on Union-occupied St. Helena Island.

1863   All-black Massachusetts 54th leads the assault on Fort Wagner. Sgt. William Carney awarded Congressional Medal of Honor.

1865   Civil War ends. Thirteenth Amendment abolishes slavery.

1868   Fourteenth Amendment makes ex-slaves citizens; in decade following, Robert Smalls and Thomas Miller serve in Congress.

1870   Ku Klux Klan becomes active.

1895   State constitution deprives most blacks of voting rights.

1954   U.S. Supreme Court finds segregation in public schools unconstitutional.

1960s   Civil rights movement begins. Harvey Gantt becomes first black student to attend an all-white college in South Carolina; public facilities desegregated; right to vote insured.

1968   Three black students are killed and 40 injured as students integrate Orangeburg bowling alley.

1970   Three blacks elected to state house of representatives.

1974   First black woman elected to the state house of representatives.

something that occurred a century earlier. In 1862, soon after the Union occupied Beaufort, Quakers from Philadelphia opened the first school for freed slaves in the South at Penn Center. It became the cultural and community center of the freedmen on St. Helena Island. The school closed during the 1950s, but Penn Center remains a living museum preserving the language, culture, and history of the Sea Island's Gullah population. The museum is open from 11 A.M. to 4 P.M., Tuesday through Friday (838-2432).

There are no beaches on St. Helena Island, but several can be found at the eastern end of US 21 on Hunting and Fripp islands.

That route reaches the ocean just across the marshes of Johnson Creek at another unique version of the Sea Islands—**Hunting Island.** During the past two decades, the state converted almost all of this large island into a state park. Within the park are more than 5,000 acres of wide, "boneyard" beaches (named for the bonelike driftwood sculptures left by cypress and pine limbs and trunks), one of the best areas in the southeast for shelling, as well as a maritime forest, sand dunes, and salt marshes with a boardwalk. Hikers may see many small game animals, birds, and giant sea turtles, protected now that hunting is no longer allowed.

Hunting Island is far from crowds, noise, and nighttime lights. It offers rental cabins and hundreds of campsites, and has a nineteenth-century lighthouse with a spectacular view from the top. (For more information, call 838-2011).

Fripp Island, just south of Hunting Island, is entirely private, with one inn—The Fripp Island Inn—for visitors.

Closer to Charleston is another such Sea Island development, **Seabrook,** with its Bohicket Marina Village of upscale shops, restaurants, and townhouses. Next to Seabrook is the widely known (among golf zealots) **Kiawah Island,** whose Ocean Course hosted the 1991 Ryder Cup matches.

■ KIAWAH ISLAND

The colonization of Kiawah began in the 1690s when the English Lords Proprietors bought it from its namesake Indian tribe, mostly in exchange for cloth, hatchets, and beads. The lords granted the 2,700-acre island to Capt. George Raynor, believed to be one of the many pirates who sometimes sailed for the English against the Spanish, and sometimes sailed for themselves against all others. In the 1730s, John Stanyarne, a wealthy merchant and planter, bought Kiawah to raise cattle and grow indigo. For the next 120 years, Kiawah was owned by Stanyarne's descendants, the Vanderhorsts, who also used it to raise cattle and grow crops.

In 1953, the Vanderhorst estate sold Kiawah to a wealthy timberman from Aiken, C. C. Royal, who used the island for logging and as a family vacation retreat. Royal also built the first bridge linking Kiawah to neighboring Johns Island, which already had bridges linking it to the mainland and Charleston. In 1974, in a deal that shocked the Sea Islands, the Royal family sold Kiawah to an investment group led by the oil-rich sheikdom of Kuwait, which for 14 years developed Kiawah as a golf, tennis, convention, vacation, and retirement resort. In 1988, the Kuwaitis sold out to a Charleston development group, which in turn the next year sold Kiawah's three golf courses, resort inn, tennis courts, and convention facilities to Landmark Land Company, a classic example of the greedy, go-go 1980s.

Landmark used its New Orleans subsidiary, Oak Tree Savings and Loan, to finance the purchase and development of resorts around the nation, including Kiawah, and then landed in bankruptcy court. In 1993, the Resolution Trust Corp. put Kiawah's resort amenities, including the famous Ocean Course golf

Martina Navratilova in action at a tournament on Hilton Head.

Greg Norman at the Heritage Golf Classic.

links, up for public auction. At that point, the strange tale became simply bizarre. Seventeen of the 18 holes on the Ocean Course are protected under the federal Coastal Barrier Resources Act, giving environmental groups the right of first refusal to buy the property.

In one of the most puzzling moments in the history of the nation's environmental movement, the Audubon Society of New York bid $27 million for the golf course. Audubon wanted to impose environmental restrictions on the golf course, then turn it over to a private management group to operate. The Internal Revenue Service initially ruled Audubon would not lose its nonprofit status in doing so, but the Resolution Trust Corp. (RTC) demanded the property be used as a wildlife refuge for natural resource conservation and recreation—not golf. Then the federal district court ruled that the Audubon Society may *not* administer the area as a golf course without losing its nonprofit status, and the future of the area is in limbo.

Sea Island communities such as Kiawah affect the fragile ecology not only with their populations, but also with their golf courses. In addition to the enormous quantities of fresh water needed for golf courses, the fertilizers used to maintain the lush greenery American golfers expect and demand (as opposed to the English, Scottish, and many Europeans who play on fairways resembling pastures) pollute the salt marshes that not only enhance the natural beauty of the Sea Islands but also give life to the region.

To partisans of the Sea Islands' uninhabited marshes, still wild beaches, and nature preserves, the electric-cart lifestyle of islands such as Kiawah may seem incomprehensible. To others, it is heaven.

■ EDISTO ISLAND AND EDISTO BEACH

So far, very few persons other than South Carolinians visit or live on these two islands. The two Edistoes retain so much of their pre-boomtime character in part because their residents rejected massive development. The small island town of Edisto Beach still has a small fleet of shrimp trawlers. The much bigger community of Edisto Island, just inland from the beach town across the salt marsh and tidal creeks, still has family descendants living on Colonial-era plantations and attending the same historic Edisto Island churches their ancestors did.

True, there is a new bridge across the Atlantic Intracoastal Waterway from the mainland to Edisto Island, but it is named for McKinley Washington Jr., the state senator from the local district. He is an African American, and his position, as well as the new bridge, is an example of change.

Still, for the most part, Edisto has resisted development. There is not yet a motel or hotel in Edisto Beach or on Edisto Island. There are accommodations for visitors, and the very nature of those seems to imply that passing acquaintance, or the fast buck, are of no interest here.

In Edisto Beach, the accommodations mostly are dozens of modest, one-story, single-family, and fully furnished houses rented by the week through local realtors. They are the kind of houses built before the golf- and federal-flood-insurance-fueled boom on the Sea Islands beaches, built with an acceptance of the probability that nature will come along one day and blow it all away. Meanwhile, let's have some fun.

There also is one golf course development, Fairfield Ocean Ridge, with rental fairway villas in the interior of Edisto Beach Island, and one condominium complex, Bay Creek Villas, with weekend and weekly rental units, at the south end of the island. **Edisto Beach State Park** offers more than a hundred oceanside campsites at the north end of the island, and five fully furnished, heated, air-conditioned cabins overlooking the marsh. On the big island, there is one bed and breakfast inn, Cassina Point Plantation, overlooking the North Edisto River's confluence with the Atlantic Ocean.

Casual seafood restaurants at Edisto Beach serve what the local trawlers and fisherman just caught, and a gourmet restaurant, the **Old Post Office** on Edisto Island, is as renowned as any in Charleston or Hilton Head. Retail fresh seafood markets and roadside fresh vegetable stands provide epicurean delights for preparation in your own rented kitchen.

■ SEA ISLANDS' FUTURE

The momentous social change throughout the Sea Islands in recent years has not changed every community and island within the region. Bluffton is essentially unchanged, Beaufort remains a comfortable small town, Hunting Island preserves Sea Island ecology, and to the delight of many South Carolinians (pronounced locally "Sow-Ka-lineans," as in "Sow-Ka-lina") there is Edisto Beach and Edisto Island.

(following pages) Edisto Island remains one of the least developed of South Carolina's Sea Islands.

Cotton pickers return from the fields on a Mt. Pleasant plantation carrying the day's harvest on their heads, ca. 1875. (South Carolina Historical Society, Charleston)

COASTAL PLANTATIONS

FEW CHAPTERS IN AMERICAN HISTORY arouse the intense interest, and often emotional obsession, stirred by the plantation culture of the Old South. It was a way of life that flourished in South Carolina—a way of life that, long after it passed, became wrapped in myth and enshrined in a fairy tale (or a nightmare depending on your point of view).

The colonial and antebellum rice, indigo, and cotton plantations of South Carolina grew fat on the fruit of a tragedy: the enslavement of one race by another for profit. Without slavery, *Gone With the Wind*'s Rhett and Scarlett still might have quarreled and loved, but they would have done so in a simple frame house with one good suit and one fine dress between them.

Yet despite the prominence of the myth, very few Southerners, other than slaves, ever lived on a plantation. What's more, that *Gone With the Wind* style of duels, dances, manners, and honor was not something the wealthy planters created themselves. They borrowed it, as we shall see, from romance and adventure novels as popular in their time as *Gone With the Wind* is today, another example of life imitating art, especially when people have way too much free time.

As is often the case in human history, tragic, wretched, sometimes comical excesses leave behind an architectural grandeur, a physical beauty, which cannot be denied and might as well be enjoyed. On many of South Carolina's old plantations, this legacy is open to the public, a visible splendor today.

■ SLAVES, RICE, AND INDIGO

In September of 1670, five months after the first English settlers landed at Albemarle Point, a ship from the British colony of Bermuda sailed into Charleston Harbor. On board were the first African slaves to be recorded by name in North America.

The Carolina colony was the only English colony on the continent where African slaves were introduced virtually at the outset. This was a varied group, lumped together simply as "African," but including people from the Congo, Ibos, Coromantees from the Gold Coast, Gambian Muslims, and others. Placed together on plantations, these disparate groups eventually formed an entirely new culture—a mixture of language, custom, and ethnicities paralleling that of the Europeans in its complexity. By 1708, the colony's population included 3,960 free white men, women, and children; 4,100 African slaves; and 1,400 American Indian slaves.

The Africans were enslaved, and the plantations created, to produce a seed imported from Madagascar in 1672 by one of the colony's most respected and learned settlers, Dr. Henry Woodward. His agricultural experiment promised to give the colony its first export product more lucrative than deerskins. The product was rice.

For the next three decades, Dr. Woodward's bonanza crept up the tidal rivers of the Low Country. To do the work, planters sought slaves from rice-growing areas of West Africa who were not only experienced with the crop but themselves resistant to the malaria endemic to both regions. River swamps were cleared and drained. Marshes were enclosed and divided by earthen dikes into square fields watered by a series of trunks and sluices. The seeds were planted in spring and the fields subsequently flooded. Throughout the summer, the rice grass was stimulated and insects controlled by periodic draining, flooding, and hoeing. In early

*A diorama of a rice barge on the Magnolia Plantation not far from Charleston.
(Photo by Lyle Lawson)*

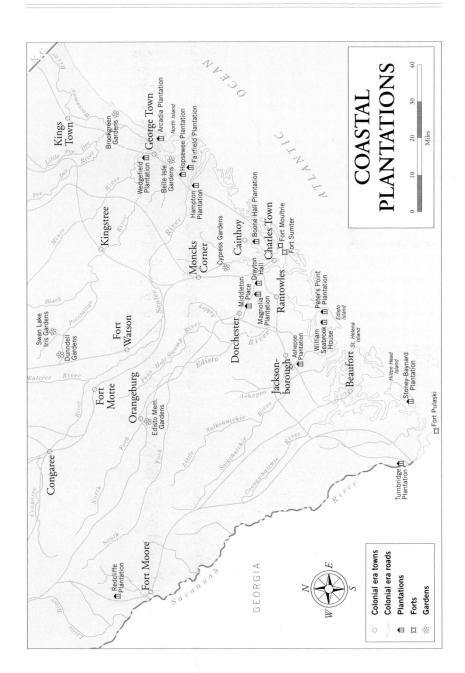

COASTAL PLANTATIONS

Miles

0   10   20   30   40

Colonial era towns
Colonial era roads
Plantations
Forts
Gardens

N.C.

OCEAN

ATLANTIC

Kings Town

Brookgreen Gardens

George Town

Arcadia Plantation

North Island

Wedgefield Plantation

Belle Isle Gardens

Hopsewee Plantation

Fairfield Plantation

Kingstree

Hampton Plantation

Cypress Gardens

Cainhoy

Boone Hall Plantation

Moncks Corner

Drayton Hall

Charles Town

Fort Moultrie

Fort Sumter

Middleton Place

Magnolia Plantation

Rantowles

Peter's Point Plantation

Dorchester

Edisto Island

Swan Lake Iris Gardens

Dunndell Gardens

Fort Watson

William Seabrook House

Ashepoo Plantation

Jacksonborough

St. Helena Island

Beaufort

Hilton Head Island

Stoney-Baynard Plantation

Congaree

Fort Motte

Orangeburg

Edisto Mem. Gardens

Fort Moore

Redcliffe Plantation

GEORGIA

N
W   E
S

Fort Pulaski

Turnbridge Plantation

Little Pee Dee River

Pee Dee River

Waccamaw River

Lynches River

Black River

Pocotaligo

Santee River

Wateree River

Congaree River

South Fork

North Fork

Little River

Edisto River

Four Hole Swamp River

Salkehatchie River

Little Salkehatchie River

Coosawhatchie River

Savannah River

Ashepoo

Broad River

autumn, when the stalks turned golden brown, they were harvested by sickles, tied into bundles, and transported on flatboats to plantation rice mills for threshing.

By the 1730s, rice had made the Carolina planters the richest men in America, and then, indigo made them richer. The indigo plant can be processed to yield a dye that colors cloth indigo blue—between blue and violet in the color spectrum. England's rapidly expanding textile factories were launching the Industrial Revolution and clamoring for more indigo dye. In 1749, Parliament began awarding a bounty, a kind of bonus, to indigo suppliers.

Indigo is a difficult crop to cultivate and even more so to process, but during the 1740s, a Carolina plantation mistress, young Eliza Lucas Pinckney, developed an efficient method of processing the whole plant to yield the valuable dye. She let it ferment in a vat of water for 12 hours. The liquid was then drawn off into a lower vat, stirred vigorously with paddles for several hours, and when it turned the desired color, lime was added to stop the fermentation and fix the color. The heavier dye settled to the bottom, and the water was drawn off, leaving a paste. That was strained to remove excess water, cut into cubes, then set out in the sun to dry.

River systems, along with slaves, were the lifeblood of the rice and indigo plantations. Linear neighborhoods formed along the tidal streams, most notably along the Ashley, Cooper, Wando, and Stono rivers near Charleston, the Pee Dee, Waccamaw, Black, Sampit, and Santee rivers near Georgetown, and the Edisto, Ashepoo, and Combahee rivers near Beaufort. Twice a day, ocean tides forced the rivers to back up, while plantation tidal gates let in freshwater for irrigating the fields. Down the same rivers came the crop, on shallow draft flatboats, en route to the docks and ships of Charleston and Georgetown. As the crop went downstream to port, up the river came supplies, lavish furnishings for new mansions, and slaves.

Imports of slaves rose faster than exports of rice, and the planters usually paid for their slaves with rice, or on credit until the rice was shipped to Charleston. Import duties on slaves, paid to the colonial treasury, financed nearly half the annual budget of the colonial government in Carolina during the 1730s. Not until after the American Revolution did South Carolina stop importing slaves. The international trade ceased in 1787, then resumed in 1803. In the four years following, nearly 40,000 more slaves were imported, until, in 1808, the United States Congress outlawed the importation of slaves. Slavery itself continued for nearly six more decades.

Slaves and the tools they used for working indigo fields are depicted in this 1770 lithograph by Beauvais de Raseau. Indigo was South Carolina's second great cash crop. (South Caroliniana Library, Univ. of S.C.)

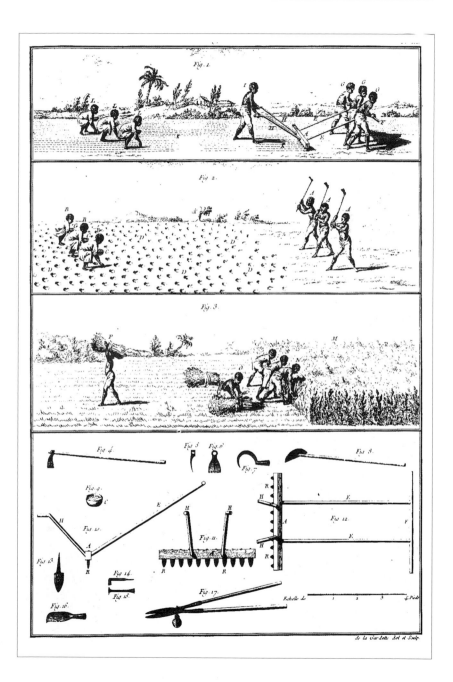

■ ANTEBELLUM MANSIONS

The plantation system made possible the plantation mansions and gardens that today, preserved or restored, offer a glimpse into this world.

It is remarkable that any of the houses are left standing. Accidental fire was the most frequent cause of destruction on the plantations of South Carolina's Low Country and Sea Islands, but war was a close second. In 1715 the Yemassee Indians destroyed nearly all of the plantations south of Charleston, as the owners abandoned their mansions and fled to the safety of the port. During the Revolutionary War, and again during the Civil War, more plantations were burned. Hurricanes, earthquakes, termites, heat and humidity, and then the neglect born of poverty and despair during the Reconstruction Era and the Great Depression all wore on the old buildings.

The mansions which escaped violent destruction or merely withstood the ravages of time did so in part because cypress was the favored building material. It is resistant to rot and termites, and shrinks little over time. Heart pine was used for flooring; poplar and mahogany for trim. In the colonial period, masonry was the preferred exterior, and bricks were usually made at the site. Wood was the popular antebellum siding.

The Planter's House *by an unknown artist. (South Caroliniana Library, Univ. of S.C.)*

The beautiful gardens of the Magnolia Plantation.

The famous Greek Revival style of Tara in *Gone With the Wind,* with its columned porch and portico, was the least popular architectural style. The planters themselves, not trained architects, usually designed the mansions, and they most often chose Georgian, Federal, Gothic Revival, and early Colonial styles.

■ ASHLEY RIVER BARONS

As rivers go, the little Ashley isn't deep, or wide, or long—about 30 miles as the gull flies from its headwaters to its mouth in Charleston Harbor. Every foot of its banks, however, is rank with pivotal figures in the early history of both South Carolina and the nation.

The fabulously wealthy rice and indigo planters of the Ashley River included men who overthrew the English Lords Proprietors, signed the Declaration of Independence, served as members of the Continental Congress (including the president of the first such congress) and as governors and chief justices of South Carolina, and signed the Ordinance of Secession to launch the Civil War.

They also included more than a few wretched excesses.

Consider John Drayton, who built Drayton Hall between 1738 and 1742, and whose descendants kept the mansion in the family through the next seven generations. John built his palace as a place where he could recline in state while slaves fanned him with peacock plumes. He died one of the wealthiest men in colonial America, leaving behind 500 slaves, several rice and indigo plantations, and an epitaph: "Such was his character, he lived in riches, but without public esteem. He died in a tavern, but without public commiseration."

Or take another Drayton, William Henry of Magnolia Plantation, who in 1769 rebelled against new taxes imposed by England. At the same time, downriver in Charleston, some middle-class shopkeepers wanted to join the protest. William Henry considered that a bit too much, on grounds that men of his class should not have to "consult on public affairs with men who (know only) how to cut up a beast, cobble an old shoe or to build a necessary house." William Henry called them the "profanus vulgus."

Drayton Hall, Magnolia Plantation and Gardens, and a third extraordinary plantation and gardens, Middleton Place, come one after another in a 10-mile stretch of **SC Scenic Highway 61,** which parallels the Ashley River from Charleston to the headwaters. Together, the three provide a composite picture of the grandeur the Ashley River barons lavished upon themselves. All three houses are on the National Register of Historic Places, Drayton and Middleton also being National Historic Landmarks. All three are open to the public.

Today, **Drayton Hall** is a museum of the National Trust for Historic Preservation, owned jointly by the trust and the state of South Carolina. It is the only Ashley River plantation mansion to survive the Civil War, spared by Union troops because it was being used as a smallpox hospital for the just-freed slaves of the Drayton plantations. Considered the finest early Georgian house in the nation, its massive Palladian portico is believed to be the first of its kind in America. Inside are rich, hand-crafted details, delicate mahogany carvings, painted cypress paneling, a hand-molded drawing room ceiling executed in wet plaster, and, in keeping with historic preservation, no running water, electric lighting, or central heating. (For information, call 766-0188.)

Magnolia Plantation and Gardens was the first home of the Draytons, established by Thomas, one of the wealthy planter-colonists from Barbados, whose son built Drayton Hall. Its 50 acres of lawn and gardens, with 250 varieties of azalea and 900 of camellia, were begun in the 1840s by Dr. John Drayton and have been open to the public since 1870. Dr. Drayton was an anomaly among the Ashley

River barons. He became an Anglican priest, and despite state laws against it, taught his 300 slaves to read and write.

He also invited artist John J. Audubon to visit and obtain water bird specimens. A recent addition to Magnolia, the **Audubon Swamp Garden,** rises from 60 acres of black water in a cypress and tupelo swamp adjoining the plantation. Board-walks, dikes, bridges, rental canoes, walking and biking trails make both gardens accessible. (Call 571-1266.)

Middleton Place, the nation's oldest landscaped gardens, was for three centuries, like Drayton Hall, owned by one generation after another of the same family—in this case, the Middletons. Of course, the Ashley River barons intermarried so much, it is hard to say which family name applies. Henry Middleton established this duchy in 1740. He built his holdings into 20 plantations, 50,000 acres, and 800 slaves, and was president of the First Continental Congress. His children married a Drayton, a Pinckney, a Rutledge, a Manigault, an Izard, a Smith, and a Parker. His son, Arthur, signed the Declaration of Independence, and Arthur's children married into almost all the same families, as did their children—suggesting that if the Civil War and the end of slavery had not done in the Ashley River barons, in-breeding might have.

Henry the First's plantation mansion was burned to the ground by unimpressed Union troops in the final days of the Civil War. The family then moved into what was built as a gentlemen's guest wing in 1755 but seems today to be as immense and elegant as any mansion should be, with Empire furnishings, Aubusson carpet, and a portrait of Czar Nicholas I. (Henry the Second served 10 years as the nation's minister to Russia.)

The main draw at Middleton Place, however, is the grounds. The formal gardens and butterfly lakes were modeled after seventeenth-century European gardens. They blaze with color almost year-round, camellias in winter, azaleas in spring, kalmia, magnolia, crepe myrtle, and roses in summer. These are not merely well-tended grounds; they are closely barbered. There are scrubbed and brushed cows lowing (the word *moo* seems inappropriate for such a setting) and sheep grazing right there on the huge front lawn, munching grass on a greensward which rivals the putting greens of the best Sea Island golf course and surely costs more to maintain.

These three cathedrals of the Old South—Drayton, Magnolia, and Middle-ton—can produce a kind of sticker-shock over the wealth of the Ashley River barons, but just up the road is a perfect spot to put it all into perspective, perhaps over a picnic.

Old Dorchester State Park is the site of what once was the frontier outpost, and then the colony's third largest town, **Dorchester.** Founded in 1697 by Congregationalists from Dorchester in the Massachusetts colony, it was the limit of navigation on the Ashley and the beginning of a major Indian trading trail.

Dorchester's colonial merchants traded finished goods shipped upriver from Charleston for plantation products such as rice, indigo, and naval stores. Its craftsmen included carpenters, tailors, and blacksmiths. A small fort guarded the town, but it and Dorchester were seized by the British during the Revolution. By the end of that war, Dorchester was abandoned. Today, only the tabby walls of the fort, the ghostly remains of a church bell tower, and the tombstones of an old cemetery remain, sheltered by huge live oaks and stately pines. Archaeological excavations are ongoing, and outdoor kiosks detail the town's history. Picnic tables and outdoor grills on the banks of Boo-Shoo Creek and paths along the Ashley offer respite to minds reeling from the long gone world of a time, and a style, that really happened.

To get to **Old Dorchester State Park,** go north on SC 61 about five miles beyond Middleton Place to SC 165, turn right and drive north about one mile to SC 642, then right again and drive about a mile. Old Dorchester is a day-use park, open 9 A.M. to 6 P.M. free of charge, closed Tuesdays and Wednesdays.

Middleton Place (above) contains the nation's oldest landscaped gardens, owned by the Middleton family for three centuries. (Photo by Lyle Lawson) The manicured plantation grounds are a contrast to the Audubon Swamp Garden (right) which rises from a cypress and tupelo swamp adjoining the Magnolia Plantation.

■ GOOSE CREEK BARBADIANS

While the Ashley River barons' plantations today are the most public and best known in South Carolina, the Goose Creek barbadians were the men who launched the plantation system in the colony. They imported the first African slaves, enslaved Yemassees despite protests from England, and controlled government in the Carolina province throughout its early decades.

Goose Creek branches off the Cooper River on the other side of the Charleston peninsula from the Ashley River in what today is a center of industrial development and suburban sprawl. In the 1670s, during the first decade of the colony's existence, each year brought more immigrants from the West Indies, especially from the British colony of Barbados. Edward Middleton, whose son built Middleton Place on the Ashley, was among these early Barbadians who settled on Goose Creek and the Cooper River.

So was William Rhett, or "Colonel Rhett" as he put it, who led the expedition of planters and Charleston merchants that put an end to pirate raids on plantation shipping through the port (see the "CHARLESTON" chapter). Rhett probably was as confusing to his contemporaries as he was 250 years later to the South Carolina historian David Duncan Wallace, who wrote: "There are few men in South Carolina history of such contradictory character as this greedy, violent, vulgar, lawless, brave, impulsive, generous, loyal churchman, and pirate fighter. Greedily violating law and propriety for bigger profits, insulting the noble and courteous Governor Craven too vulgarly for quotation, trying to kill Governor Daniels in a quarrel over authority . . . he represents the raw material of violent passions, powerful personality, and untamed willfulness."

The Barbadians brought to the colony, in addition to slavery and the plantation system, a culture combining Old World elegance and frontier boisterousness. By the time of the Revolution, their influence was no longer distinct within the planter-merchant oligarchy of the Low Country and Sea Islands. Today, their plantations are home to subdivisions, shopping centers, and industry.

Colonial and antebellum rice plantations spread further up the Cooper River from Goose Creek, and one of those was Dean Hall. The plantation was settled by a family of Scottish baronets, the Nesbetts of Dean, then sold to William Carson in 1821. For his son, the plantation was not a happy place. Writing after the Civil War, he said, "My father, William A. Carson, was a rice planter who wore out his life watching a salty river, and died at the age of 56, when I was 10 years old."

In 1909, Dean Hall plantation was sold to Benjamin Kittredge, who had no interest in planting the land, but instead conceived of a garden of azaleas, camellias, and other flowers rising out of the cypress and tupelo swamps of the plantation. Dean Hall is now called **Cypress Gardens,** donated to the city of Charleston in 1963 and open to the public.

■ GEORGETOWN RICE PLANTATIONS

By 1840, plantations along five rivers in the Georgetown region, 60 miles north of Charleston, grew almost half the rice produced in the nation. During the 1840s and 1850s, more rice was shipped from the port of Georgetown than from any other port in the world, and nearly all of the crop was grown by 91 planters, who until the Civil War lived as richly and lavishly as the Ashley River barons of the colonial period.

Four rivers empty into Winyah Bay at Georgetown: the Sampit, Black, Great Pee Dee, and Waccamaw; a fifth, the Santee, empties into the Atlantic Ocean 15 miles south of the port. The first plantations in the region were near the mouth of the Santee, where Huguenots seeking religious freedom, after being forced from France by the Edict of Nantes, began settling in 1689.

Within a decade, about 70 French Huguenot families were diking the marshes of the lower Santee, producing rice and indigo, and that stretch of the river became known as "French Santee." The legendary guerrilla raider of the Revolutionary War, Gen. Francis "Swamp Fox" Marion, was born into this French Huguenot community in 1732.

A few miles further up the Santee, equally illustrious figures in South Carolina and American history were born into "English Santee" plantation families. Thomas Lynch, a delegate to the Continental Congress, founded **Fairfield Plantation.** His son, Thomas Jr., a signer of the Declaration of Independence, lived across the river at **Hopsewee Plantation** (see "Plantations to Visit" in this chapter).

Perhaps the most influential of all the Santee River settlers, however, was a young English millwright, Jonathan Lucas, who emigrated to the colony shortly before the Revolution. The ship Lucas was aboard ran aground on sand bars at the mouth of the Santee River, and so the Santee and its rice plantations were the first experiences the inventive immigrant had in his new homeland.

The laborious mortar-and-pestle method used to clean the hull from the rice struck Lucas as a waste of labor. Around 1787, he invented a pounding mill, a machine powered by the rising and falling tides of the river, and revolutionized the processing of rice. Lucas became wealthy, with a townhouse in Charleston, a summer retreat in the fall line town of Aiken, and a 4,000-acre rice plantation with 500 slaves on Murphy Island not far from where his ship ran aground.

A large portion of rice grown in South Carolina was produced on tidal deltas. Here a sluice is opened to flood a rice field at high tide. (South Carolina Historical Society, Charleston)

The Grove Plantation house in the Sea Islands is privately owned but open to the public.

■ HAMPTON PLANTATION

Perhaps the most celebrated—certainly the most accessible—of all the Santee River rice plantations is just north of US 17, and about 15 miles south of Georgetown at **Hampton Plantation State Park.** Begun in 1700 by Elias Horry, a Huguenot, and expanded shortly before the Revolution (with a massive, columned Adams portico and a ballroom with a sky-blue ceiling), the mansion and plantation were home to Horrys, Pinckneys, and Rutledges.

Harriott Horry, daughter of the renowned Eliza Lucas Pinckney, who perfected indigo processing, brought Hampton to its architectural glory and greatest prosperity. She owned it and managed it, as a widow, from the 1780s until her death in 1830. President George Washington came there in 1791 and was greeted by Harriott and Eliza, who wore sashes painted with his likeness (the Washington Oak is planted in front of the house). Harriott's daughter had married a Rutledge, and it was a descendant born two generations later who became Hampton's most famous resident.

Archibald Rutledge was born at Hampton in 1883, grew up hunting, fishing, and playing on the plantation, then left as a young man to pursue a teaching career at private schools in Pennsylvania. For 15 years, after the death of his parents in 1921 and 1923, the mansion stood empty and slipped into disrepair. But it was not left entirely alone.

Young Archie Rutledge grew up with a childhood best friend, Prince Alston, who also lived at Hampton. The Alstons were descendants of the slaves who had worked Hampton's rice fields, and after the Civil War and freedom, had simply stayed where they were.

Upon his retirement from teaching in 1937, Archibald Rutledge came home. "When I came to where the gate used to be, I could hardly see the house for the tall weeds and taller bushes. It was as if the blessing of fecundity had been laid on everything natural, and on everything human, the curse of the decay," he later wrote.

Rutledge and his old friends the Alstons set to work restoring the mansion and grounds as a labor of love. In the mansion's front room, Rutledge sat before the fire late in the days, a board laid across the arms of his big chair, and wrote. He became South Carolina's first poet laureate.

A second and more scientific restoration of this National Historic Landmark was completed during the 1980s by the state Department of Parks, Recreation, and Tourism. In rebuilding the interior of the mansion, cross-sections of walls were left open to show visitors colonial and antebellum construction techniques. The Hampton house is open to visitors Thursdays through Mondays from 1 to 4 P.M., and the plantation grounds are open from 9 A.M. to 6 P.M. on the same days. For more information, call 546-9361.

■ WACCAMAW NECK

North of Georgetown, the rice plantations spread along the Black, Waccamaw, and Great Pee Dee rivers. The most accessible to visitors, and easily the most interesting simply because of what became of them, are along US 17 in the short peninsula between the Waccamaw River and the Atlantic Ocean. The southern end of the peninsula is called **Waccamaw Neck,** and next to it, where Winyah Bay enters the ocean, is **North Island.** When the Marquis de Lafayette sailed to America to join the revolution against the English, he landed at North Island, to be welcomed by Maj. Benjamin Huger, one of the Waccamaw Neck rice planters.

PLANTATION LIGHTS AND SHADOWS

*B*owered in its reticent grove of massive old live-oaks, there stands the ancient Southern colonial home, beautiful, wistful, almost like some dreamy fair memory of days long gone . . . . Architecturally, the place stands revealed; but subjectively it is veiled and mysterious. Only by actually living near such a place, by reading its history—if any is recorded—and, best of all, by gossiping with the oldest and most alert of the neighbors can one secure stories of an intimate nature regarding such a remote and magnificent edifice, tales of the more vivid of its inhabitants in far-off times, glimpses of those who now call it home. As I was born and reared in a plantation region, and as I always have taken a certain strange delight in the semi-legendary tales of these ancient picturesque estates and a deep interest in their more modern lore, perhaps it may be possible for me to set ajar certain doors of the enchanted Past, thereby calling to memory life as it was on the old Carolina plantations . . .

The setting for this strange yet delightful culture was romantic and picturesque to an extraordinary degree. There were the immense tracts of lonely woods, timbered with virgin pine and oak; dark, misty, impenetrable swamps, the haunts of many wild and some savage creatures; noble rivers, difficult to navigate and harder to bridge; sunny shrubberies of a tropical luxuriance of growth; solitary reaches of melancholy coastline, beautiful with the forbidding charm of a spiritual autumn. Nowhere else in the world has nature been so kind to her children as in those regions where the plantations were formed out of the Edenlike wilderness of the Low-Country. And that charm is an eternal one; though the civilization that it cradled and nourished has passed away, the charm survives. The home remains lovely after the guests are gone.

—Archibald Rutledge, *The Carolina Low-Country*, 1931

The colonial and antebellum planters made fortunes growing rice on the Neck, and they also spent summer months at the beach here, away from the swamps and marshes where "the fever"—malaria—struck from May through September. North Island was one such planters' resort, until September of 1822, when a hurricane swept over the island and drowned 40 members of plantation families and their servant-slaves. Pawleys Island, 10 miles north of the devastated resort, and well known today for its rope hammocks and beach houses, drew the antebellum plantation families next.

Prospect Hill, Clifton, Arcadia, and Litchfield rice plantations stretched from ocean to river across the peninsula, but the biggest of them all was the barony given Lord Carteret, one of the original Lords Proprietors, in 1718 by King George II. Carteret, never much interested in the colony, soon sold it, and eventually the barony was sold off in plantation parcels of 1,000 to 3,000 acres. Between 1790 and 1900, as many as 10 rice plantations thrived on the barony, which covered all of Waccamaw Neck. Then, in the winter of 1905, a young native of Camden came back to South Carolina on a hunting vacation to a place of his childhood memories, Waccamaw Neck. His name was Bernard Baruch.

As the first half of the twentieth century progressed, Baruch became the nation's premier private financier, an advisor to presidents, a friend of Prime Minister Winston Churchill and President Franklin Roosevelt. But, that winter of 1905, already a wealthy stockbroker in New York, Baruch had more personal plans: buying Waccamaw Neck. Within two years, he had it all, 17,500 acres of pristine beach, marsh, rice fields, and maritime forest, more land than Lord Carteret was given by the king.

Baruch named his vast estate **Hobcaw Barony,** from a Waccamaw Indian word meaning "between the waters." He used a small cabin for hunting trips and winter retreats, then in 1931 built a mansion on the bluffs overlooking Winyah Bay, where he hosted Churchill, FDR, and other world leaders.

Baruch's daughter, Belle, also loved life at Hobcaw, and in 1936 built her own mansion on a plantation-sized parcel of the barony she named Bellefield. She acquired all of Hobcaw after her father's death, and after her own death in 1964, a trust she established, the Belle W. Baruch Foundation, which owns the old barony, entered into agreements with Clemson University and the University of South Carolina.

Clemson scientists study the maritime forest on the barony's high ground, Carolina scientists the salt water marsh and estuarine area. **North Inlet,** about 9,000 acres of beach, tidal wetlands, oyster reefs, old rice fields, and waterways on the barony, is one of just 21 pockets of pristine nature in the nation set aside as benchmarks to measure environmental changes in a program managed by the National Science Foundation and National Oceanic and Atmospheric Administration.

Summer Day Under Spanish Moss *by William de Leftwich Dodge captures the feeling of a past era of gracious living in the rural South. (Greenville County Museum of Art)*

The **North Inlet-Winyah Bay National Estuarine Research Reserve**, the **Bellefield Nature Center, Hobcaw Barony**, and the **Baruch mansions** all are open to the public for a variety of van and walking tours, seminars, lectures, and short-course field studies. The programs are so popular that reservations are recommended several months in advance. (For program information and reservations, phone 546-4623, or write to Bellefield Nature Center, Route 5, Box 1003, Georgetown 29440.)

■ B R O O K G R E E N   G A R D E N S
A few miles north from Hobcaw on US 17 is another old rice plantation—Brookgreen Gardens—which also evolved into unexpected ends. Joshua Ward, the immigrant who brought the Industrial Revolution to the rice plantation with his water-powered and later steam-powered rice-threshing mill, once owned this huge ocean-to-Waccamaw River tract. During the 1920s, novelist Julia Peterkin used it as the setting for *Scarlet Sister Mary,* winner of the 1928 Pulitzer prize for fiction. In the 1930s, the wealthy New York art patrons Archer and Anna Huntington bought the old plantations and began transforming them into formal gardens and an outdoor museum for sculpture.

Today, Brookgreen Gardens is home to more than 350 pieces of nineteenth- and twentieth-century American and foreign sculpture, as well as a restaurant and visitors center. For more information, call 237-4218 or (800) 849-1931.

■ GEORGETOWN
There are dozens of old plantations along the five rice rivers of Georgetown, and for the ones less open than Bellefield, Brookgreen, or Hampton, the best (often the only) way to see them is via boat or van tours from Georgetown.

Every April since 1947, the women of Prince George Winyah Parish Episcopal Church hold a two-day tour that includes private mansions and gardens. Throughout the year, tour boats from marinas in Georgetown and the Waccamaw Neck peninsula cruise the rice rivers for views from the water. For more information about the plantation tours, call 546-4358. (Also see "PRACTICAL INFORMATION" for more on boat tours.)

The old rice port of Georgetown itself, founded in 1729 on the banks of the Sampit River and Winyah Bay, has several dozen residential, religious, and public

The coastal area along portions of Waccamaw Neck contains some of the last pristine stretches of beach to be found in the state.

structures from the eighteenth and antebellum nineteenth centuries in its down-town National Register historic district. There are guided walking and van tours of the district available.

Among the notable buildings are the **Prince George Winyah Episcopal Church,** and the **Rice Museum,** with its maps, dioramas, and artifacts illustrating the heyday of the plantations. A renovated Front Street and Harbor Walk along the docks, with galleries, boutiques, and restaurants along a six-block stretch of Front Street, invite idle strolling, and the shady, quiet streets of the residential portion of the historic district are within a few blocks.

■ SEA ISLAND COTTON

After the American Revolution, the cultivation of rice became almost exclusively the domain of the Georgetown region, because a new crop took over the planta-tions south of Charleston on the Sea Islands. By 1800, Sea Island cotton had transformed the coastal economy, creating more antebellum millionaires.

The first seeds for the prized cotton—whose silky fibers grow up to two inches in length, twice that of cotton grown inland—were imported from Bermuda, the Bahamas, and other British colonies in the Caribbean. It was a perfect cash crop for the islands, needing only relatively small fields to produce enormous profit and only the nutrients of marsh mud for fertilizer.

Two of the Sea Islands, Edisto, an hour's drive south of Charleston, and St. He-lena, just east of Beaufort, became rich and famous in their plantation heyday. Today, both islands provide not only a window upon what happened then, but also examples of how it all turned out, nearly two centuries later, for the descen-dants of the two races which created the Sea Island cotton plantations.

On Edisto, among the many plantation mansions now on the National Register of Historic Places, is the William Seabrook House (private), built in 1810 by the first Sea Island cotton planter to make a fortune on the crop, and the first to use marsh mud as fertilizer. Seabrook's son, William, in 1851 at the World's Fair in London (where McCormick won a medal for his reaper, Colt for his revolving pistol, and Goodyear for his India rubber) won a medal for his Sea Island cotton.

The cotton, the climate, and slavery on Edisto Island produced an isolated society of—by 1808—236 free whites and 2,600 African slaves. This was the norm on the Sea Islands, and it seems impossible today to understand how either race went through the day. On the eve of the Civil War, in 1860, the dependency upon slavery and fervor to secede from the Union was so intense on Edisto Island that its planters began calling it "the royal principality of Edisto." One of them, Col. Joseph E. Jenkins, told a secessionist meeting, "Gentlemen, if South Carolina does not secede from the Union, Edisto Island will." The colonel had no idea that, in its mind, South Carolina already had.

That same year, there were nearly 10,000 slaves on Edisto's plantations. Today's African-American community on the island numbers about 1,300, and the white

Wagons carry cotton from the ginning mill to be baled for transport out of state or overseas. (South Carolina Historical Society, Charleston)

Martha Dewese, a costumed interpreter in the kitchen at Middleton Place Plantation, demonstrates early cooking methods.

population about 300. Most of them are descendants of the masters and slaves who owned and worked the same colonial and antebellum plantation lands they all live on today, family descendants still attending the same historic churches their ancestors founded, some living in the mansions their ancestors built.

The Emancipation Proclamation brought an end to any pretensions of being a "royal principality" at Edisto. Sea Island cotton continued to be cultivated on Edisto and other Sea Islands until a 1921 infestation of the boll weevil insect throughout the islands finally wiped out the last of the crop. The old Sea Island cotton fields now produce large crops of vegetables and melons, fresh produce sold daily at roadside stands usually set in the shade of the twisted, gnarled limbs of a live oak canopy.

The physical remnants of the Sea Island cotton plantations are neither as numerous nor as accessible to visitors today as the plantations of the Georgetown rice rivers or the Ashley River barons. Various church and civic groups organize guided or self-guided tours of the privately owned Sea Islands cotton and Low Country rice plantations on occasional weekends throughout the year, especially during the fall and spring. A check with the local chambers of commerce in Edisto and Beaufort will yield the most recent information on these changing dates and tours.

■ THE MYTH OF THE OLD SOUTH

What seems to be far more lasting and influential than the physical remnants or restorations of any of South Carolina's plantations is an emotional legacy, one which is part gift, part contagion, and part religion. This is the Old South image, and it is revered or vilified—in short, seems to make a difference to people—far more so today than it ever was then.

Curiously, that cavalier tradition of chivalry and romance (made possible only by wealth and leisure founded on slavery) was not something the plantation aristocracy created themselves, but instead was something they borrowed from a book. Or rather, several books, all imported from England, all by Sir Walter Scott, from his 1810 poetry in "Lady of the Lakes" to the 1818 *The Bride of Lammermoor,* and especially from 1819's *Ivanhoe.*

In retrospect, it almost seems as though Scott's novels were passed from plantation to plantation, up the Waccamaw and down the Santee, along the Ashley and Edisto, with an accompanying note saying, more or less: "Let's be like this." Few fads in human history have lasted as long.

Planters put aside the old Indian and Carolinian names they used for their estates and adopted the names of castles in Scotland and England—Arundel, Annandale, and Dirleton plantations on the Pee Dee River to name just three. In time, all of this, from chivalry and romance to dueling dilettantes, became the white South's idea of itself. In time, this notion became fixed. With more time, it became corrupted. The symbols of the Confederacy—the song "Dixie" and the Confederate battle flag—were taken over not by admirers of the Old South myth but by Ku Klux Klan defenders of racism.

South Carolina is the last southern state still flying the Confederate flag atop its capitol in Columbia, though this is being challenged and may soon change. A surprising number of white southerners remain convinced, as South Carolina's Sen. Strom Thurmond told his colleagues in the U.S. Senate in 1993, " . . . they treated the slaves well," and "Southerners didn't bring them here. Northerners brought them here. Slave traders in Boston." As we shall see in the following chapter, the principal slave importers and profiteers of colonial and antebellum South Carolina were a few Charleston merchants whose ancestral names are today among the most socially prominent of the city.

■ SLAVE UPRISINGS

Although no more than perhaps two percent of all white South Carolinians lived on a plantation and owned numerous slaves, all whites in the colony and later the state lived in constant fear of a slave uprising, of violent reprisals for the abuses—in addition to the status as slaves—endured by the Africans. Whippings for the most trifling provocation were routine, often ending in death. Even white children had personal slaves on the wealthy plantations, and those slaves often were tyrannized and abused for sport. The penalty for escape was 40 lashes for the first offense. Branding, mutilation, or public execution could be applied to repeat offenders.

In 1737, Lt. Gov. Broughton warned the colony "our Negroes are very numerous and more dreadful to our safety than any Spanish invaders."

Broughton was right. Two years later, on Sunday morning, September 9, 1739, at the Stono River bridge 20 miles south of Charleston, the bloodiest slave revolt in the history of colonial America erupted. About 50 slaves attacked a store and nearby plantation homes, murdering more than a dozen whites and burning their houses. The band of slaves then set out on foot through the Low Country in hopes of reaching Spanish Florida, where runaways were given freedom by Spanish forces hoping to weaken the Carolina plantation economy.

A force of armed and mounted planters caught up with the slaves near Jacksonboro at the Edisto River on what today is US 17. Fourteen slaves were shot on the spot, while the others fled into the woods. Within weeks, the militia had arrested and killed more than 40 more runaway slaves accused of taking part in the rebellion.

One year later, up the Cooper River at Goose Creek, a similar slave revolt was betrayed by other slaves before it began. Scores of slaves were tried in the plot. Some were hanged, some had ears sliced off, others were branded or whipped.

Fears of violent slave uprisings and retribution preyed upon the white population throughout South Carolina, perhaps more so in this state than in other slave states simply because slaves so greatly outnumbered whites, and whites, as well as blacks, knew the brutality of slavery. Attempts today to refute or revise the realities of slave days seem but a vain exercise in truly awesome denial.

Some former slaves continued to serve their masters after the Civil War, as illustrated in this photo from a Carolinian family album of the 1870s. (South Carolina Historical Society, Charleston)

■ PLANTATIONS TODAY

The end of slavery and the ravages of the Civil War itself devastated South Carolina's rice and Sea Island cotton plantations. A bumper crop was produced in 1920, but by 1921 the boll weevil infestation finally finished off the maritime cotton kingdom. A series of hurricanes around 1900, especially a 1911 storm, finally brought an end to commercial rice production near Georgetown, where gaping holes were ripped in the dikes and the rice fields were soaked in saltwater.

Bernard Baruch's purchase of Hobcaw (the vast land parcel on Waccamaw Neck) set off a real estate boom on the old rice plantations. A new aristocracy—mainly wealthy northerners—bought the old fields and mansions for use as hunting preserves and winter retreats. By the 1940s, more than half the 38 major rice plantations of Georgetown County and another 159 Low Country rice or cotton plantations were in the hands of out-of-staters and used exclusively as hunting retreats. Birds and deer flock to the old fields to feed and nest.

Carolina Gold, the strain of rice which made millionaires along the plantation rice rivers from Waccamaw Neck to the Savannah River, today is grown only at Turnbridge Plantation (private), on the Wright River inland from Daufuskie Island near Hardeeville. A Virginia native and Savannah eye surgeon bought the 300-year-old plantation in 1976 and began planting Carolina Gold in 1988 to lure ducks for hunting. As it turned out, ducks are not that fond of rice, but Dr. Richard B. Schulze continues to harvest two six-acre fields of Carolina Gold as a hobby.

In recent years, using the old plantations for deer and bird hunting has gone beyond the circle of wealthy, individual owners and their friends and become a multi-million-dollar business in the Low Country and Georgetown areas. Commercial hunting clubs own or lease thousands of acres and often convert old plantation homes into lodges for visiting hunters. In many cases, the commercial hunt clubs are owned by major timber and pulpwood corporations who also harvest the pine forests which are home to wildlife.

Through the spring and summer months in the old plantation countryside from Georgetown to the Savannah River and inland for 30 miles or more, the thick, sweet scent of pine sap and freshly cut trees is a reminder of what most of the old plantations are used for today. Forestry is the largest segment of South Carolina's agriculture. Most of the trees (usually pines) are used not for lumber but for pulp and paper products.

An aerial view of the Hunting Island inland waterways which are part of the ACE Basin conservation area.

Not all of the old plantations have become the domain of the chainsaw and double-ought buckshot. One of the unique and most innovative conservation programs in the nation was begun by wealthy, out-of-state owners of historic rice and cotton plantations along three Low Country rivers between Charleston and Beaufort.

In 1966, Gaylord Donnelley, retired chairman of a Chicago printing concern, bought the 10,000-acre Ashepoo Plantation (private) at the mouth of the Ashepoo River along St. Helena Sound near Beaufort. He and his family used the land for their own pleasure, allowing only friends and business associates to hunt there. Donnelley and other wealthy owners of the long-dormant plantations, some of them descendants of the original plantation families, most of them from out-of-state, opposed development, and also sought a way to protect their lands for future generations.

In 1988, Donnelley and other private owners including the media entrepreneur Ted Turner formed the ACE Basin Task Force, a coalition that includes the Nature Conservancy, Ducks Unlimited, the South Carolina Wildlife and Marine Resources

Department, and the U.S. Fish and Wildlife Service. The private plantation owners are making conservation easements a permanent part of their deed restrictions, as well as donating some land for use as research reserves and future scientific and educational centers.

The basin is bordered on the north by the Edisto River, on the south by the Combahee River, on the west (inland) by an irregular pattern of watersheds, uplands, and highways, and on the east by St. Helena Sound, where all three rivers converge. The basin's 850,000 acres make it one of the largest, most pristine estuarine ecosystems in North America, home to 17 endangered or threatened species, including the wood stork and loggerhead sea turtle. About 25 private plantations along the Ashepoo, Combahee, and Edisto rivers account for the bulk of the land in the area and form the core of the conservation project. A similar program of protective easements recently began on private plantations along the old rice rivers near Georgetown.

PLANTATIONS TO VISIT

Many of the seventeenth- and eighteenth-century plantations that once abounded in South Carolina were destroyed during the Civil War when the Union army came through the state. Some survive today as private residences, and some have been converted into state parks and gardens (see "State Parks" and "Historic Sites" in "PRACTICAL INFORMATION").

■ ASHLEY RIVER PLANTATIONS

Drayton Hall. Considered an exceptionally sophisticated example of early Georgian architecture in America. A red-brick structure with a massive Palladian portico, Drayton Hall is the only plantation house on the Ashley River to have survived the Civil War. (John Drayton informed Union soldiers his house was a hospital for smallpox patients.) Open daily. 3380 Ashley River Road off Route 61, nine miles from downtown Charleston; 766-0188.

Magnolia Plantation and Gardens. Not much remains of the Drayton family's original plantation house (owned by John Drayton's father), but the lush grounds and beautifully tended gardens are well worth a trip. Visitors may rent canoes and tour the waterfowl refuge, walk or bicycle along several acres of nature trails, and traverse bridges and boardwalks to explore the vast Audubon Swamp Garden. Open daily. Ten miles northwest of downtown Charleston on Route 61; 571-1266.

Middleton Place. When Union troops burned down the plantation mansion the Middleton family moved to the adjoining guesthouse. Now open for viewing, the guesthouse contains a fine collection of period furnishings, silver, and artwork. The main attraction at Middleton Place are the splendidly landscaped gardens. Grounds open daily; house closed Mondays. Route 61, 14 miles northwest of Charleston; 556-6020.

■ SANTEE RIVER PLANTATIONS

Hampton Plantation. Built ca. 1735, the original structure had only six rooms but mid-century Daniel Huger Horry expanded the house by adding a two-story ballroom and several large bedrooms and sitting rooms. The six-column Adams portico was completed in 1791 shortly before George Washington's visit. The plantation was also home to Archibald Rutledge, poet laureate of South Carolina. Call for times. Eight miles north of McClellanville off US 17; 546-9361.

Hopsewee Plantation. Overlooking the North Santee River is the home of Thomas Lynch, a South Carolina delegate to the Continental Congress and signer of the Declaration of Independence. The mansion's interior charms include a fine Georgian staircase and hand-carved Adam candlelight moldings. Twelve miles south of Georgetown; US 17; call for times, 546-7891.

■ NEAR CHARLESTON

Boone Hall. A stunning avenue of moss-draped live oaks line the entrance to Boone Hall. The house standing today is a 1935 reconstruction of the original mansion but the nine slave cabins date back 250 years. Other features include the original cotton gin house and smokehouse. Still a working farm, the plantation harvests pecans and raises cattle and sheep. Open daily. Six miles northeast of Charleston, just off US 17; 884-4371.

■ INLAND

Redcliffe Plantation. One of the few preserved inland plantations, Redcliffe was the home of South Carolina senator James Henry Hammond and, later, John Shaw Billings, editing director of Time, Inc. Beech Island, seven miles southeast of North Augusta off Route 278; call for times, 827-1473.

CHARLESTON

NATIVES OF CHARLESTON NEVER TIRE of repeating three quips about themselves and their unique and historic seaport city:

"We, like the Chinese, eat rice and worship our ancestors."

"The Ashley and the Cooper rivers come together in Charleston Harbor to form the Atlantic Ocean."

"I'd rather be dead in Charleston than alive in Columbia or rich in Greenville."

South Carolinians who don't live in Charleston sometimes wonder whether those epigrams are self-deprecating humor or simple arrogance.

Whatever the case, this city—this gothic, bodice-ripping, historical romance of sugary myth and pivotal (sometimes appalling) reality—is the jewel of South Carolina. When Edgar Allan Poe in his poem "Annabel Lee" wrote of a "kingdom by the sea," Charleston was the place he described.

From a distance, the peninsular city between the Ashley and Cooper rivers resembles an antebellum watercolor come to life in pastel shades. Its low profile skyline is pierced by the spires and steeples of 181 churches, a phenomenon of urban architecture and religion leading natives to call Charleston "the holy city."

After 300 years of epidemics, wars, pirates, fires, earthquakes, hurricanes, and hubris, Charleston remains one of the nation's best preserved cities. Along Battery (Street) at the point of the peninsula, elegant, airy old homes influenced by the style of eighteenth-century West Indies planters face the harbor where the Civil War began.

To walk the streets of Charleston is to stroll not only in antebellum but also in colonial times, down narrow cobblestone lanes, past wrought-iron gates, and under the gaze of tiers of great verandas, which Charlestonians call piazzas.

All this architectural charm is a result of the peculiar combination of Charleston's antebellum wealth and postbellum poverty. The city simply was too poor to tear down its old homes and public buildings and replace them with later styles.

There are many levels to Charleston, of course. For example, there is the sensuous and epic old seaport, now beautified and bespangled like never in its history, attracting travelers and aficionados from around the world. Then there is the Charleston seen only by those born into it, or invited by name, the old aristocratic Charleston whose ancestors created this splendor, ancestors still hovering, or

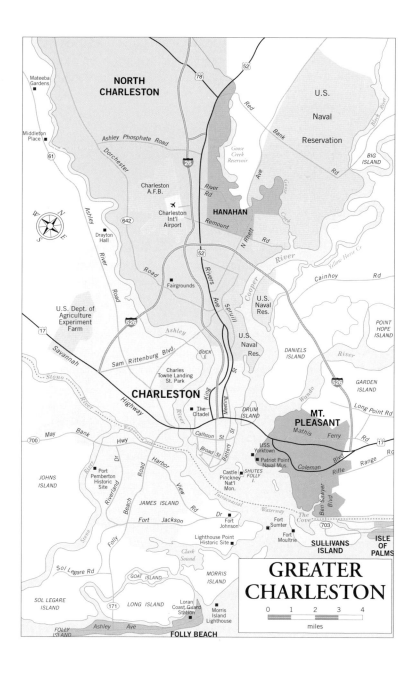

GREATER CHARLESTON

haunting, today's aristocracy like ghosts at the dinner table. And there is the tale of how this "kingdom by the sea" came to be, and how it persists today, from the Battery mansions to the parade ground of The Citadel military college, from the old slave marts to the Wando River docks.

For most of its long history, Charleston was South Carolina's only city. To this day, she remains the state's only city with a real character of its own.

■ COLONIAL PORT

Nine years after the first English settlers landed a few miles up the Ashley River at Albemarle Point in 1670, the Lords Proprietors, ruling the Carolina colony from London, decided that location wasn't adequately defensible. They preferred the tip of the peninsula, then called Oyster Point, now the Battery and White Point Gardens. So, in 1680, the little settlement packed its bags and sailed back down the Ashley to an enormous mound of oyster shells left like picnic litter by generations of Native Americans.

It was a prescient change of plans.

The new location, Charles Town, was an immediate success. Deerskins and furs were the settlement's early exports, soon followed by naval stores such as tar, turpentine, and timber from the vast coastal pine forests, shipped to England for the mother country's navy and merchant fleets.

The harbor became thick with sailing ships. The town's dirt streets sported a mixture of sailors, Royal Marines, prostitutes, river planters and farmers, merchants, fur traders, African slaves, indentured white servants, and an occasional Indian chief in ceremonial dress trailed by a band of his tribe.

The first planters, Barbadians who settled up the Cooper River at Goose Creek, then up the Ashley River, soon were joined by new planters and religious refugees from Europe. Protestant French Huguenots, Quakers, Presbyterians, and Baptists from England, Scotland, and Ireland established plantations along the coastal rivers north and south of Charles Town, and the port became much like a Greek city-state, the plantations its surrounding province.

It also became a pirate's prize.

Charles Town lay between two major pirate haunts—the West Indies and the hiding places up the inlets of the North Carolina coast. At first, the merchants of the port welcomed freebooters, privateers, and pirates for their free spending.

Then, in June of 1718, the notorious Edward Teach, "Blackbeard," led four ships and 400 men in plundering merchant vessels anchored in Charles Town Harbor. Teach seized passengers, held them for a ransom of medical supplies, and departed when paid.

Two months later, in late August, Stede Bonnet, "the gentleman pirate," seized and plundered merchant ships off the entrance to the harbor. This time, enraged merchants led by Col. William Rhett, one of the Goose Creek Barbadian planters, struck back. With two sloops and 130 men, Rhett's force captured Bonnet up the Cape Fear River near what today is Wilmington, North Carolina.

Bonnet and dozens of other pirates were hanged during the fall and winter of 1718 in Charles Town, and pirates no longer attacked merchant ships entering or leaving the harbor.

By the end of the 1730s, with a population of more than 6,000, Charles Town was the fourth largest town in British North America, after Boston, New York, and Philadelphia.

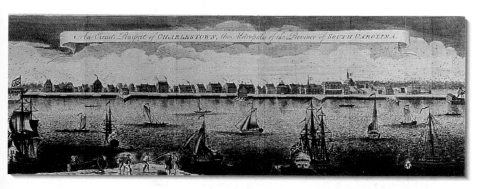

An early view of Charles Town Harbor. Seaborne trade caused the city to grow into one of the four largest in America by the beginning of the eighteenth century, the others being Boston, New York, and Philadelphia. (South Carolina Historical Society, Charleston)

■ REVOLUTIONARY WAR

The first British attempt to capture Charles Town began in May 1776. A sea and land force attacked Sullivan's Island while the Patriot rebels scurried to complete Fort Moultrie, guarding the northern side of the harbor entrance. While British troops advanced ashore, British ships opened fire, but the new fort had been built with a material virtually impervious to cannon shot—palmetto logs. The spongy, freshly cut logs absorbed most of the shots without effect, and the Patriot return fire from behind Moultrie's walls proved too fierce for both the British naval and land forces. The British withdrew, turning their efforts toward Gen. George Washington's army in the North, and the palmetto tree became the state symbol, incorporated on the blue background of the state flag.

In the spring of 1779, the British, unable to defeat Washington in the northern colonies, launched a southern strategy intended to rally the considerable number of British Loyalists in the South. By May, they were plundering the Ashley River rice plantations and were on the outskirts of Charles Town. By early 1780, the entire rebel army of South Carolina, about 5,000 men, was walled inside the town without an escape route.

Led by Lord Cornwallis, a massive land-sea force bore down on Charles Town. Fort Moultrie on Sullivan's Island fell May 7, 1780. On May 12, after a 42-day siege, the British captured the colonies' last open seaport and the only Patriot army in the southern theater of the war, their greatest victory.

Loyalists to the English crown streamed into Charles Town. Cornwallis and his armies marched inland, to Camden, then on to the surprising British losses at Kings Mountain and Cowpens (see "PIEDMONT" chapter).

A ruthless guerrilla and civil war raged beyond Charles Town in the interior of the colony, from the swamps of the Low Country rivers to the hills of the Piedmont. One by one during 1782, British outposts fell to Patriot forces led by Gen. Nathanael Greene, and by spring of 1782, Greene's army was within 15 miles of Charles Town, threatening to trap the British inside the town.

Cornwallis' defeat at Yorktown the year before had left Charles Town as the only major British outpost in the war. That summer of 1782, the British commander at Charles Town fled, and negotiations began for the surrender of the port.

On October 27, 1782, a convoy of 40 ships departed Charles Town with most of the British army. With them went more than 3,700 civilians loyal to the crown and 5,000 of their slaves. Many of these white and black civilians ended up settling on the islands of the northern Bahamas, where their descendants live today. The remaining British troops formally surrendered and evacuated Charles Town on December 14, 1782, and Greene's army took possession of the seaport after two and a half years of British occupation and rule.

In August 1783, the new South Carolina legislature, convening in the port city, changed its name from Charles Town to Charleston.

■ SLAVE TRADE

Many African-American historians today characterize slavery as the African holocaust. Hundreds of thousands of persons were taken from Africa to what is now the southern United States from the late seventeenth century until the early nineteenth century, and by the time of the Civil War the U.S. slave population numbered four million persons. Of those born in Africa who made the crossing, thousands died during the cattleship ocean voyage, and those who survived soon began a life of unremitting toil.

(left) A view of the British siege of Charles Town in the spring of 1780. The American force of 5,500 men under Gen. Benjamin Lincoln surrendered in May 1780. (South Caroliniana Library, Univ. of S.C.)

Of those who came to North America, about a third entered first through Charleston. They were quarantined in pens on Sullivan's Island, and most then were sold in the slave marts of Charleston.

Enormous personal fortunes were made by the slave traders of the port city. During the 1730s, for example, nearly 20,000 slaves, most of them from Angola, were imported through the city, almost a third of them by Joseph Wragg & Co., the biggest slave trader in town.

Merchant vessels calling at Charleston included a fleet of 140 British-owned ships doing trade only between England and Charleston. More than 800 vessels a year were using the port shortly before the Revolutionary War, and Charleston's annual import-export tonnage exceeded that of New York, even though the southern city had only half the population.

Ships entering the port from England brought consumer items and wines, while ships entering from the West Indies brought sugar and rum. Ships leaving the colonial port carried tar, pitch, turpentine, leather, deerskins, corn, peas, beef, pork, and rice.

Slave quarters on Boone Hall Plantation.

A slave auction in the streets of Charleston is depicted in this issue of The Illustrated London News *in 1856. (South Caroliniana Library, Univ. of S.C.)*

By far, rice was the most profitable export, and by far, the labor which grew the rice—slaves—was the most profitable import.

During the early 1770s, the slave trade through Charleston boomed. More than 65 vessels with more than 10,000 Africans came through the port during 1772–73 alone. It was the core of the shipping trade and the economic foundation upon which Charleston grew.

The traffic in humans officially ended in January 1808, when Congress outlawed the importation of slaves, but another 250,000 African slaves were smuggled into the nation, many via Charleston, from 1808 until the Civil War.

Visitors to Charleston, and many residents, mistakenly believe that City Market, a two-block-long structure on Market between Meeting and East Bay streets, was the city's slave mart (slaves were never sold there). In fact, there was no single slave mart, but instead a number of vacant buildings or lots, sometimes simply in the street, where slavers sold their wares.

Advertisements announcing auctions were placed in the Charleston newspapers, and most of the auctions were held in various locales along Chalmers and State streets near the Exchange (East Bay at Broad) where South Carolina's delegates to the First Continental Congress were elected in 1774.

Despite the fact that the ancestors of so many of today's American citizens reached this nation through Sullivan's Island and the slave marts of Charleston, there is no museum, not even an historical marker, memorializing—or admitting— the enormous tragedy.

One former slave mart site, on Chalmers Street one block north of Broad, was bought by the city in 1993 as a potential site for a museum of the African-American history of Charleston.

Pieces of the history of slavery and of black life in Charleston can be found in the exhibits, galleries, and archives of the Avery Research Center for African-American History and Culture, operated by the College of Charleston. In 1993, nearly 400,000 persons visited the Avery.

A rare and extraordinary collection of "hire badges" at the Charleston Museum reveals a strange aspect of "the peculiar institution" of slavery. These thin pieces of copper listing the slave's occupation, badge number, and year of issue, were worn (beginning in 1751) by artisan slaves hired out by their owners to work for others.

Very few members of Charleston's powerful aristocracy opposed—or dared to voice opposition to—the slavery of antebellum and colonial times or the racial segregation of the twentieth century. Some Charlestonians did oppose slavery, however, and their breach of custom struck the elite as both philosophically and socially aberrant.

Sara Grimke, eldest daughter of an eminent Charleston jurist, left town in 1821 to join the abolitionist movement in Philadelphia. Her sister, Angelina, soon joined her. The two women, also advocates of women's suffrage, opposed slavery on humanitarian grounds.

Other Charleston women of the slave-owning class quietly opposed it for the opportunity it offered their husbands for extramarital sex. An excerpt from the writings of Mary Boykin Chestnut of plantation and Charleston elite circles:

> Like the patriarchs of old, our men live all in one house with their wives and their concubines; and the mulattos one sees in every family partly resemble the white children. Any lady is ready to tell you who the father is of all the mulatto children in everybody's household but her own.

Unlike other Southern states, South Carolina did not prohibit interracial marriage until after the Civil War. In Charleston, mulatto women and well-regarded white men occasionally married during antebellum years. The city had a free black population of more than 3,000 (rivaled in numbers only by New Orleans) and within that group was an elite of about 500 free mulattos.

By 1820, about 58 percent of the city's population was black. White residents were anxious about the large numbers of slaves living in town and about the large number of other slaves who came to Charleston on Sundays to celebrate a day off (and sometimes to runaway and disappear among the large number of blacks in the community).

Romanticists and apologists for the Old South who portray the slaves as happy, singing, dancing "darkies," little more than children unable to care for themselves, should ponder the story of Denmark Vesey.

Rumors, almost always unfounded, of slave uprisings were a staple among the fears white Charlestonians faced. The most notorious of these rumors was the Denmark Vesey affair of 1822.

Denmark, owned by Capt. Joseph Vesey, could read, write, and speak several languages by the age of about 30. Vesey used him on a ship shuttling between Charleston, St. Thomas, and Santo Domingo in the West Indies. Denmark bought a chance in the popular Charleston East Bay Lottery, won $1,500, and promptly bought his freedom for $600.

Taking the name Vesey, he became a skilled and prosperous carpenter. His property in Charleston included a home at 20 Bull Street. Vesey helped found the African Methodist Episcopal (AME) Church, became well known among town and plantation slaves, and was admired as well as envied for his powerful personality, quick mind, and sophistication.

In June of 1822, rumors swept through the white community of a slave rebellion planned for the night of June 16. That night, 2,500 armed whites patrolled the city, and in the days following, 10 blacks were arrested as leaders of the alleged plot, including Vesey.

On July 2, Vesey and five other blacks were hanged.

Terrified slaves began turning in others, and in the end a total of 35 blacks were hanged. The AME church, at Reed and Hanover streets, was demolished, suspected of being a hotbed of rebellion. While the plotted rebellion was never actually proved, Vesey is considered a hero by many, and a new AME church was constructed at 110 Calhoun in 1865.

In December 1822, the legislature passed a law requiring all free black males over the age of 15 to take a white guardian or risk being seized and sold into slavery.

In Charleston, the repression went further. A "workhouse" on the southwest corner of Magazine and Mazyck streets was created for the purpose of giving uppity slaves "a little sugar" on a tortuous treadmill. The arms of men and women were fastened to an overhead rail and a treadmill put in motion beneath their feet. Those unable to keep pace suffered a constant beating of legs and knees against the treadmill steps while "drivers" also flogged them with a cat o' nine tails whip.

The abolition of slavery would take decades longer, but it was foreshadowed in 1833 when the English Parliament outlawed slavery in the British West Indies, and, in Philadelphia that same year, the American Anti-Slavery Society was founded.

■ CIVIL WAR

Secessionist fever inflamed Charleston and the rest of the state for at least two years before the first shots of the Civil War were fired. One of the few Unionists left in Low Country plantation and Charleston aristocratic circles, James Petigru, advised a secessionist meeting in Charleston that "South Carolina is too small to be a republic and too large to be an insane asylum."

Frederick Law Olmstead, visiting Charleston in 1859, wrote, "the cannon in position on the parade ground, The Citadel . . . with its martial ceremonies, the frequent parades of militia . . . the numerous armed police, might lead one to imagine that the town was in a state of siege or revolution."

The most strategic fort in Charleston, Fort Sumter covered all of a tiny island almost in the middle of the entrance to Charleston Harbor from the Atlantic Ocean.

At 4 A.M., April 12, 1861, cadets from The Citadel military academy fired a cannon at the fort. By 5 A.M., 43 batteries and mortars were bombarding Fort Sumter from Fort Moultrie on Sullivan's Island, Fort Johnson on James Island, and other impromptu sites. Fort Sumter's Maj. Robert Anderson, a Southerner but a Union army commander, refused to surrender.

Charlestonians rushed to the Battery, to wharves and rooftops, for a view of the pyrotechnics. By nightfall, 2,500 rounds of shot and shell had been fired onto the fort. Major Anderson's cannon, meant only to engage ships in the harbor entrance, lacked the range to inflict damage on the rebel cannon. On the afternoon of April

13, after 34 hours of almost continuous bombardment, and with his isolated outpost ablaze, Anderson surrendered.

By mid-July, 11 warships of the Union's Atlantic Blockading Squadron were cruising off Charleston, Savannah, and the North Carolina coast in an effort to disrupt all trade with the South's richest city. On November 7, 1861, a Federal fleet swept into Port Royal Sound, launched an amphibious assault, and captured Hilton Head, Port Royal, Beaufort, and the nearby Sea Islands. The occupation shocked Charleston, and tightened the blockade.

At first, blockade-running ships regularly slipped through the Union fleet off Charleston Harbor. They made for Bermuda, Nassau in the Bahamas, and Liverpool in England, taking cotton bales out, bringing back military and medical supplies, dry goods, groceries, and occasional luxury items. Estimates are that about 80 percent of all blockade runners based in Charleston eluded capture. Their captains, crew, and investors reaped huge profits, but the overall tonnage was minuscule in comparison with pre-war commerce.

By early 1863, more than 10,000 Rebel troops were encamped in and around the city, which by then had changed dramatically. Streets were almost deserted, stores closed, as the Union's naval blockade drove up prices and made even ordinary goods such as shoes unobtainable in stores.

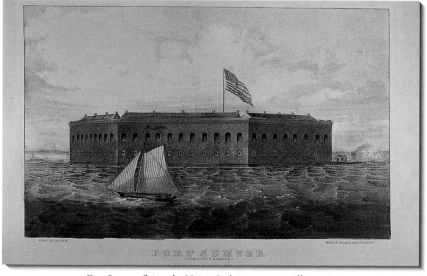

Fort Sumter flying the Union Jack in a pre-war illustration.
(South Caroliniana Library, Univ. of S.C.)

The Union made three attempts to capture Charleston.

The first came on June 15, 1862, on James Island. More than 6,000 troops landed on the island and began an assault across a narrow peninsula against a fortified Confederate breastwork where cannon awaited them. After three charges and two and a half hours of fierce hand-to-hand fighting, the Union withdrew.

The second attempt came April 7, 1863, when nine Union ironclads steamed into the harbor mouth and shelled Fort Sumter. After heavy damage inflicted by Confederate cannon from the fort and shore batteries, they withdrew.

The third assault came in July 1863 by a combined land and sea force. It too failed, but is notable as the first time black soldiers—commanded by white officers—fought in the Civil War. The 54th Massachusetts Volunteer Infantry Regiment assaulted Battery Wagner on Morris Island. They were repulsed, but the Confederates eventually abandoned the outpost.

After those three failures, the Union settled for laying siege to Charleston and its port. Bombardment began August 27, 1863, and continued until the city was abandoned by Confederate troops a few months before the end of the war. During one nine-day period in January 1864, about 1,500 Union shells were fired onto Charleston, but because the city south of Broad Street was nearly deserted, there were few casualties.

A curiosity of the war in Charleston occurred later in 1864, when the Confederate submarine *Hunley* sank the Union sloop *Housatonic* in the harbor. It was the first submarine to sink an enemy vessel in history, and in so doing, the *Hunley* itself went down with all hands.

The Union's Gen. William Tecumseh Sherman, with 60,000 battle-toughened soldiers, marched through Georgia and took Savannah December 22, 1864. Expecting Charleston would be next, about 16,000 Rebel troops were deployed around the city. In January 1865, Sherman crossed the Savannah River into South Carolina. He kept his enemy guessing as to his intentions, but told his aides to march north to Columbia. Charleston, Sherman said, was "a mere desolated wreck hardly worth the time it would take to starve it out."

Outflanked by Sherman's march north, the Confederate army abandoned Charleston February 17–18, 1865, marching up the peninsula, then toward the North Carolina border. On the morning of February 18, 1865, Union troops landed at the foot of Broad Street near East Bay Street, established headquarters in

RHETT BUTLER

*E*veryone knew now that the fate of the Confederacy rested as much upon the skill of the blockade boats in eluding the Yankee fleet as it did upon the soldiers at the front.

Rumor had it that Captain Butler was one of the best pilots in the South and that he was reckless and utterly without nerves. Reared in Charleston, he knew every inlet, creek, shoal and rock of the Carolina coast near that port, and he was equally at home in the waters around Wilmington. He had never lost a boat or even been forced to dump a cargo. At the onset of the war, he had emerged from obscurity with enough money to buy a small swift boat and now, when blockaded goods realized two thousand percent on each cargo, he owned four boats. He had good pilots and paid them well, and they slid out of Charleston and Wilmington on dark nights, bearing cotton for Nassau, England and Canada. The cotton mills of England were standing idle and the workers were starving, and any blockader who could outwit the Yankee fleet could command his own price in Liverpool. Rhett's boats were singularly lucky both in taking out cotton for the Confederacy and bringing in the war materials for which the South was desperate. Yes, the ladies felt they could forgive and forget a great many things for such a brave man.

—Margaret Mitchell, *Gone With the Wind*, 1936

The Citadel, declared martial law, and ordered the stars and stripes hoisted over all public buildings and fortifications.

Thousands of now-freed slaves deserted plantations all around Charleston, pouring into the city to celebrate, to search for family members, and to enlist in the Union army.

For nearly two centuries, Charleston had been the most prominent, and certainly the most politically important, city in the South. Her aristocracy controlled South Carolina's politics, and South Carolina led southern politics.

Then, in just short of four years, the "kingdom by the sea" lost forever both its fabled wealth and its influence.

■ CHARLESTON ARISTOCRACY

Three of the most revered (at least by their social peers) old Charleston family names are Porcher, Huger, and Petigru. The first two are pronounced "Por-*shay*" and "Hugh-*gee*," making things rhyme in the antebellum doggerel that explains just how important family ancestry is to Charleston's aristocracy:

> *I* thank Thee, Lord, on bended knee,
> I'm half Porcher and half Huger,
> For other blessings thank Thee too,
> My grandpa was a Petigru.

In the larger scheme of life north of Broad Street—for example, the Earth—that's an amusing quatrain. In Charleston, south of Broad Street in the peninsula city's elite historic district which extends to the Battery, and which is "the only" place to live, there is nothing funny about it.

INDELICACIES OF WAR

August 29, 1861

. . . *We* are Americans as well as the Yankees—& Russell cannot do us justice—he even repeats those hateful & *hideous* falsehoods as to our treatment of wounded & prisoners, when their own officers write such different stories—& one of the head surgeons writes to thank our surgeons. It is really amusing to see the accounts of the way Mrs. Gwin & Phillips & Greenhow are treated—houses guarded. Our women are now in a nice condition—traveling, your false hair is developed & taken off to see if papers are rolled in it—& you are turned up instantly to see if you have pistols concealed—not to speak of their having women to examine if you are a *man*—in disguise. I think *these* times make all women feel their humiliation in the affairs of the world. With *men* it is on to the field—"glory, honour, praise, &c, power." Women can only stay at home—& every paper reminds us that women are to be *violated*—ravished & all manner of humiliation. How are the daughters of Eve punished.

—The diary of Mary Boykin Chestnut, daughter and wife of U.S. senators, 1861

*Henry Laurens, a promi-
nent Charleston aristocrat
and Huguenot of the eigh-
teenth century. Originally
a merchant and planter,
Laurens served in the state
assembly, and was president
of the Continental Congress
from 1777 to 1779. He
was captured by the British
during the Revolutionary
War while on a diplomatic
mission and imprisoned in
the Tower of London, then
traded for Lord Cornwallis.
Upon his release, Laurens
was billed for meals.
(South Caroliniana
Library, Univ. of S.C.)*

For two centuries, from its founding until the 1900s, the same families controlled virtually everything in Charleston, from membership in the St. Cecelia
Society (Scarlett probably would not have made it) to who gets to be mayor next.
While its influence beyond its own small social circle no longer approaches political or financial supremacy, the old aristocracy remains a power to be reckoned with
in Charleston.

The elite were responsible for the preservation movement which saved the city's
architectural beauty, as well as the buildings their ancestors constructed.

By the 1730s in colonial Charles Town, the aristocracy had established itself.
Prominent mercantile families were marrying into prominent coastal plantation
families, and a plutocracy emerged. Merchant and planter families intermarried so
thoroughly that they became "one great tangled cousinry."

Almost from the city's beginnings, the aristocracy set out to entertain itself in style. In 1703, Charles Town had what generally is considered to be the first professional theatrical performance in North America. Formation of the South Carolina Jockey Club in 1735 and the club's annual "race week" in February gave definition to a social season which began in November and ended in May.

The Charles Town aristocracy created the colonies' first natural history museum, first public library, first theater, first musical society, and first scientific society. For all that, however, the cultivation of good times, as opposed to the culture of enlightened learning, was the elite's raison d'être.

By the 1770s, more than 23 singing and dancing masters offered lessons in Charles Town. Unlike Boston, Philadelphia, or New York, however, Charles Town had no institution of higher learning. The College of Charleston was founded in 1770 and claims to be the oldest municipal college in the nation. However, in its early decades, the college was actually a high school, and often closed. On the eve of the American Revolution, fewer than 20 Charles Town *and* coastal plantation Carolinians held college or university degrees.

Historian Walter J. Fraser Jr., in his history of the city, *Charleston! Charleston!*, explains: "It was a society that placed a premium on good looks, good companionship, bright conversation and a rounded personality. It embraced the sparkling dilettante, avoided the solitary thinker."

It also was a society whose fortunes were based not merely upon slavery, but also upon the slave trade.

The three wealthiest men in colonial Charleston were Henry Laurens, Gabriel Manigault, and Benjamin Smith, and the fortunes of all three came from the slave trade. Laurens, said to be the richest man in colonial America, was the principal partner in the firm of slave importers owned by Laurens, George Austin, and George Appleby, three family names still prominent in Charleston society.

The Civil War devastated the Charleston aristocracy, both financially and emotionally. Many were forced to take in boarders, and sewing, merely to live.

Still, the same families who ruled antebellum Charleston continued to rule the city after the war—Gibbes, Huger, Middleton, Pinckney, Ravenel, and Rhett among them. Unlike the emerging "New South" cities such as Atlanta, Nashville, and Charlotte, where in the absence of an old aristocracy there was room for a vibrant civic leadership to emerge, in Charleston, nothing changed.

"Conviviality over diligence, dilettantism over specialization, and leisure over work," as Fraser put it, continued to be the Charleston style.

The usual business day barely had time for business, what with the long, mid-morning coffee break, the long dinner (known elsewhere as "lunch") from two to four o'clock in the afternoon, with several courses, wine and liquor, then back to the office for no more than an hour or two.

Charleston's old plutocracy purposely prevented railroads from entering the city limits, and restricted the building of steam-powered mills and factories to outside the town, in part to keep out free white laborers seen by the elite as "antagonistic to our institutions."

The loss of the manufactured dream, the mythical world supposedly analogous to Sir Walter Scott's novels, and the defeat in the Civil War became a case of mass denial by an entire class of Charlestonians. Nostalgic and inaccurate recollections of the Old South as the best of times, and of the Civil War as the "Lost Cause" became by the 1880s the basis for a subculture.

One of the most extraordinary and ("south of Broad") scandalous episodes in the aristocracy's forced entry into the modern era began in 1947. One of their own, J. Waites Waring, federal district court judge and member of a prominent, old Charleston family, outlawed the exclusion of blacks from the state Democratic Party primary elections.

Soon after Judge Waring's decision, both his family and the aristocracy began to ostracize him. To this day, some claim the shunning was due to Waring's divorce from a member of another elite family and his rapid marriage to a Northern divorcée.

Waring ended segregated seating in his courtroom and ordered all court personnel, including attorneys, to address blacks as "Mister, Missus, and Miss."

His second wife, Elizabeth, invited black civil rights activists to the Waring home on fashionable Meeting Street south of Broad. On February 11, 1950, Mrs. Waring appeared on NBC television's "Meet the Press" and spoke in favor of a complete end to racial segregation in the South, as well as of racial intermarriage. About the same time, Judge Waring said in a speech to a New York City church group, "We don't have a Negro problem in the South; we have a white problem."

Early in March 1950, a cross was burned in front of the Waring home. The judge resigned his membership in the St. Cecelia Society, his captaincy in the elite Charleston Light Dragoons, and his affiliation with the local Episcopal church. On January 29, 1952, Waring announced his retirement from the federal bench, and he and Elizabeth left immediately for New York. They returned, alive, to Charleston only once more.

(following pages) Cadets practice drills in the courtyard at The Citadel, one of America's foremost military institutes.

Waring's written opinions in a public school desegregation case from Clarendon County in 1950 eventually became much of the legal reasoning for the Supreme Court's 1954 decision that racially separate educational facilities are inherently unequal, and thus, unconstitutional. After the high court's decision, more than 500 members of the local, state, and national NAACP gave a testimonial dinner for the Warings at a black church in Charleston.

The couple returned to New York immediately after the banquet. On January 17, 1968, J. Waites Waring was buried in Charleston's Magnolia Cemetery.

A further crumbling of the elite's traditions—albeit one unlikely to result in social ostracism—came July 22, 1994, when the 152-year-old, men-only admission policy of The Citadel military college was ruled unconstitutional by U.S. District Court Judge C. Weston Houck. The college, with Virginia Military Institute the last two state-supported military colleges in the nation, was a creation of Charleston's aristocracy. From its founding in 1842, The Citadel has reflected the Charleston aristocracy's love for military trappings and ceremony. It remains to be seen whether the college will continue as a private or publicly funded institution. Friday afternoons, from September through May, the cadet corps marches on its parade grounds, and the public is invited to observe them.

Perhaps inevitably, the young woman who successfully sued for admission not only to the college but also to the corps of cadets, came from Simpsonville, an Up Country mill town just south of Greenville—that same part of South Carolina that has always challenged the institutions of the aristocracy.

■ MODERN SEAPORT

Until the 1820s, the single most important and dominant seaport in the nation was Charleston. Then, the advent of steam-powered vessels meant merchant ships from England and Europe no longer had to follow the trade winds route via Bermuda, the Bahamas, or West Indies. With steam, the merchant ships took the direct route to Baltimore, Philadelphia, and New York.

About the same time, fertile, new lands for growing cotton were opened to migrating farmers in Alabama, Mississippi, Louisiana, Arkansas, and Texas. Mobile and New Orleans emerged as major cotton ports, surpassing Charleston.

After nearly a century of decline, in 1912 the Navy created its base up the Cooper River, and it grew to be one of the largest in the nation through World Wars I and II and the Korean War. It also became a Polaris and ballistic missile submarine base. The military complex includes a large army "point of embarkation" for troops, supplies, and equipment. During the 1970s, as many as 90 ships with nearly 20,000 officers and men called Charleston their home port, and 11,000 civilians were directly employed at the naval base.

It was at this time that the port of Charleston again began to achieve national status. Today, it is one of the nation's top seaports for container cargo, second to New York on the East Coast, and sixth nationally. The state Port Authority's huge new container cargo terminal on the Wando River, a tributary of the Cooper River just northeast of the city, is among the largest in the nation.

Although merchant shipping is thriving, the future of the naval station remains unclear. In 1993, Charleston's economy and tradition were rocked when the Navy

Cotton piled on a Charleston wharf in 1870 awaiting shipment.
(South Carolina Historical Society, Charleston)

CHARLESTON ARCHITECTURE

Popular styles of architecture in the historic district include:

COLONIAL
(1690–1740)
Defining features:
Low foundations
Clapboard sidings
High, pitched roofs

*John Lining House at
106 Broad at King.*

GEORGIAN
(1700–1790)
Defining features:
Hipped roofs
Box chimneys
Flattened columns
Raised basements

*Miles Brewton House
at 27 King Street.*

FEDERAL
(1790–1820)
(also known as Adam)
Defining features:
Geometric rooms
Iron balconies
Exterior trip, spiral stairs

*Nathaniel Russell House
at 61 Meeting Street.*

GREEK REVIVAL
(1820–1875)
Defining features:
Large heavy columns
and capitals
Gabled or hipped roof
Wide band of trim

*Beth Elohim Reform
Temple at 90 Hasell Street.*

GOTHIC REVIVAL
(1850–1885)
Defining features:
Pointed arches
Buttressed stone tracery

*French Huguenot Church
at 136 Church Street.*

ITALIANATE
(1830–1900)
Defining features:
Balustrades
Low, pitched roofs
Verandas

*Col. John Ashe House at
26 South Battery.*

VICTORIAN
(1860–1915)
Defining features:
Multi-gabled roofs
Gingerbread trim
Turrets

*Sottile House at Green Street
on the College of Charleston
campus.*

CHARLESTON SINGLE HOUSE
(late 1700s)
Defining features:
Single room width
Set at right angles
to the street

*Col. Robert Brewton
House at 71 Church.*

announced it would close the huge and historic Charleston Naval Station and Charleston Naval Shipyard in early 1996, a loss of about 30,000 jobs.

It will be years before new civilian uses are found for the old Navy base. Some Navy units will remain, such as the naval hospital and a communications unit. The Army is basing a fleet of 15 freighters at the old Navy base, the ships loaded with ammunition and supplies at all times and ready to sail immediately to wherever Army troops are deployed.

Charleston has become accustomed to the payroll, and the uniforms, of the Navy, to the sight of ships gliding by on the Cooper River—guided missile frigates, nuclear subs, and destroyers—all gone now.

■ ARCHITECTURE

The historic streets of Charleston, where nearly every structure has a plaque facing the sidewalk—church, home, courthouse, or office—seem at first to be not a living part of the city but a museum neighborhood. It is both.

Marriages, funerals, and worship services routinely go on in St. Philip's Episcopal. Families, some old Charleston aristocracy, many others well-to-do newcomers, bathe, dine, quarrel, and love inside the old homes on Tradd or Legare streets. Mundane records are still filed at the county courthouse at Broad and Meeting streets, and shipping agents consign cargo to ports around the world from offices on East Bay Street.

There are more than 1,000 residential, commercial, civic, and religious structures within Charleston's sprawling historic district, including 73 from the colonial period, 136 from the late eighteenth century, and more than 600 built prior to the 1840s. Inside almost all of them, while hundreds of thousands of visitors stroll by outside, the details of daily living continue.

In addition to its historical appeal and uniquely bucolic urban charm, the old streets are a living museum for admirers and students of architecture and design. The many architectural styles found in Charleston, including the city's own "single house," are discussed in "Charleston Architecture" in this chapter.

Many of Charleston's Colonial houses used yellow pine and cypress from trees felled in the coastal forests only in wintertime, when the sap was down. They were cut into 40- to 70-foot lengths at river sawmills then floated to Charleston. Cured in saltwater, then air dried, the wood became nearly iron-hard, almost impervious to termites or fungus, enduring today after centuries of exposure.

Ornamental wrought iron is another creative aspect of architecture that can be seen throughout the historic district, nearly all of it created by black artists, first as slaves, later as freedmen, and today as nationally recognized treasures such as Phillip Simmons. Born in 1912, Simmons began as a blacksmith at the age of 13. Over the years, his work evolved from farm implements to car bodies to ornamental iron. More than 200 of his gates, fences, balconies, and grills adorn homes in the historic district.

Simmons's gates are ornate designs sometimes 10 to 15 feet high, decorated with fauna, fish, snakes, and palmetto trees. In the early 1990s, Simmons was named by the Smithsonian Institution as a National Heritage Fellow and commissioned to produce a gate for display. He has also been recognized by the Folk Arts Program of the National Endowment for the Arts as a master traditional artist.

Simmons is the living descendant of Charleston's tradition of black artisans whose skills made their owners rich. At one time, nearly 200 black cabinetmakers practiced their craft in Charleston, serving the city and plantation elite.

Some of the artisans became wealthy themselves, such as Thomas Elfe, a slave whose cabinetry from the 1760s and 1770s now is eagerly sought by collectors.

That anyone can still live in or see the architectural and design beauty of historic Charleston today is the result of a meeting held on April 21, 1920, in a home at 20 South Battery. The city was about to widen its streets to accommodate automobiles that year, and that meant the destruction of historic structures throughout the lower peninsula, a prospect that moved 32 of Charleston's aristocratic families to attend that April meeting.

From it came the Charleston Society for the Preservation of Old Dwellings, later renamed the Preservation Society of Charleston.

Still running most of the city in those days, the aristocracy pressured the city council in 1929 to pass the nation's first zoning ordinance to protect historic structures. In 1931, the city council set aside 23 square blocks of the lower peninsula— today's principal historic district—as an architectural preserve, limiting owners in what they could do with their property and establishing a Board of Architectural Review.

Charleston's historic preservation laws became models for historic districts across the nation. In 1946, the Historic Charleston Foundation was created and assumed the lead in the city's preservation movement.

That movement, however, is not limited to the wealthy, nor aimed at the gentrification of low-income areas. Historic Charleston is rehabilitating vintage buildings in economically depressed neighborhoods and helping low-income Charlestonians finance ownership. The foundation also administers a crafts program that trains young adults in carpentry and masonry restoration.

Charleston's municipal government, with the help of the city's architects, is building several hundred small-scale public housing facilities. The program refused to use the usual (and usually, eventually, trashed) standard design of brick duplexes or high-rise apartments. Instead, it builds single-family units on vacant lots.

■ TOUR OF HISTORIC CHARLESTON

The 1923 musical *Runnin' Wild* introduced one dance number that swept the nation in the 1920s "flapper" heyday. It was "the Charleston," a knee-knocking, palm-slapping, leg-kicking forerunner of the jitterbug.

There is absolutely nothing that quick—human or motorized—in today's historic Charleston.

The historic districts of the city's lower peninsula, and for that matter most of the residential and commercial neighborhoods without the "historic" designation, are a theater of detail. The best of Charleston can be noticed best at foot speed and eye level.

Visitors to Charleston eager to orient themselves and understand the old city should stop first at the new Charleston Visitors Reception and Transportation Center in the heart of the commercial district, north of the historic district, at 375 Meeting Street. Parking is a problem anywhere, anytime, any day, in the historic district; however, it is simple to park at the visitor center lots and then take a trolley south to the historic district.

Inside the center is an overview of the city and surrounding area in the form of a large diorama and multimedia videos, as well as a comprehensive collection of brochures, maps, fliers, and other notices. Free shuttle buses leave the visitors center at 15- to 20-minute intervals to and from the Old City Market on Market at East Bay streets, on the northern edge of the historic district. The center is open 8:30 A.M. to 5 P.M. daily.

Guided tours in air-conditioned buses or horse-drawn carriages are available at the visitors center and other locations in the historic district. (There are so many

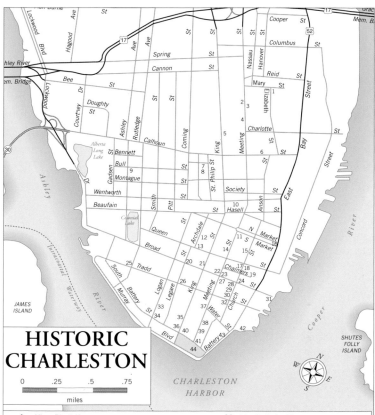

HISTORIC CHARLESTON

```
0        .25      .5       .75
                 miles
```

CHARLESTON
HARBOR

1 Aiken-Rhett House	20 John Rutledge House
25 Alston House	4 Joseph Manigault House
6 AME Church	11 Market Hall (Confederate Museum)
10 Beth Elohim Synagogue	35 Miles Brewton House
39 Calhoun Mansion	42 Missroon House
24 Chamber of Commerce	37 Nathaniel Russell House
3 Charleston Museum	5 Old Citadel Building
23 City Hall	16 Old City Market
29 Col. Charles Brewton House	31 Old Exchange
41 Col. William Washington House	15 Old Power Magazine
7 College of Charleston	36 Patrick O'Donnell House
22 County Courthouse	30 Robert Brewton House
17 Dock Street Theater	19 Slave Market
43 Edmondston-Alston House	8 Sottile House
14 Gibbes Museum of Art	12 St. John's Lutheran Church
34 H. A. Middleton House	27 St. Michael's Church
28 Heyward-Washington House	26 Stuart House
38 Huger House	13 Unitarian Church
18 Huguenot (French Protestant) Church	2 Visitor Information Center
32 Jacob Motte House	44 White Point Gardens
40 John Ashe House	9 William Blacklock House
21 John Lining House	33 William Drayton (Manigault) House

horse-drawn carriage tours in historic Charleston that the horses wear diapers. If there is an "accident" the carriage driver drops a marker at the spot and special trucks clean the street, then spray it with a perfumed disinfectant.)

Not far from the visitors center in the historic district are a number of fascinating old buildings worth exploring.

The **Aiken-Rhett Mansion** is located at 48 Elizabeth Street. When Gov. William Aiken inherited the house from his father in 1833, he added Greek Revival features to the original Federal-style design. Aiken spent three years in Europe collecting furniture and chandeliers for his home. In 1863 Jefferson Davis spent a week as Aiken's house guest and Confederate general P. G. T. Beauregard used the house as his headquarters during the Civil War. Aiken lost his fortune during the war and Federal troops ransacked his house.

The **Charleston Museum** at 360 Meeting Street, founded in 1773, is the oldest museum in the United States. It includes artifacts, treasures, and exhibits on the history of the Low Country, as well as an inventive "Discover Me" room for children.

Across the street is the **Joseph Manigault Mansion.** This splendid Federal-style mansion was built in 1803 by a wealthy planter, Joseph Manigault, and designed

The dance known as "the Charleston" swept the country during the boom years of the 1920s. (Underwood Photo Archives)

by Joseph's brother Gabriel Manigault, a lawyer fascinated with architecture. Educated in Europe, Gabriel brought elements of the Franco-English villa style into his design, seen best in the elegant breezeway and graceful staircase. The original gatehouse stands in the garden, and represents a small Roman temple.

Further down Meeting Street is the **Old Citadel Building,** built in 1822 at Marion Square to house state arms and troops. It was here that the famous South Carolina Military College—The Citadel—first began. (The new site is at Hampton Park, on Moultrie Street off Ashley Avenue.) A portion of the tabby wall that once marked the town's northern fortifications can still be seen.

At 110 Calhoun Street is the **Emanuel African Methodist Episcopal Church,** home of the South's oldest AME congregation, which had its beginnings in 1818 at another location. In 1822, authorities demolished the original church, claiming it was the sanctuary where Denmark Vesey planned the slave insurrection of that year. The congregation's new location opened in 1865.

At this point visitors might want to make a tour of the shops on **King Street,** long a center of commerce for the city. The **Patrick O'Donnell House** at 21 King Street (private) was built in the 1850s in the Italianate style. O'Donnell was an Irish immigrant and master builder who undertook the building of this house for his fiancé. Unfortunately, the building took so long that she married someone else.

At 27 King Street, visitors can see the handsome brick **Miles Brewton House** (also private). With its two-tiered piazza, the house is an elegant example of the Charleston double house in the Palladian style. It was completed in 1769 for Brewton, a colonial merchant and leading slave trader who was lost at sea with his family in 1775. The house served as headquarters for Sir Henry Clinton and Lord Cornwallis during the American Revolution as well as Union generals George Meade and Edward Hatch during the Civil War.

Just off King Street, at 90 Hasell Street, is **Congregation Beth Elohim.** The original synagogue, the birthplace of American Reform Judaism, was destroyed by fire and replaced by this structure in 1840. It is considered one of the finest examples of Greek Revival architecture in the country.

East of King, at 8 Archdale Street, is the **Unitarian Church.** The oldest Unitarian church in the South, it was built between 1772 and 1787. In 1852, Francis D. Lee began extensive remodeling in the Gothic Revival style popular at the time. He added the Gothic arched window, buttresses, and a fan-tracery vaulted ceiling based upon that of Gloucester Cathedral.

The Greek Revival **St. John's Lutheran Church,** on the corner of Clifford and Archdale streets, was built in 1817. Of note is the fine craftsmanship in the wrought-iron gates and fence, as well as the 1823 Thomas Hall organ case.

Back at the intersection of Meeting and Market streets is **Market Hall,** a National Historic Landmark built in 1841 and modeled after the Temple of Nike in Athens. The **Confederate Museum** is located here; founded in 1898 by the Daughters of the Confederacy, the museum still displays flags and other Confederate memorabilia.

At 135 Meeting Street is **Gibbes Museum of Art,** an outstanding collection of American art and portraits relating to Southern history. Specialties of the museum include the collection of over 300 miniature portraits and the miniature rooms, detailed with fabrics and furnishings. The rotunda's Tiffany-style stained-glass window is also worth noting.

Nearby, at 79 Cumberland (one of Charleston's few remaining cobblestone thoroughfares), is the **Old Powder Magazine.** Built in 1713, it is the oldest public

The historic district of downtown Charleston includes a row of brightly painted homes along Tradd Street known as "Rainbow Row."

■ CULTURAL TIMELINE ■

1670 First permanent settlement, Charles Town, established.

1718 After a summer of pirate attacks by the notorious Blackbeard and Stede Bonnet, Gov. Robert Johnson and Col. William Rhett rid the Carolina coast of pirates. Bonnet and others are hanged.

1736 Dock Street Theater opens in Charles Town. Site of what is considered the first play produced in the United States: "The Orphan."

1744 Teenage plantation mistress Eliza Lucas (later Pinckney) brings a good crop of indigo seed to maturity. Develops an indigo-processing technique.

1762 St. Cecilia Society founded as a musical organization in Charles Town. Functions today as an exclusive social club.

1773 Charleston Museum—the oldest in the United States—is founded.

1780 Henry Laurens, in England as a diplomat representing the rebellious colonies during the Revolutionary War, is charged with high treason and imprisoned in the Tower of London. He is billed for meals.

1783 Name of Charles Town changed to Charleston.

1812 Theodosia Burr Alston, daughter of Aaron Burr, sails to New York and is never heard from again. Later a pirate confesses she had been forced to walk the plank.

1827 Edgar Allan Poe's artillery unit is assigned to Fort Moultrie on Sullivan's Island. Poe gets ideas for his 1843 short story "The Gold-Bug."

1880 Col. E. B. C. Cash and Col. William S. Shannon fight (with pistols) the last legal duel in the state over an inheritance. Shannon is mortally wounded.

1915 Charleston becomes the place to drink when statewide prohibition is enacted.

1920s Author DuBose Heyward writes *Porgy,* the basis for George Gershwin's operatic work *Porgy and Bess.*

1923 The musical *Runnin' Wild* introduces "the Charleston." The dance becomes a national craze.

1928 Julia Peterkin wins Pulitzer prize for her novel *Scarlet Sister Mary.*

1930s Anna Hyatt Huntington begins her collection of sculpture at Brookgreen Gardens.

1950s Teenagers on the Strand start dancing "the Shag."

1983 *The Big Chill* is filmed in South Carolina.

1990s Numerous films are filmed in South Carolina, including *The Prince of Tides, Sleeping With the Enemy, Rich in Love, Chasers, Forrest Gump,* and *Scarlett.*

building in the city, and was used during the Revolution to store munitions. It is now a museum operated by the Colonial Dames of America, with costumes, furniture, armor, and other artifacts from eighteenth-century Charleston.

Most carriage tours begin and end in the Old Market area. Visitors can explore the shops there, then walk south along East Bay Street, past the row of pastel-colored houses near **Tradd Street** (called **Rainbow Row**), or along any of the cool, palmetto-shaded streets. There are private gardens and churches hidden about, waiting to be discovered by the curious.

Returning to Church Street and continuing south, visitors will enter the neighborhood known as **Cabbage Row.** At 87 Church Street is the **Heyward-Washington House,** built in 1772 by rice king Daniel Heyward, and the setting for DuBose Heyward's *Porgy.* President George Washington stayed here during his 1791 visit.

At 51 Meeting Street is the **Nathaniel Russell House,** headquarters of the Historic Charleston Foundation. Built in 1808, it is one of the nation's finest examples of Federal-style architecture, and features a three-story staircase which spirals upwards without touching the walls, seemingly without support. Nathaniel Russell was a native of Rhode Island who arrived in Charleston in 1765 and established a mercantile empire on rice, indigo, cotton, and slaves.

Further south is the area where somewhat more lavish mansions reflect the wealth of a later era. At 16 Meeting Street is the 35-room **Calhoun Mansion,** opulent even by Charleston's standards. Built in 1876 by George W. Williams, no expense was spared. His son-in-law, Patrick Calhoun (a grandson of John C. Calhoun) inherited it, but the house passed out of the family in the 1930s and the building was on the verge of being condemned when restoration began in 1970. It is an interesting example of Victorian taste, notable for its ornate plasterwork, fine wood moldings, and a 75-foot domed ceiling. Still a private residence, the first and second floors of the mansion are open to the public (check ahead for times).

At 21 East Battery is the **Edmondston-Alston House,** built by the Scottish merchant Charles Edmondston in 1828. The financial panic of 1837 forced Edmondston to sell the mansion, and the new owner, Charles Alston, immediately set about remodeling it. The result is the handsome Greek Revival mansion with its three-story piazza and commanding view of the harbor. The house has remained in the family since its purchase, but the bottom two floors are open to the public.

A tranquil spot for relaxing is the **White Point Gardens, in Battery Park,** facing the harbor and shaded by palmettos and oak trees. Once the site where pirates hung from gallows, it is now the most romantic spot in Charleston, for several hundred couples a year. It is the number one marriage site in the city.

The park offers a spectacular view of Charleston Harbor, with Fort Sumter in the distance, and some of the historic district's finest old homes behind the park on Battery Street. Today, visitors from as far off as Oregon and New Jersey, recalling the locale from earlier visits, reserve the gazebo in White Point Gardens as much as a year in advance to get married in it. (For reservations, contact the City of Charleston Recreation Department at 724-7327.) Strolling visitors to the historic district are likely to become spectators at the nuptials.

Every October, the Preservation Society of Charleston conducts a month-long house and garden tour, and every spring, the Historic Charleston Foundation holds a mid-March to mid-April festival of houses, which includes plantation oyster roasts, symphony galas, and candlelight tours. The Ashley River plantations are located about a half hour drive away from Charleston on SC 61.

BLIND TIGERS

South Carolinians of the non-temperance temperament first made Charleston a place to visit during the 1890s. They came looking for a drink, because no government on Earth has ever succeeded in telling Charlestonians how, when, or where they should consume alcoholic beverages. When Gov. "Pitchfork" Ben Tillman tried to dry up the town in 1893, Charleston's saloon-keepers, city council, municipal court judges, and citizenry, including the aristocracy, more or less said, "You betcha, Ben," and turned a blind eye to the whole business.

The "blind tigers" thrived. These were the same old places, only now the saloon-keepers paid protection money to city police and state liquor agents. Any raids made were pro forma, usually coordinated with the saloon.

Most of Charleston, then and now, believes the role of government police forces is to prevent crime, not sin. When federal prohibition came along in 1919, Charleston and its "blind tigers" ignored that too.

So, by the time Charleston's city fathers decided during the 1920s to officially promote tourism in "America's most historic city," there already was a core of regulars visiting the port city to drink, and perhaps to commit other acts, away from hometown eyes.

CHARLESTON SHE-CRAB SOUP

This recipe calls for a *she*-crab, as opposed to a *he*-crab, because traditionally it included roe. It is illegal now to catch female crabs in the spring, when they have roe, but it is possible to buy crab roe. Most restaurants use cooked egg yolks instead.

2 cups white crabmeat

1 qt. milk

$^1/_4$ cup roe or 2 cooked egg yokes

$^1/_2$ cup cream, whipped

$^1/_4$ lb. butter

1 tbs. flour

Few drops onion juice

$^1/_2$ tsp. Worcestershire sauce

Mace, salt, pepper to taste

4 tbs. dry sherry

Melt butter and blend in flour. Add milk, crabmeat, roe, and all seasonings, except sherry. Cook slowly 20 min. over hot water. Pour $^1/_2$ tbs. warmed sherry into individual bowls. Add soup. Top each bowl with a serving of whipped cream (milk or half and half can be substituted). Serve piping hot.

A chef prepares a portion of she-crab soup. (Photo by Lyle Lawson)

SWEETGRASS BASKETS

In South Carolina, sweetgrass basketry was first practiced in slave quarters by West African women accustomed to weaving grass baskets at home. In the Carolinas they used sweetgrass—not to be confused with the cord grass, spartina—a long-stemmed plant which once grew plentifully in the Sea Island and mainland marshes from South Carolina into north Florida.

Basketmakers coiled sweetgrass with strips of leaves from the palmetto tree and with pine straw from longleaf pines. (Coiling is a process of sewing or stitching, once done with a bone, now with a metal spoon handle.)

Today sweetgrass baskets are becoming scarce and valuable. Fewer people make them—basketmakers once numbered about 1,200, now it's closer to 200—and the supply of sweetgrass has diminished due to development. An attempt to renew the supply is underway on James Island in the suburbs of Charleston, financed by the Agricultural Society of South Carolina (founded 1785) as well as the Sea Grant Consortium and the Historic Charleston Foundation.

"Basket ladies" today are almost exclusively African-American women, who display their skills and sell their wares in roadside stands along US 17 east of Mt. Pleasant. In Charleston, they are found at the Old City Market (Market and East Bay streets) and "the Four Corners of the Law" at Broad and Meeting streets. One of the most well known is Mary Jane Manigault, a 1984 National Heritage Fellow.

A craftswoman prepares the foundation for a sweetgrass basket.
(Photo by Lyle Lawson)

Boat tours to Fort Sumter and through the fort leave frequently each day from docks at the Battery. Fort Moultrie on Sullivan's Island is also open to the public.

■ OUTSIDE CHARLESTON

In addition to the plantations along the Ashley River (described in "COASTAL PLANTATIONS"), there are other sites near the city of Charleston worth seeing. Fine beaches, the Cape Romain National Wildlife Refuge, and the Francis Marion National Forest are all located outside of the city.

■ BEACHES

Three hundred years before George Gershwin wrote "Summer time, and the living is easy..." savvy beach-goers from the Bohicket tribe of Native Americans were summering at the ocean near Charleston. Their regular camping destination was **Folly Beach,** just south of Charleston Harbor's mouth.

Gershwin himself stayed at Folly during the 1920s while writing his hit musical *Porgy and Bess.* During the 1930s and '40s, Folly's Pier Pavilion and Atlantic Boardwalk drew big crowds and big bands such as Tommy Dorsey, Artie Shaw, Harry James, Guy Lombardo, and Vaughn Monroe.

Today, Folly Beach is elbow-to-elbow with an eclectic mix of old and new single-family houses, small apartment and condo complexes, a few motels, and a permanent population of about 1,000 which swells during the summer. It also is an East Coast surfing mecca.

To reach Folly Beach from Charleston, take the James Island bridge and expressway (SC 30) from Calhoun Street to SC 171, which crosses James Island, a residential suburb, and leads to Folly.

Charleston's other suburban, island beach communities are north of the harbor entrance on Sullivan's Island and Isle of Palms. All three islands have beach houses for rent through local realtors. (See "Accommodations" in "PRACTICAL INFORMATION.")

Edgar Allan Poe spent 13 months during 1827–28 on **Sullivan's Island,** where he absorbed images he later used in his blood-curdling short story of buried pirate treasure, "The Gold-Bug."

Poe, then 18, was in an army artillery unit assigned to Fort Moultrie, guarding the entrance to the harbor. He described Sullivan's Island in the story: "This island is

George and Ira Gershwin's presentation photo to DuBose Heyward upon completion of Porgy and Bess. *Gershwin wrote a portion of the hit musical while staying at Folly Beach. (South Carolina Historical Society, Charleston)*

a very singular one. It consists of little else than the sea sand, and is about three miles long . . . . It is separated from the mainland by a scarcely perceptible creek, oozing its way through a wilderness of reeds and slime, a favorite resort of the marsh-hen."

Charlestonians began building summer homes on Sullivan's in the nineteenth century. Neighboring **Isle of Palms** began to develop as a family summer-house beach after World War II. Today, its Wild Dunes Beach and Racquet Club rental condos, golf course, and marina add to the vacation facilities.

Sullivan's and Isle of Palms are in the other, northeast, direction from Charleston via US 17 and the Cooper River bridge. The route passes through historic **Mt. Pleasant,** where colonial Charlestonians first began summering around 1700. Turn right off US 17 just beyond the bridge onto SC 703, passing by Mt. Pleasant's Shem Creek, where a small shrimp boat fleet and a number of charter deepsea fishing boats are based, and where some of the area's most popular seafood restaurants are located.

DIGGING FOR TREASURE ON SULLIVAN'S ISLAND

*I*dug eagerly, and now and then caught myself actually looking, with something that very much resembled expectation, for the fancied treasure, the vision of which had demented my unfortunate companion. At a period when such vagaries of thought most fully possessed me, and when we had been at work perhaps an hour and a half, we were again interrupted by the violent howlings of the dog. His uneasiness, in the first instance, had been, evidently, but the result of playfulness or caprice, but he now assumed a bitter and serious tone. Upon Jupiter's again attempting to muzzle him, he made a furious resistance, and, leaping into the hole, tore up the mould frantically with his claws. In a few seconds he had uncovered a mass of human bones, forming two complete skeletons, and intermingled with several buttons of metal, and what appeared to be the dust of decayed woollen. One or two strokes of a spade upturned the blade of a large Spanish knife, and, as we dug farther, three or four loose pieces of gold and silver coin came to light . . . . We now worked in good earnest, and never did I pass ten minutes of more intense excitement. During this interval we had fairly unearthed an oblong chest of wood . . . . It was firmly secured by bands of wrought iron, riveted and forming a kind of open trellis-work over the whole . . . . Luckily, the sole fastenings of the lid consisted of two sliding bolts. These we drew back—trembling and panting with anxiety. In an instant, a treasure of incalculable value lay gleaming before us. As the rays of the lanterns fell within the pit, there flashed upwards a glow and a glare, from a confused heap of gold and of jewels, that absolutely dazzled our eyes.

"What are we to make of the skeletons found in the hole?"

This is a question I am no more able to answer than yourself. There seems, however, only one plausible way of accounting for them—and yet it is dreadful to believe in such atrocity as my suggestion would imply. It is clear that Kidd—if Kidd indeed secreted this treasure, which I doubt not—it is clear that he must have had assistance in the labor. But this labor concluded, he may have thought it expedient to remove all participants in his secret. Perhaps a couple of blows with a mattock were sufficient, while his coadutors were busy in the pit; perhaps it required a dozen—who shall tell?"

—Edgar Allan Poe, "The Gold-Bug," 1843

With a rental boat from the Wild Dunes marina, it is a short trip via the Intracoastal Waterway or along the beach past Dewees Island (under development for private homes) to **Capers Island,** a state Heritage Preserve. Capers' long beach is usually deserted, but overnight camping is available by permit.

There are no facilities on Capers, fishing is allowed only from the beach, and campers should bring their own water, food, and charcoal or firewood. Pets are not allowed. Reservations should be made a week in advance: S.C. Department of Natural Resources, Fort Johnson, P.O. Box 12559, Charleston, SC 29422. Phone 762-5043.

One of the nation's largest nesting grounds for sea turtles exists on Cape Island.

■ CAPE ROMAIN NATIONAL WILDLIFE REFUGE

One of the most pristine stretches of South Carolina's Atlantic coast is 30 miles northeast of Charleston in the Cape Romain National Wildlife Refuge. Access is tightly controlled to the refuge's 60,000 acres of open water and saltwater marsh and 4,000 acres of high land, but day visitors will find the trip worth it.

Cape Island on the northeast boundary of the refuge is one of the nation's largest nesting grounds for sea turtles, and **Marsh Island** in Bulls Bay is a rookery for brown pelicans. Fishing, birding, and hiking trails are available on **Bull Island.** The Seewee tribe harvested oysters and clams here in pre-colonial times, and visitors today can do the same.

Access to the refuge is by boat only. Look for refuge headquarters signs on US 17 at Awendaw. Private boats can be launched at high tide only from Moore's

IS CHARLESTON DISASTER PRONE?

Apocalyptic events (other than losing "The War") from pestilence to fire, earthquakes to hurricanes, are as much a part of Charleston's history as the "south of Broad" single house. With all its bad luck, the city's survival is a wonder.

PESTILENCE

1698   Smallpox epidemic kills 300.

1699   "Swamp fever," or malaria, kills about 180.

1738   Smallpox and whooping cough kill 10 percent of the colonial port's population.

1760   Smallpox epidemic kills nearly 730.

1918   Spanish flu kills 450 in Charleston.

FIRE

1740   On December 18, fire destroys about 300 buildings in four hours.

1861   On December 11, fire destroys 575 homes, five churches, and numerous commercial and government buildings.

EARTHQUAKES

Charleston is in a little-known but high-risk earthquake zone centered beneath the Ashley River showplace, Middleton Place. More than 300 earthquakes, almost all of them of little consequence, have been recorded in the area since early colonial settlement.

1886   On August 31, a major earthquake kills nearly 100 persons, leaves hundreds homeless, damages or destroys 2,000 buildings. Regarded as the most powerful earthquake on record for the eastern United States.

HURRICANES

Then, there were four major hurricanes (so far).

1752   On September 15, a hurricane puts Charles Town under nine feet of water. Within a 30-mile radius of the city, plantations are ruined and valuable pine forests are flattened.

1885   On August 25, a hurricane kills 21. Ninety percent of Charleston's private homes are damaged or destroyed.

1893   On August 27, the worst hurricane on record kills four in Charleston, and nearly 2,000 on the Sea Islands from Charleston south to Hilton Head.

1989 On September 21, Hurricane Hugo hits the coast between Charleston and McClellanville. McClellanville is almost leveled, much of Francis Marion National Forest is flattened, and 26 are killed. More than $4 billion in damage reported in the state. Remarkably, Charleston's historic district suffers little damage.

St. Philip's Church was extensively damaged during the great earthquake of 1886. (South Carolina Historical Society, Charleston)

Landing at refuge headquarters on the Intracoastal Waterway. A public ferry from Moore's Landing takes day visitors (no vehicles) to Bull Island at 9 A.M. Tuesday, Friday, and Saturday, returning at 4 P.M. No overnight camping is permitted within the refuge. For details, call the refuge headquarters: 928-3368.

■ **FRANCIS MARION NATIONAL FOREST**
About 40 miles north of Charleston via US 52, this site comprises 250,000 acres of swamps, vast oaks and pines, and little lakes thought to have been formed by meteors.

Home to Indians for 10,000 years, the area was settled by the English (primarily in Charleston) and French Huguenots (on plantations along the Santee River). One of the latter, Gen. Francis Marion, "the Swamp Fox," battled British Col. Banastre Tarleton in the forest during the Revolutionary War.

After the Civil War, the land was bought up by lumber companies, who established logging camps and laid down railroads for transporting timber to Charleston and other cities. The lumber companies in turn sold the land to the government in the 1930s, and the area was declared a National Forest in 1936. Today, the forest encompasses numerous campsites as well as a few small towns.

Buck Hall, located just off US 17, is the largest and most developed campground in the forest. It includes full facilities and is the only campsite for which there is a fee. The **Guilliard Lake campground** is in the Guilliard Lake Scenic Area on the Santee River. There are also **"hunt camps,"** unimproved camping areas which do not require a fee. Among these are Elmwood, Canal, Halfway Creek, and Honey Hill. In addition, camping in the general forest is allowed with a permit, obtainable at the two district offices (see below).

Huger Recreation Area is open for day use only, and is a good place for picnicking. It has a boat launch on the nearby creek, and is one of the most popular spots in the forest.

The Wambaw District office of the Francis Marion National Forest is located in McClellanville, at 887-3257. The Witherbee District office is in Moncks Corner, at 336-3248. Permits, needed only if visitors plan to camp in the forest outside of camping areas, can be obtained at these two locations.

Brown pelicans are one of many species of birdlife which may be seen along the shoreline of the Cape Romain National Wildlife Refuge.

MYRTLE BEACH
AND GRAND STRAND

MORE VISITORS COME TO SOUTH CAROLINA'S Grand Strand than to any other vacation destination on the eastern seaboard of the nation, with two exceptions; Atlantic City's gambling casinos, where dreams of the fast buck beckon, and Florida's Walt Disney World, where suspended disbelief replaces dreams. Most of these visitors are not travelers exploring new places but vacationers looking for things to do.

Officially, the Strand (meaning shore) begins at Winyah Bay and Georgetown in old rice plantation country and runs northeast for 60 miles to Little River Neck, on the North Carolina state line. Unofficially, but perhaps more realistically, the Grand Strand is Myrtle Beach, heart and soul of one of the nation's more eclectic places.

More than a dozen beach towns and scores more communities are packed to capacity during the height of the summer season at the Grand Strand. The town of Pawleys Island, the colonial and antebellum summer retreat of plantation families, anchors down the south end of the Strand. Little River, on the north end, is a town of wall-to-wall, all-you-can-eat seafood restaurants. What's in between Pawleys and Little River is a hodgepodge, including Myrtle Beach, a sprawl of boardwalks, arcades, amusement parks, roller coasters, cotton candy, candy apples, and more waterslides and miniature golf courses than trees.

A bit further north, around the town of North Myrtle Beach, there are more real golf courses than any single duffer could play in a month.

Just north of the golfers' heaven, there is Ocean Drive Beach—OD to the cognoscenti. Here, for almost a half century and still going strong, generations of teenagers learned the steps to, and picked up the aloof, bored, Ms. Cool facial deadpan style of South Carolina's official state dance, the Shag, usually in an open-air dance hall trembling with testosterone and boogie beats, smelling of Shalimar, Schlitz, and sweat.

During the high school and college spring break vacations, and all summer long, there are thousands of greased hard-bodies broiling on the sand or by the motel pool, and cruising Ocean Boulevard and US 17.

There are venues for that shop-'til-you-drop state of mind in outlet malls and basic, ordinary shopping malls. There are huge country-music emporiums with shows, dinners, and star performers. There are fishing piers extending more than 1,000 feet into the ocean, and fleets of charter and party fishing boats. There are RV parks right on the dune line, without a shade tree in sight, and belly-bombing fast food outlets without cease.

There is a beach, too, sometimes out of sight, just on the other side of the row of high-rise time-share and retirement condos which thickens every year.

In short, there are several hundred thousand persons in the summer, and several score thousand during fall, winter, and spring, who appear to be having one hell of a time along the Grand Strand, and it seems likely many of them actually are.

■ EARLY VISITORS

While rice, indigo, and cotton plantations were creating lavish wealth in Georgetown, Charleston, the Sea Islands, and along Low Country rivers, the eastern corner of colonial and antebellum South Carolina was a place most settlers avoided. The Great Swamp kept them away.

A watery morass of tupelo gum and cypress made the region nearly impenetrable. Rice plantations spread up the Waccamaw River only as far north of Georgetown as today's Brookgreen Gardens (see "COASTAL PLANTATIONS" chapter), and planter families summered on the beach only as far north as Pawleys.

No river empties into the Atlantic Ocean along the Grand Strand as rivers do elsewhere on South Carolina's coast. Without river-borne sediments, no coastal islands other than Pawleys (which essentially is just a big sand dune) were created. The **Atlantic Intracoastal Waterway,** inland a few miles from the beach, runs

---

BEASTS OF PREY ON THE SANTEE

*W*e were awaken'd with the dismall'st and most hideous Noise that ever pierc'd my Ears . . . our Indian Pilot (who knew these Parts very well) acquainted us that it was customary to hear such Musick along that Swamp-Side, there being endless numbers of Panthers, Tygers, Wolves, and other Beasts of Prey, which make this Swamp their Abode . . . making this frightful Ditty 'till Day appears.

—Explorer John Lawson on the Santee, 1701

almost 30 miles from Little River Inlet south to the Waccamaw River in a stretch known as the **Pine Island Cut**. The waterway and the Waccamaw today make it appear the entire Grand Strand is a 60-mile-long island, but the waterway was not dug until World War II.

Colonial settlers, most of them one-mule, Scotch-Irish farmers, first trickled into this area from North Carolina. They built small cabins and houses, farmed a few acres, established a settlement at Little River, and were ignored or forgotten by the rest of the region. A French Huguenot planter, Peter Horry, and a Charleston entrepreneur, Robert Conway, settled in the area during the Revolutionary War. Horry County (pronounced 'ore-ee'), which includes Myrtle Beach, was named for the former, and the county seat, Conway, for the latter. Both men became large landowners, largely of swamps.

Until the 1890s, Horry County remained mainly in the hands of small farmers and the Great Swamp. During that decade, F. G. Burroughs of Conway began timbering the swamp. He bought land as he cleared his path, built a lumber mill at Pine Island, and laid railroad tracks to the sea—the Conway Seashore Railroad —

OCEAN FOREST HOTEL, MYRTLE BEACH, S. C., "AMERICA'S FINEST STRAND"

670 MILES SOUTH OF NEW YORK, 735 MILES NORTH OF MIAMI   5B-H3:

The Ocean Forest Hotel, built in 1926, was Myrtle Beach's first grand hotel.
(South Carolina Historical Society, Charleston)

to ship his wood and turpentine to Conway, and from there down the Waccamaw to Georgetown.

The seashore terminus of the railroad was called New Town for a few years, until 1900, when Burroughs renamed it **Myrtle Beach,** for the evergreen shrub with small, dark leaves and scented, white flowers once abundant along the shore, but now found mostly in Myrtle Beach State Park. Farm families and small-town storekeepers began riding Burroughs' lumber train to Myrtle Beach, and in the summer of 1901, he opened the resort's first hotel, the Sea Side Inn, as well as a commissary and pavilion. A sandy dirt road from Conway to the lumber village of Socastee was extended to the beach in 1914, and a few more farmers and shopkeepers began vacationing at Myrtle Beach. Most of them pitched tents on the beach and in the dunes. (There are more than 10,000 campsites in public or private parks along the Strand today.)

Then, in 1926, a cotton mill magnate from the Piedmont, John T. Woodside of Greenville, led a group of investors in building a huge, grand hotel—the Ocean Forest—at Myrtle Beach. Woodside and his associates bought most of the town, laid out streets, and began selling lots. It was a

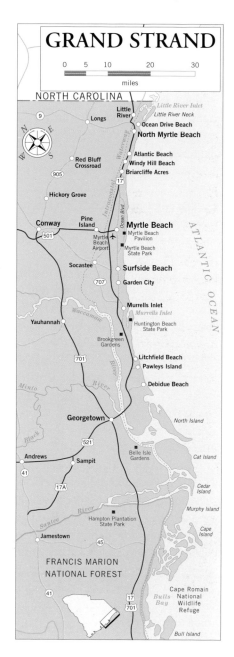

banner year for the Strand. Beach communities were founded, incorporated, and began developing with small inns, casual seafood cafes, and beach houses at Garden City just south of Myrtle Beach and at Ocean Drive and Cherry Grove to the north. (The Ocean Forest Hotel is no longer there.)

The Great Depression of the 1930s, then World War II, halted the boom launched by Woodside until the post-war boom of the 1950s. The Strand, however, never severed its Greenville connections. Its visitors were primarily vacationing textile executives and cotton-mill hands from Greenville and other upstate communities until the 1970s. Even today, the daily Greenville newspaper, published 242 miles from Myrtle Beach, includes the "Grand Strand Forecast"— but that of no other beach—in its weather report.

The Strand also became known as "the beach" for much of North Carolina, since it is as close or closer than any other seashore for all of North Carolina west of Raleigh.

In the late 1960s and early 1970s, Myrtle Beach and the Grand Strand were put on the national map (serendipitously or disastrously, depending upon one's point of view) by a snowstorm, the Middle East oil embargo, and a golf visionary. After that, the summer regulars and small-town ambience became just a burp in an all-you-can-eat saturnalia.

In 1967, the late George "Buster" Bryan, a Myrtle Beach businessman, envisioned his hometown becoming a mecca for golf. He built two courses, no big deal so far, then came up with the clincher—packaged golf-weekend vacations and "golfotels," providing special lodging just for golfers. Bryan predicted golfers would come between Labor Day and late spring, when Myrtle Beach and the Strand were like a ghost town.

A few winters later, a snowstorm closed the famous golf courses 100 miles up US 501 at Pinehurst and Southern Pines, so the North Carolina resorts sent their vacationing golfers to Myrtle Beach. For a few days, golfers filled hotels, restaurants, and courses; and the rest is history.

At the same time during these winters, Canadians and residents of the Middle Atlantic and New England states traditionally jammed Interstate 95 for the drive south to the Florida sun. In 1973, as the oil embargo sent gasoline prices soaring, winter travelers checked their roadmaps for destinations closer to home and discovered that by hanging a left off I-95 just as it enters South Carolina, they could drive to the Strand.

Summer no longer was the only season.

■ BIG BOOM AT MYRTLE BEACH

Bolted to the planks in chrome loneliness on the fishing pier at Myrtle Beach State Park, at the southern city limits of Myrtle Beach, is a quarter-in-the-slot for a 60-second-view, binocular machine, a hardy leftover of 1950s tourism technology. Through the swiveling lenses the beachfront view is balcony-to-balcony, belly-to-belly, high-rise condominiums. To the south, in Surfside Beach and Garden City, construction cranes 15 stories tall erect more new nests.

Development, much like some marriages, can be good or bad, depending upon where you come from and how long you plan to stay. Still, a place must be getting crowded when the Federal Aviation Administration has to warn banner planes (flying low and slow up and down the beach trailing banners: "Bikini Contest Trader Bubba 9 Tonight") to watch out for parasail riders ($20 a tourist, sign the release form). And warn *both* groups to stay away from the flight paths of scheduled jetliners using the Myrtle Beach Airport.

In a major, national-map, family-vacation, oceanside resort such as Myrtle Beach, the 30,000 or so year-round residents come to expect and adjust to a steady 10,000 to 20,000 vacationers from September into April. They even deal with 350,000 visitors, more than 10 times the locals' numbers, during the summers.

What seems to have caught Myrtle Beach and the Grand Strand by surprise is how many visitors came and never left.

From 1980 to 1990, the population of Horry County increased by 42 percent, a phenomenal rate of growth, the fastest in the state. Nearly 150,000 permanent residents now live in the county, and an estimated two-thirds of them live in the narrow strip between the Atlantic Ocean and the Intracoastal Waterway on the Grand Strand. By the year 2020, that population is predicted to more than double, and Myrtle Beach alone should have more permanent residents than all of Horry County does today.

Before the 1970s, nearly everyone who retired in Horry County had also spent most, usually all, of his or her life here. Now, 20,000 residents of the county are age 65 or older, and half of them live east of the waterway on the Strand. All through the year, older men wearing earphones connected to metal detectors patrol the beach, their trousers rolled. Classified ads in the local newspaper ask for part-time motel desk clerks and say, "Ideal for retirees." Nearly anything seems better than Lake Erie in January.

Within Myrtle Beach, where summer traffic backs up for miles on both business

and bypass routes US 17, there are hopes for an eight-mile monorail transit system through the heart of the north-south, linear city. Soon a 28-mile bypass will take traffic from the North Myrtle Beach area inland over the waterway, around Conway, to US 501, the feeder highway from I-95 to the Strand, avoiding Myrtle Beach entirely.

In the course of this big boom, Horry County became a place of two sharply differing personalities. Drive over the waterway and 15 miles inland, and the rhythms of life are not those of the winter and summer tourist season, but of spring planting and late summer harvesting. Horry's farm production ranks second in value among the state's counties. Two-thirds of its $72 million crop comes from the sale of tobacco.

Until the boom, men in bib overalls driving tractors on farms around hamlets named Cool Spring, Galivants Ferry, and Hickory Grove had as much influence in county politics and government as the restaurant and motel owners of Myrtle Beach. Now, that $72 million crop and the farming way of life pales compared with a $2 billion-a-year economy created by more than 11 million visitors a year.

Egos get riled, sensibilities bruised, and disparaging words exchanged, when, for example, the county council and the Myrtle Beach city council feud over what to do with **Myrtle Beach Air Force Base.** Built during World War II between business and bypass US 17 just south of Myrtle Beach, the base was the county's biggest single employer until it closed in 1992 in the nationwide wave of defense cutbacks. The base once had a fighter wing of 70 jets, and its last squadron of A-10 "Warthog" anti-tank planes flew 1,492 combat missions during the Gulf War.

The jets are mothballed in an Arizona desert now, and the future of the air base could take years to settle. It doubles as the Grand Strand's commercial airport, and the county commission, whose members run the airport, want to expand it. Myrtle Beach politicians see no need for that—most of the Strand's visitors arrive by car—and want to sell or lease pieces of the base to light industry, a proposed mammoth theme park, and a retirement village.

The local squabble seems irrelevant to the millions of visitors already driving in from elsewhere, wondering when the fields of tobacco end and the smell of salt air begins. Few people feel as personally about land as do farmers, and few view land with such dispassion as do developers.

The beaches of the Grand Strand are now among the
most developed on the entire Eastern Seaboard.

"Spanish Galleon" is billed as one of the area's top "Shaggin'" venues.

■ COUNTRY MUSIC

There is something about country music, unlike most other kinds of music, that makes most people either like it a lot or not one bit. It touches the heart or grates on the nerves, and almost no one seems to be neutral about it.

Mostly, it makes me chuckle. Lyrics lamenting the loss of "her" to my best friend, both of whom are making the babies we should have, while I'm getting so drunk in this bar I'll probably lose my job, and wouldn't care except my dog ran off and my pickup truck needs tires, bring to mind the old saying: Get a life!

Today, a number of country music theaters are open in Myrtle Beach and on the Strand, plus a **dinner theater** featuring "a horse racing, whip cracking, wagon busting good time," a creation of Dolly Parton's Dollywood Productions. Performed in huge, new auditoriums and theaters, country music is bringing a new life to old Myrtle Beach.

In retrospect, country music seems to be a natural for Myrtle Beach. The golf complexes around North Myrtle Beach, and the social airs, real or imagined, of Pawleys and DeBordieu, attract mostly upscale visitors. Myrtle Beach, however, always has been a blue-collar family resort of two-week vacationers driving campers, cooking their own meals, and listening to "The Grand Ole Opry" on the radio.

Until 1986 there was little vacationers could do together, as a family, once the sun set. That was the year Calvin Gilmore, an entrepreneur from the Ozarks of Missouri and frequent vacationer at Myrtle Beach, opened his 2,200-seat **Carolina Opry.**

Some of the biggest names in country music joined in what Gilmore began. Gilmore himself followed his Carolina Opry with the 1,000-seat **Dixie Jubilee,** in North Myrtle Beach, and the 1,000-seat **Southern Country Nights** in Surfside Beach. The mega-group Alabama, which once played for tips in Myrtle Beach nightclubs, opened the **Alabama Theater** at Barefoot Landing in North Myrtle Beach. **The Gatlin Brothers** opened their theater in Myrtle Beach in 1994, and almost every week another rumor hits Myrtle Beach about another country music star said to be following the crowds: Lee Greenwood, Garth Brooks, Mel Tillis, Crystal Gale, Conway Twitty, Travis Tritt, Barbara Mandrell, and Mickey Gilley among them.

A country rock band at work in the Alabama Theater.

GRAND STRAND MUSIC VENUES

■ MUSIC THEATERS

Alabama Theater. 4750 US 17 South, North Myrtle Beach; (800) 342-2262. Celebrity concerts each week and a musical variety show six nights a week. Special appearances throughout the year by owners, the musical group Alabama.

Carolina Opry. 82nd Ave., North Myrtle Beach; 238-8888. The first in a trend of Grand Strand music theaters, this popular music hall hosts a talented cast of country-western singers and dancers.

Dixie Jubilee. 7101 Main St., North Myrtle Beach; 238-8888. Variety shows featuring country, rock 'n' roll, bluegrass, and gospel music.

Dixie Stampede. N. junction of US 17 and US 17 Business. 497-9700. Dolly Parton's dinner theater presents music, comedy, rodeo, Wild West performances, and a four-course, country-style meal.

Southern Country Nights. US 17 Business, Surfside Beach; 238-8888. Musical and comedy performances nightly. Sunday nights headline Mark Twain.

■ NIGHTLIFE

The Afterdeck. US 17, Restaurant Row; 449-1550. An open-air club with live music, dancing, and comedy.

Atlantis Nightlife. Hwy. 501; 448-4200. Three clubs in one: a fast-paced dance floor, live bands and entertainment, and a quiet patio lounge.

The Coquina Club. Best Western Landmark Resort Hotel, 1501 S. Ocean Blvd.; 448-9441. Host to shaggin' on some nights.

Crazy Zach's. Hillside and Second Ave., North Myrtle Beach; 249-2404. The biggest club on the strand, with Top-40 music and multiple bars.

Duck's. 229 Main St., North Myrtle Beach; 249-3858.

Fat Harold's. 212 Main St., North Myrtle Beach; 249-5779

Sandals. Sands Ocean Club; 449-6461. Live entertainment in a lounge.

Spanish Galleon. 100 Main St., North Myrtle Beach; 249-1047. Shaggin' also offered, some nights.

Studebaker's. 2000 N. Kings Hwy.; 626-3855

None of this country music boomlet is ever likely to usurp Nashville, but the Grand Strand, and especially Myrtle Beach, is enjoying visions of Branson, Missouri, which has at least 34 theaters, more seats than Broadway, and a steady stream of country music customers, despite being in the middle of nowhere, without a beach. The Strand is already considered the Number Three locale in the nation for country music, behind Nashville and Branson.

■ SHOPPING AND DINING

For all the excitement over country music in Myrtle Beach in recent years, two old Grand Strand standbys still draw crowds by the thousands. One is eating and the other is shopping.

A section of US 17 just north of the Myrtle Beach city limits has been known locally for decades as **Restaurant Row.** The two-mile strip no longer has the best nor the most restaurants on the Strand, but it has some good ones (Cagney's and Gullyfield among them).

The specialty in this area is seafood, and some favorite Low Country dishes are she-crab soup, various deep-fried or sauteed entrees, and crab cakes. Many restaurants offer all-you-can-eat buffets at reasonable prices, and some combine dining with entertainment.

The huge **Waccamaw Pottery/Outlet Park** on the waterway and US 501 just outside Myrtle Beach dwarfs everything else on the Strand. The complex consists of three large malls covering 500 acres and drawing more than five million shoppers, browsers, and curiosity-seekers a year.

On US 17 at the turnoff to Pawleys Island, there are nearly 20 shops and boutiques in a complex centered around the original **Pawleys Island Hammock Shop,** where locals still make the rope hammocks.

Barefoot Landing at North Myrtle Beach is an unusual outdoor mall on the waterway which features upscale boutiques. Other Grand Strand shopping centers are Myrtle Beach Square Mall, Inlet Square at Murrells, Briarcliffe Mall, and the Galleria along US 17 north of Myrtle Beach.

SHAGGIN'

On New Year's Day, 1740, at a colonial tavern near Cedar Creek, not far from what today is Ocean Drive Beach, George Whitefield, a fiery Methodist disciple, swept down upon a group of dancers. The preacher told the dancers they were committing a sin. The tavern patrons stopped dancing. The preacher baptized one child, went to bed, and the dancing resumed.

It might be a good thing Whitefield isn't around now. Dancing, especially dancing the shag, just might never stop along the Grand Strand. The dance is a shuffling, four-step hybrid of the Jitterbug and the Lindy Hop, performed to Carolina beach music, which is not at all the same as the music of California's Beach Boys. It's a rhythm and blues sound made famous by songs such as "Give Me Just a Little More Time" and "Sixty-Minute Man."

Teenagers from South and North Carolina began practicing the Shag during spring and summer vacations from school in hangouts along the Strand during the 1950s. There's a shag hangout in every beach community here, from **Ocean Boulevard,** a kind of teenager's Bourbon Street in Myrtle Beach, to the birthplace of the shag, **Ocean Drive Beach.**

At OD, in the legendary shag hangout, The Pad, countless middle-class, white Southerners discovered black rhythm-and-blues bands.

The Pad closed in 1987 after being damaged in a fire. Its remains were demolished in January 1994 as nearly 200 of its old regulars, many now in their 40s and 50s, looked on.

Shaggin', however, remains so popular that it has its own preservation society, the **Society of Stranders,** who gather in other OD and Strand hangouts every April and September, in numbers nearing 10,000 strong, to lay down some steps to the Temptations' original version of "My Girl."

(right) While the young shaggin' set dances freely to the original '50s and '60s upbeat R&B tunes, as well as to updated covers (and sometimes new R&B material) by today's crooners, an older crowd prefers four-stepping with partners to the tried-and-true versions. Here, a couple shags at Fat Harold's.

■ PRINCE GEORGE TRACT

The last major chunk of land on the entire South Carolina coast that was undeveloped, and not part of a state, federal, or privately owned park, refuge, or preserve, was sold for development in 1994. Known as the Prince George tract, its nearly 2,000 acres stretch from the beach to the Waccamaw River just south of Pawleys Island.

Archaeologists found evidence of temporary camps used by passing Native American tribes in pre-colonial times. Hickory, red maple, cypress, gum, and pine trees cover much of the tract, and traces of the **old Kings Highway,** which George Washington rode on his triumphal tour through South Carolina after the Revolutionary War, still can be found on the hilly terrain.

After the Revolution, parts of Waterford and Hagley rice plantations were here. Remnants of steam-powered rice mills remain, and a canal and dike system between the rice mill and river is still intact. There are remains of a boat landing used by passengers between Georgetown and Pawleys.

In 1909, as wealthy Northerners began buying the failed rice plantations for use as hunting preserves and winter retreats, Isaac E. Emerson of Baltimore bought the property and named it **Arcadia Plantation.** It was inherited in 1931 by his grandson, George W. Vanderbilt, son of the industrialist Cornelius Vanderbilt. In 1961, Lucille Vanderbilt Pate inherited the tract.

In 1971, she sold some of the beachfront to developers who built a posh resort they named **DeBordieu Colony,** in part because the local name of that beach — Debidue—didn't sound swell enough to attract buyers. In 1985, some of the DeBordieu developers bought the rest of the Prince George tract from Mrs. Pate for $17.5 million. By 1988, however, both the Prince George project, which never got off the ground, and the DeBordieu Colony fell victim to a Texas savings and loan, and ended up in the hands of the Federal Deposit Insurance Corporation and Resolution Trust Corporation.

DeBordieu was successfully revived. The FDIC put the Prince George tract up for auction, nearly 2,000 acres of the absolute last pristine land on the state's coast. Lips were smacking both near and far.

The Melrose Corporation, one of the developers of Daufuskie Island and Hilton Head, hooked up with the Georgetown County Council. The county and the developers proposed golf courses, hotels, restaurants, and marinas for most of the 2,000 acres, with 250 set aside for a state park. Their bid was $5.7 million, on land appraised at $9.8 million and bought by the FDIC for $12 million.

The plan just might have worked, except the University of South Carolina and its developer partners offered $10.5 million, and a different land-use plan. About 1,300 acres would be set aside as a coastal research center, a habitat for the endangered red-cockaded woodpecker and as protected wetlands, with the rest of the tract cut into lots and sold for houses, to finance the deal.

The university's developer partners are two of the same investors who now run DeBordieu Colony. The luxury lots they're selling are on the beach.

■ PAWLEYS ISLAND

There was a time, not too long gone, when the certain prospect of social ostracization would have stopped even a parvenu from installing air conditioning in a Pawleys Island house. Everyone left their windows open, and what the ocean breeze didn't cool, ceiling fans would.

Families returned year after year, generation to generation, to the same ramshackle cottages and gently dilapidated, two- and three-story old beach homes. Ownership, as well as summer reservations, went through the hands of relatives or friends—the same family got the same month year after year.

They came to the tiny, 3.5-mile-long island for the only amenity it offered: laid-back, simply beyond modern conveniences, relaxation on an unspoiled family beach, without arcades, theme parks, restaurant rows, condo rows, traffic, nightclubs, noise, or even—yes, truly—a golf course.

The permanent islanders, about 100 of them, happily coexisted with the 4,000 or so mid-spring to early fall visitors, most of them regular renters. Everyone purred, and why not? Everyone had the same plan, which was to make no plans. The day's options included the uncrowded beach, crabbing in the tidal creeks of the saltwater marsh separating Pawleys from the mainland, a big midday Carolina dinner of, perhaps, fresh broiled flounder, corn fritters, yams, biscuits, lima beans, and ice tea, and a nap on a cool, yawning porch in one of the wide, and now-famous, Pawleys Island rope hammocks.

To the north, Myrtle Beach and the Grand Strand went commercial, the Pawleys regulars told each other with a shudder. No one ever drove up US 17 to see it. To the south, there were the spiffy new golf course resorts such as Kiawah, and the pressure-cooker sea island of Hilton Head, and nobody ever went there either. Nobody cared to see a million-dollar mansion on the beach.

The Pawleys regulars were (let's face it) a little smug about Pawleys, about the beach traditions begun two centuries ago by wealthy rice plantation families. Several years ago, one of them began handing out bumper stickers: "Pawleys Island, Arrogantly Shabby."

You could cut the reverse snobbism with a knife. You also had to admit it: Pawleys was all that it crowed about.

The good news is, a lot of Pawleys still is. The bad news is—parvenus moved in, built houses they wanted others to notice, and Julian Kelly, a year-round resident and the mayor, as well as a wit, had a new set of bumper stickers printed: "Arrogantly Shabby," with the "shabby" X-ed out.

There is air-conditioning in the showplaces erected by the new crowd. There is, let it be said, a creeping element of DeBordieu on Pawleys.

The Pawleys year-rounders and property owners, most of whom live elsewhere, voted to incorporate the island in 1985 to prevent Grand Strand commercialism in any form, from luxury condos to boutique mini-malls. The only commercial property on the island today remains an aging, small condo and two small, almost historic beach inns, the **Pelican** and the **Sea View.** A duplex is the only

Hurricane Hugo caused massive destruction along the coast from
Charleston to Myrtle Beach in 1989.

new multi-family housing town zoning ordinances permit. Even soft drink machines are banned.

The plan, the only plan ever accepted by the islanders, seemed to be working. And then, in 1989, Hurricane Hugo's outer reaches hit Pawleys. Hugo sliced a new inlet through Pawleys, and leveled 90 houses, most of them ramshackle cottages in the south end known as "Bird's Nest."

This happened to Pawleys before, in 1822, when only the rice plantations families and their house slaves summered on the island. The difference this time was that Pawleys had become one of the most prized possessions in the pantheon of the American Dream: "beachfront property," at roughly $350,000 a lot.

On those lots were constructed beachfront homes valued at about $500,000 each, plus the lot, and in rebuilding from Hugo, what was the "Bird's Nest" became a peacock's strut. That's when Mayor Kelly had the new bumper stickers printed, because as it turned out, the "parvenus" who built the new houses were the same island regulars who'd been living there before!

Barry McCall, magistrate of the island and year-rounder, suspects the protective motives which led to the island's incorporating itself into a town, might have altered the spirit of what was supposed to be protected.

An aerial of Murrells Inlet, home of crime novelist Mickey Spillane.

The magistrate told an interviewer: "It's regressed from what it was 20, 30 years ago. There was a bowling alley, trampolines, miniature golf, raft rentals, the Pavilion. Now, it's so residential people have become possessive of their property. It never used to bother us when young people parked in our yard to get to the beach."

■ MURRELLS INLET

Murrells Inlet, halfway between Pawleys and Myrtle Beach, is a holdout of feisty individualists, including two-fisted, blonde-bombshell-loving, commie-hating, private-eyeing, Mike Hammer-creating, detective-novel-writing Mickey Spillane, and some much tougher women, all battling the spread of commercial development.

When Mickey Spillane married Jane at the old and legendary restaurant **Oliver's Lodge,** his words were, "I do; let's eat."

More than likely, none of the wedding guests, at least none who call "The Inlet" home, thought that at all strange, probably including the bride. Murrells Inlet always has been, and still mostly is, about seafood, the skill, hard work, pleasure and secret recipes of cooking it, and the slow, grinning pleasure of eating seafood prepared by masters.

There are more than 40 restaurants in Murrells Inlet today: Mexican, Japanese, Italian, Cajun, and seafood. Until World War II, when the air base was built 10 miles north, Oliver's was the only one, a boarding house for weekenders who went charter fishing with Capt. Mack Oliver and then feasted in the dining room.

Except for a screen porch built during the 1960s, Oliver's hasn't changed. The long, old, swaybacked joggling board first used for crossing ditches on rice plantations is still a seat on the porch for diners waiting to be seated inside. Oliver's does occasionally make adjustments, not changes, such as the time the menu listed something called "Scallops Leon," a mushroom, shrimp, and scallops combination served in a cream sauce over pastry, a regrettable surrender to the unfathomable customers who think fresh seafood is eaten with sauce.

There have been a few other, probably inevitable, changes at The Inlet.

The Murrells Inlet Historic District, locally known as "Little Marion," isn't there anymore. Dozens of families from the farm town of **Marion,** about 60 miles inland on US 501, once summered at The Inlet and built their cottages in the same neighborhood. Jane Spillane's was one of them.

There were about 20 white clapboard summer cottages with large screen porches in the neighborhood, most of them overlooking the tidal creeks and saltwater marshes which gave The Inlet its name, and led to the creation of a fleet of commercial and charter fishing boats.

Hurricane Hugo damaged or destroyed most of the old summer places, and when the neighborhood was rebuilt, fancier, bigger, and pricier homes replaced "Little Marion." The only old summer cottage left is the Bates house. The Marionites, the kitchen crew at Oliver's, and anyone else who wanted to, also used to go

SALTWATER FISHING

"Snagging lip (stuffed, baked flounder) does not come from the cabbage patch."

Every day of the year, in one of humanity's more fervent displays of optimism, saltwater anglers are out there, surf casting from the beach, fishing from piers, prowling the coastal inlets and waterways, and riding deep-sea charter boats far off shore toward the Gulf Stream. (The Gulf Stream flows from 50 to 75 miles off the coast of South Carolina.)

Fleets of the big, shining, chrome charter boats, as well as "party boats" carrying a score or more of strangers, are based in every section of the coast. The major sportfishing marinas for these fleets are at Little River and Murrells Inlet on the Grand Strand; Georgetown and Mt. Pleasant's Shem Creek across the Cooper River from Charleston; and Edisto Beach, Beaufort, and Hilton Head Island in the Sea Islands.

The prime fishing season is from March to November, when the catch includes king and Spanish mackerel, flounder, spot-tail bass, cobia, bluefish, sheepshead, Atlantic croaker—and from June to October, Florida pompano in coastal waters (off piers or in the surf). Spotted sea trout, pinfish, kingfish, and whiting are taken year-round in the same waters. The usual baits are live shrimp, minnows, small live fish, dead shrimp, sand fleas, and cut bait.

Various sport fishing clubs and the state Marine Resource Division have created 34 artificial reefs, sinking cast-off tug boats, landing craft, Liberty ships, barges, and old bridges from 10 to 20 miles offshore to attract fish. Maps with loran coordinates for the artificial reefs, as well as the *Seasonal Guide to Saltwater Fishing in South Carolina,* both published by the South Carolina Marine Resources Division are available from MRD, P.O. Box 12559, Charleston, SC 29422. (803) 795-6350.

Big-game fishing for sailfish, tuna, and shark on charter boats in waters near the Gulf Stream have yielded several world-record catches in recent years. Check local marinas and bait-and-tackle shops for dates and entry information regarding big-game fishing tournaments.

right into The Inlet's tidal creeks for fresh oysters and clams, and there were cinder block, roadside oyster bars serving nothing but oysters, shrimp, and crackers along the highway.

The oyster shacks are gone now, and yellow pollution-warning signs dot the old oyster beds, victims of growth in and around The Inlet.

On the other hand, The Inlet still has plenty of stubborn, salty, independent, and unincorporated individualists determined to keep at least something of the old ways.

In 1991, for example, a proposal was made to merge Murrells Inlet with Garden City and Surfside Beach, just to the north, into a single artificial place to be named South Myrtle Beach. The plan had a precedent in North Myrtle Beach. Before the big boom, there was no such place as North Myrtle Beach; there were Cherry Grove, OD, Crescent, Atlantic, and Windy Hill beaches along the north end of the Strand. When people went there, they went to a place with one of those names. After the boom, a referendum put them all inside an artificial place named North Myrtle Beach.

Jane Spillane, Maxine Oliver Hawkins (who owned Oliver's Lodge), and

While the boom of North Myrtle Beach has attracted the young at heart . . . .

Genevieve "Sister" Peterkin (a retired librarian who grew up in The Inlet and is the daughter-in-law of the novelist Julia Peterkin) drafted a petition against the merger. The three women got 1,400 signatures of property owners agreeing with them, and that was the end of that.

■ STATE PARKS

In the development boom that washed over the Grand Strand, and which shows no signs of slowing, two oases of relative solitude and natural beauty were saved. Simply by entering either Myrtle Beach or Huntington Beach state parks, visitors get a respite from the traffic and noise of hectic beach life.

The Grand Strand, with the exception of some golf courses, is least crowded during the winter. Even in January and February, daytime high temperatures in the upper 60s (F) and low 70s are not uncommon. It's the kind of weather that lures the golfers, and the kind of weather that's perfect for scavenging the beach and hiking the maritime forest at these two parks.

. . . residents of southern Myrtle Beach prefer more reflective pastimes.

The 312-acre **Myrtle Beach State Park,** on business US 17 opposite the airport and old air base, includes about 100 acres of one of the last maritime forests along the Strand. The first state park opened to the public in South Carolina, it offers picnic tables, shelters, camping, playground equipment, cabins, a pool, a 750-foot pier (the Strand's oldest), and a store selling everything one needs for fishing, as well as a full-time staff naturalist who directs nature walks and craft programs.

Among the park's best features are its pristine beach, its dune line, and its myrtle bushes—big as trucks and sculpted by salt spray and sea breeze—especially when a pair of yellow-breasted Carolina wrens, the state bird, are warbling within them.

Huntington Beach State Park, about 15 miles south of Myrtle Beach on US 17, below Murrells Inlet, preserves 2,500 acres of salt marsh and tidal creeks with boardwalks to fish or catch crab. Archer Huntington and his wife, the sculptress Anna Hyatt Huntington, built their unusual, fortress-like home—**Atalaya,** the Spanish word for "watchtower"—on this land. With no detailed plans, and built in fits and starts from 1931 through 1933 by local labor, the result is a square of outer walls, 200 feet on each side, the front facing the ocean.

Within the walled structure is a large, open inner court with living quarters built in 30 rooms around three sides of the perimeter. The Huntingtons last used their beach mansion in 1947. Its furnishings were removed years ago, following their deaths, and today the unusual home has a ghostly presence and a deep quiet untouched by sounds of the surf.

The three-mile beach at Huntington is a mecca for shorebird enthusiasts. Salt marsh, tidal water, woodlands, freshwater lagoon, maritime thickets, and sand dunes attract a wide range of species, including the Wilson's plover and the painted bunting.

Across the highway lies **Brookgreen Gardens,** given to the state for use as a park by the Huntingtons, but now separate from Huntington Beach State Park. The gardens were originally built for Mrs. Huntington's sculptures, and are now home to over 500 nineteenth- and twentieth-century sculptures.

■ GOLF

In 1927, when the Greenville textile magnate, Robert Woodside, was building the first grand resort hotel at Myrtle Beach, Robert White, the Scot who was the first PGA president, began building the first golf course on the Grand Strand. It was **Pine Lakes International,** in Myrtle Beach.

Myrtle Beach has the highest ratio of golf courses to people in the nation.

Two decades later, Pine Lakes was still the only golf course on the Strand, and even by the mid-1960s, there still were only a half-dozen courses in the area.

Then along came "Buster" Bryan, his two courses, and his "golfotel" marketing concept; today there are more than 80 golf courses in the 60-mile strip from Little River to Georgetown, the densest concentration of golf courses in the nation.

Sunbathers, beach-strollers, mall shoppers, fishermen, diners, and even a lot of the country music crowd speak golf lingo nearly everywhere from Ocean Drive Beach to Winyah Bay, throwing around phrases such as "a shotmaker's course," "placement course," "long ball hitter with a hook from right to left course." I don't understand much of what they're saying, nor why they're talking about it, but I do understand clout. Golf, especially in South Carolina, especially on the Strand, has big-league clout.

South Carolina is second to Florida in the nation as the most popular golfing destination. In green fees alone during 1992, the Grand Strand courses collected $350 million from 3.2 million individual rounds of golf. For the entire state's 326 golf courses that year, green fees and maintenance expenditures pumped nearly $835 million into the economy, which doesn't take into account the restaurants, hotels, motels, and other businesses supported by the golf industry.

Golf, and homes in golf course developments, are so big in South Carolina that the single most valuable agricultural "crop" grown in the state is no longer tobacco: it's turf sod, for fairways, greens, and lawns. Annual revenues from growing sod in the state have passed $450 million.

Along the Strand, especially from fall through spring, it's routine for a package-golfotel visitor to get a tee time and play 18 holes even before checking into the hotel. Then, for the next six days, that same golfer will get in 36 holes a day, often playing on 12 different courses, then get in another 18 holes on another course after checking out but before driving home.

The Strand's dozens of courses range in quality from the average, small-town country club layout to some of the nation's most praised. (Most are open to the public through golfotel packages.) Some are luxurious, self-contained resorts and second-home developments such as **Ocean Creek** and **Kingston Plantation** in North Myrtle Beach. (See "Golf Courses" in "PRACTICAL INFORMATION.")

COASTAL PLAIN

FROM THE GRAND STRAND BEACHES, from Charleston and the historic plantation district, and from the Sea Island resorts, the Atlantic coastal plain spreads inland over South Carolina for a hundred miles. Two-thirds of the state lies within this plain, which rises so gently that when it ends at rapids on the Broad and Saluda rivers at Columbia, the plain still is only 135 feet above sea level.

This gentle terrain, created during millions of years by the advancing and retreating ocean, made the region ideal for agriculture, and the plain became the farming, and the small farm town, heart of South Carolina.

The region extends to the fall line, which in South Carolina roughly follows the routes of Interstate 20 from the Savannah River border with Georgia, then northeast through Columbia and Camden, and along US 1 from there through Cheraw to North Carolina. Northwest of the line are the textile mill towns of the hilly Piedmont region.

Geologists divide the coastal plain into four regions as it spreads inland: the lower and upper pine belts, the red hills, and the sand hills. Those living on the coastal plain see it a bit differently.

Inland from the Grand Strand beaches, the locals call the northeastern section of the coastal plain the Pee Dee, after the Great Pee Dee River running through it from Cheraw to Winyah Bay on the Atlantic. Flue-cured tobacco farming dominates the Pee Dee economy. Small curing sheds dot the landscape of farms, and huge tobacco auction warehouses are found in several towns, as is also, lately, an air of uncertainty created by the controversy over cigarette smoking.

At the Pee Dee end of the fall line, around Cheraw, huge hills of sand left by the ancient ocean create a mini-region as well as a microclimate known as the Sand Hills.

The stretch of the plain inland from Charleston along the Interstate 26 route to Columbia is old cotton country where plantations spread along the Santee and Cooper rivers during the early decades of the nineteenth century. Cotton is still a major crop here, although nowhere as dominant as it once was. Today, this stretch often is called Santee Cooper Country, after the hydroelectricity project that created two freshwater reservoirs, Lakes Marion and Moultrie, in the 1940s.

The coastal plain inland from the Sea Islands and the narrow belt of Low

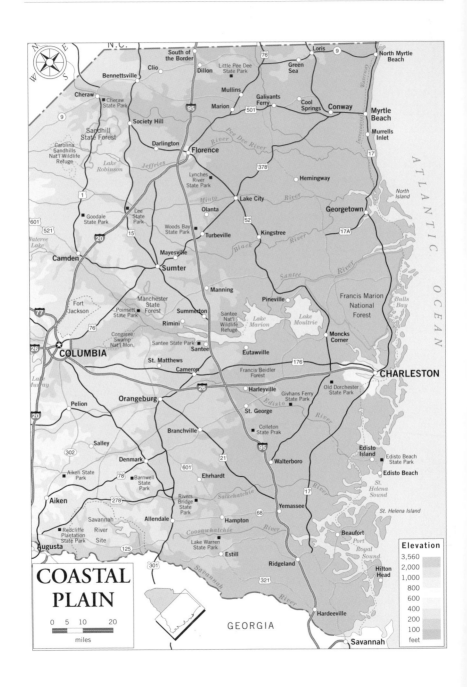

COASTAL PLAIN

0 5 10 20
miles

Elevation

3,560
2,000
1,000
800
600
400
200
100
feet

Country plantations, paralleling the Savannah River, is dominated first by tree farms, and pulpwood and lumber mills. Then, by the huge Savannah River Site, sprawling over more than 300 square miles on the Savannah River in Barnwell and Aiken counties, which has fueled the economy since the 1950s, when the federal government built five huge nuclear reactors to produce the explosive fuels, tritium and plutonium, for hydrogen bombs. "The bomb plant," as it's locally known, is South Carolina's largest single private employer.

Just beyond the plant, in the town of Aiken, mansions, horse stables, and training and racing tracks built by a winter colony of wealthy northerners beginning a century ago have led to a growing horse-raising industry, including some Kentucky Derby winners.

Along the fall line itself, the region around Columbia, the state capital, and nearby Lake Murray is known as the Midlands.

Compared with the fame, and the crowds, of South Carolina's ocean resorts, historic plantations, and Charleston, the broad coastal plain might seem at a glance to be mainly a place one drives through to get somewhere else. Travelers who take the time, and any one of many two-lane highways crossing the plain, can find contemplative glimpses into a slowly vanishing farm and farm town way of life, a culture which only seems to be asleep with crinoline memories.

The curious also can find, in between forest and farm, the majesty of a bald cypress swamp and the mystery of the huge, unexplained depressions called Carolina Bays. Aiken's spring festival of thoroughbred, steeplechase, and sulky races, as well as polo, draws tens of thousands. Bass fishing on Lakes Marion and Moultrie is famous nationwide among anglers. Columbia's Riverbanks Zoo is regarded as one of the nation's best, and the city's growing State Museum has a large following of devotees. Among stock car racing fans, there's no more historic track than Darlington Raceway.

Still, the region's principal charm may be found in simply ambling, dawdling, and stopping at a roadside stand selling fresh boiled peanuts or tree-ripened peaches, or at a farm town cafe, seeing a cotton or tobacco field in full crop, or dropping in on any of the scores of fall county fairs and year-round small-town festivals.

By late February all across the coastal plain, tractors are back on the country roads moving from field to field for plowing. There's rarely a freeze from early March to late November in this broad agricultural belt.

Tenant farming and sharecropping, systems in which laborers, usually African

Americans, lived and worked on a farm in return for rudimentary housing, a small wage, or a small share of the profit on the crop, virtually disappeared during the 1960s and '70s. In the early 1950s, there were 133,000 individual farms in the state and 12 million acres planted in crops. By the early 1990s, there were less than 25,000 farms, about 5 million acres planted, and only two percent of the state's population still lived and worked on a farm. Overall, the income from agriculture in South Carolina has been only a small part of the state's economy for decades.

As is the case with agriculture everywhere in the nation, the few family farms that survive today are usually the ones whose owners inherited their lands, adapted and diversified their skills, and expanded.

South Carolina farmers have tried a lot of unusual crops, hoping to remain on their land. Commercial catfish farming once was touted as a growth industry for the coastal plain's rural communities. Small town investors, banks, state and federal agencies lost millions on the venture, however, and the last commercial catfish processor in the state, an Orangeburg firm, closed in 1993.

In the coastal plain, however, agriculture still remains a crucial part of the economy, even though almost every year another little farm town becomes virtually deserted. Economics aside, the traditions of farm life remain strong even in the cities, as the popularity of farm town festivals among all South Carolinians shows.

■ FARM FESTIVALS

Watermelon is king in the small sand-hills town of Pageland, near North Carolina, and the equally small town of Hampton, in the pine belt near the Savannah River; both hold watermelon festivals. Other small farm towns sponsor peach festivals, tobacco days, and other special celebrations for crops that remain staples today for many South Carolinians and Southerners.

In April, the small town of St. George in Santee Cooper Country, where about 2,000 persons live, hosts more than 50,000 visitors for the World Grits Festival each year. Grits are grains of hulled corn ground into a coarse meal, cooked, and typically eaten hot with butter, salt, and pepper for breakfast. There are old-fashioned stone-ground grits cooked for an hour or more, quick grits cooked for a few minutes, instant grits mixed with hot water. In addition to the "Miss Grits" beauty pageant, the festival has the usual singing and dancing on Main Street, a carnival, and contests in grits eating.

Fruit and vegetable festivals featuring peaches (top), cabbages (below), and a host of other produce are a popular form of entertainment throughout the state. (Top photo by Tony Arruza)

COASTAL PLAINS FESTIVALS

■ CATFISH

Hardeeville: Catfish Festival. Festivities include arts and crafts, live entertainment, boat races, and sports tournaments. On I-95 near the Savannah River. In September.

Society Hill: Catfish Festival. A hometown event featuring children's games, fishing tournaments, arts and crafts, fried catfish, and catfish stew. On US 401 and 52 north of Florence. In November.

■ CHITLINS

Salley: Salley Chitlin' Strut. Featuring the deep-fried small intestines of pigs. At SC 39 and SC 394 in Aiken County. In November.

■ GRITS

St. George: World Grits Festival. In addition to the "Miss Grits" beauty pageant, the festival has the usual singing and dancing on Main Street, a carnival, and contests in grits eating. Northwest of Charleston at I-95 and US 78. In April.

■ PEACHES

Trenton: Ridge Peach Festival. Enjoy arts and crafts, a softball tournament, and peach desserts at this festival. In June.

Gilbert: Lexington County Peach Festival. A festival of arts and crafts, live music, food concessions, and peach dishes. Held at Gilbert Elementary School. In July.

■ PEANUTS

Pelion: South Carolina Peanut Party. Four and a half tons of peanuts boiled in two days. Activities include the annual blessing of the peanut pots. At US 78 and SC 302. In August.

■ POSSUMS

Barnwell: Possum Creep Festival. Eat real possum and coon and enjoy carnival rides, a horse show, and other attractions. In March.

■ RICE

Walterboro: Colleton County Rice Festival. The rice industry celebrates with dances, a parade, rice cooking contests, and the "world's largest pot of rice." On SC 64 near I-95. In April.

■ TOBACCO

Mullins: Golden Leaf Festival. Celebrating the tobacco industry with live entertainment, a husband-hollering contest, a Party after Dark, and other events. On SC 41 east of Florence. In September.

■ WATERMELON

Pageland: Pageland Watermelon Festival. Thousands come to this festival for its clogging, arts and crafts, food, seed-spitting contests, rodeo, and more. On US 601 and SC 9 near the North Carolina border. In July.

Hampton: Hampton County Watermelon Festival. A week-long festival offering free watermelon, food, parades, dances, races, and more. On US 278 near Savannah River. In June.

NEWS ITEM Aug. 15, 1935:

Marvin McIntyre, secretary to President Roosevelt, examines a 101 pound watermelon, raised in Sumter, and believed to be the largest ever grown in the South. It was presented to the President today. (Underwood Photo Archives)

In the even smaller Midlands town of Pelion, in Lexington County, about 15,000 visitors turn up each August for the annual Peanut Party. Nearly four and a half tons of peanuts are boiled in two days, producing a slightly spongy nut, slick as a raw oyster and (once boiled) officially called a goober. Activities include the annual blessing of the peanut pots.

In November, in the still smaller Aiken County town of Salley, another multitude of 50,000 shows up every year for the Chitlin' Strut. Formally called chitterlings, these gastronomic delights are the deep-fried small intestines of a pig. The aroma of cooking chitlins has stopped many a newcomer dead in his tracks.

South Carolina's fall pecan crop often contributes significantly to the state's family farms—almost all of which have a pecan grove. The state's total crop often is more than five million pounds. What began as a sideline on the Summers farm during the Great Depression today is the Golden Kernel Pecan Co., Inc., perhaps the state's biggest, certainly its oldest, pecan shelling plant. The Summers family began shelling and selling pecans from their groves in 1932 in the small Calhoun County community of Cameron in Santee Cooper Country.

Grits, goobers, and chitlin' celebrations: Is this a great country, or what?

Tobacco, however, is still the most valuable crop for South Carolina's farmers, as it has been since 1956, when it surpassed cotton. Almost all the state's tobacco crop is grown in the Pee Dee counties of Horry, Florence, Williamsburg, and Darlington. Perhaps no two crops in the history of the nation have been so associated with human misery and controversy, cotton for its spread of slavery and the economic dependence it created, tobacco for its spread of sickness, death, and addiction to nicotine.

■ PEE DEE

The pungent, almost gamy aroma of tobacco, not tobacco smoke, wafts through the small farms of the Pee Dee from mid-summer to early fall as the crop is auctioned in warehouses from Conway to Darlington.

Skilled buyers from giant corporations, who judge with a flick of an eye or brush of a fingertip the worth of the broad leaves, pass between rows of the harvested crop inside long, humid warehouses. Just as imperceptibly, the buyers bid in response to a nearly unintelligible chant from an equally skilled and specialized tobacco auctioneer.

Tobacco farming remains a mainstay of the economy of coastal plain counties.

The scene is repeated from late July to mid-September at tobacco auction ware-houses in Conway and Loris in Horry County, where 25 percent of South Carolina's tobacco is grown, and a bit further west in Hemingway and Mullins, and in three more tobacco auction markets in the US 52 towns of Kingstree, Lake City, and Darlington. Most of the **tobacco warehouse auctions**, held from late July to mid-September, are open to the public. Check local newspapers and chambers of commerce for dates, times, and directions.

South Carolina never had the huge cigarette factories found in North Carolina and Virginia, but still, nearly 15,000 persons are employed by the tobacco industry in the state, and the annual economic impact of tobacco in South Carolina, the smallest of the Southern states and still one of the poorer in the nation, is esti-mated at $750 million.

Tourism on the Grand Strand alone is worth more than twice that amount, but not everybody can live at the beach.

In January, all across the Pee Dee's farm lands, the tiny seeds of what become four- or five-foot-tall tobacco plants go into growing beds. In spring, the shoots are transplanted to the open fields. Trimmed and topped as the season passes, they are harvested from the bottom up at intervals through the summer, with the most valued leaves taken last from the top.

On some of the few small family farms still growing tobacco, the ripe leaves are tied onto sticks, then hung in a barn and cured for nearly a week as the farmer constantly monitors and adjusts the heat inside the barns with a system of flues—hence the term for cigarette tobacco, flue-cured.

Migrant laborers do most of the summer harvesting, and like most agricultural and industrial laborers, face hazards peculiar to their crop, in this case: cuts from the tobacco knives used to slice a leaf at its stem; impalement on sticks used to hang the tobacco in barns; falls from the barn rafters; and a little-known hazard called green tobacco sickness.

Pure, concentrated nicotine is as poisonous as the venom of the deadliest snake. During harvest, field laborers often carry wet tobacco leaves under their arms, and the solubilized nicotine from the leaf is absorbed through the workers' skin. The resulting green tobacco sickness produces symptoms akin to a severe case of the flu and is regarded as part of the job.

A very fit and fast tobacco picker might make up to $20 an hour, but most make closer to $8, and most are slowly being replaced by mechanization. The leaf-sticker machine has made it easier to sew leaves together to hang on sticks, and a machine pulled behind a tractor, called a setter, has sped the transplanting and watering of seedlings. The biggest changes in recent years were a mechanical harvesting machine to pick the ripe leaves, and a new method of curing in large quantities. Twenty acres was once all a farm family could harvest. Now, three times that amount can and must be planted to justify the costs of mechanization.

As a result, the small tobacco farmer is disappearing. As another result, the greater efficiency has brought so much greater production that the market price often drops under pressure of the surpluses.

Still, a farmer can net as much as $3,500 an acre on tobacco, far more than on any other crop most tobacco farmers either are equipped to, or know how to, grow.

Tobacco growers were in trouble before the recent controversies over cigarette smoking erupted. More than half of South Carolina's crop is sold abroad, and that market is dwindling. Although the number of cigarette smokers is increasing worldwide, so is the number of countries producing cheap tobacco. And U.S. cigarette makers are importing more foreign tobacco, mostly from Brazil.

The issues in the national debate over cigarette smoking, almost a social movement, are familiar to most readers—new taxes, labeling nicotine as addictive, banning smoking in most public places. In the fields and warehouses of the Pee Dee, where money from tobacco buys food, clothing, and shelter for thousands of South Carolinians, that debate is every day's biggest news.

As Marion Fowler, 81, patriarch of South Carolina's tobacco community and sales supervisor of the Lake City auction market, put to his fellows at a 1993 convention: "Tobacco is in trouble. I've been told by a top tobacco official that unless we can work out these problems, we might as well rent out our warehouses as skating rinks."

The tobacco economy, like the one before it based upon cotton and slavery, already knows that while it may continue to exist in some form, its heyday is over. In the fields of the Pee Dee, there's talk of learning how to grow asparagus, or maybe ornamental shrubbery and fresh flowers.

■ CAROLINA BAYS AND SAND HILLS

As tobacco, cotton, and other crops spread across the Pee Dee, farmers, and later naturalists, came across more and more mysterious, huge, elliptical depressions, some covering almost 2,000 acres. Every one of these egg-shaped formations, noticed and puzzled over for a century or more, lay on the land with one tip pointing northwest, the other southeast.

Some of the mysterious depressions are dry, some are shallow lakes, some are wet, dense swamps, but all have the same northwest-southeast alignment. They are found on the huge Atlantic coastal plain from New Jersey to Florida, but most of them, and the most defined ones, are found in the coastal plain of the Carolinas. At one time, 2,600 such depressions—called **Carolina Bays**—were documented in South Carolina's coastal plain, but agriculture, timbering, and development reduced that number to about 200 today. The most widely accepted theory for why Carolina Bays exist is that a meteorite shower millennia ago impacted the coastal plain.

Carolina Bays, depressions in the soil, are believed to have been created by a meteorite shower thousands of years ago. (Photo by Robert C. Clark)

One of the largest has been preserved in a state park just east of I-95 and north of US 378 near the Florence County town of Olanta. **Woods Bay State Park** is South Carolina's first all-nature state park, with no camping or playgrounds. There are picnic tables, a large aerial photograph of the three-mile-long, mile-wide bay, canoe rentals, a canoe trail into the shallow black water of the swamp, and a 500-foot boardwalk reaching into the wetland.

Stone tools and bits of pottery almost 10,000 years old have been found on the rim of a Carolina Bay inside the huge federal reservation used by the Savannah River Site "bomb plant" in Aiken and Barnwell counties.

Another unusual, although not mysterious, feature of the Pee Dee terrain is the ancient sand hills, which rise some hundreds of feet above the northern edge of the Pee Dee where the plain meets the fall line. These are the remains of sand dunes left when the ocean reached here 65 to 136 million years ago. The old dunes exist here and there all along the fall line from near Fayetteville, North Carolina, to Columbus, Georgia; they are best seen and most exposed along US 1 for 30 miles south of Cheraw.

Reckless timbering and farming of the sand hills here from 1900 to the 1930s left the dunes bare and eroded. The federal government bought nearly 90,000 acres of it during the 1930s as a relief program under the Resettlement Administration, resettling local landowners on more fertile lands elsewhere, then reforesting and restoring the land.

Today, the **Carolina Sandhills National Wildlife Refuge** and the **Sand Hill State Forest,** opposite each other on US 1, are examples of how much social and ecological programs can succeed, as well as of a unique habitat. Longleaf pine forests, commercially logged, dominate the state forest. On the wildlife refuge the pines often give way to stretches of prickly pear, yucca, and Spanish bayonet.

Ducks and geese begin migratory stays on the refuge in late September, remaining through early April, and there are observation towers and a photo blind at two lakes on the refuge. The preserve also hosts one of the largest remaining populations of the relatively nondescript, but also endangered, red-cockaded woodpecker, which nests only in living pines suffering from red heart disease. Winter is the best time to visit the sand hills because this place has a summer microclimate all its own. In daytime, the sand heats more rapidly than surrounding clay soils. Days are hot. At dusk and into the evening during the summer, the sands release their stored thermal energy into the atmosphere, producing more thunderstorms than nearby areas on either side of the sand hills.

■ PEE DEE TOWNS

The little towns of the Pee Dee are often thick with well-kept antebellum and Victorian homes and historic districts. For example, a 100-mile day trip off I-95 at Florence, then north on US 52 to Cheraw, and returning via SC 9 to the interstate highway at Dillon, offers a close look at the 250-year-old agricultural society of the Pee Dee.

Florence, in the center of the Pee Dee and with a population of fewer than 30,000, is the shopping, financial, and entertainment center of the region. Its growth began during the 1850s when three railroad lines converged on the settlement and made it a shipping hub to cotton docks at ports in Charleston and Wilmington, North Carolina.

No other town in the Pee Dee has as many as 10,000 residents, a few have about 5,000, and most have less than 1,000, which is part of its appeal.

Darlington (population about 7,000) gets the publicity for its twice-a-year, 500-mile stock car races, but that is a fans' event. The famous raceway is bolstered by the largest collection of stock car racers in the world inside the **Stock Car Hall of Fame/Joe Weatherly Museum.** (Both are off SC 34 in Darlington. For race times call 393-4041.) The 60-acre **Williamson Park** on Spring Street in Darlington has a five-mile boardwalk and trail through moss-draped swamplands planted in azaleas and camellias.

Just north of Dillon, on I-95 at the state line, a dubious notoriety beckons devotees of garish glitz to the hamlet of **South of the Border,** which began in the 1950s as a motel named Pedro's on the old US 301 route to Florida. Fed by dozens of I-95 billboards, it long has been noted also for its we-never-close wedding chapel. There is no mandatory blood test, and only a one-day waiting period, for a marriage license in South Carolina, which attracts amorous couples from throughout the South and up the Eastern Seaboard states to Dillon County.

Fifteen miles north on US 52, **Society Hill** (population 900) typifies the communities settled by Welsh Baptists during the colonial era in South Carolina. The little town, established in 1747 on a hill overlooking the Great Pee Dee River, is known for its **1822 library** and **1834 Trinity Church.**

Ten miles further north, **Cheraw State Park** is one of the oldest and largest in South Carolina and is noted for its 18-hole golf course, seven fully furnished rental cabins, lakes for swimming, boating, and fishing, and campsites.

The historic town of **Cheraw** (population 6,000) is five miles beyond the park. Founded as a trading post around 1740, it became a commercial and shipping center owing to its location at the head of navigable water on the Great Pee Dee. Today, Cheraw is known for its antiques market and a downtown historic district of more than 50 antebellum mansions, gardens, and colonial buildings.

The old farm town of **Bennettsville** (population 9,000, founded 1819) is about a 15-mile drive south from Cheraw on SC 9. Once wealthy from cotton, the town is known today for its shaded neighborhoods of Victorian and antebellum homes.

The nearby village of **Clio** (population 1,000), founded in the early nineteenth century, reached its golden age when cotton was king and its barons built palaces here. Many of these mansions remain, as does **A. L. Calhoun's Store**, built in 1905 and seemingly frozen as it was in 1925, when the Depression first hit the Pee Dee.

■ SANTEE COOPER COUNTRY

To see a field of cotton in fall bloom, like ponds, lakes, and small seas of white across the land, is also to behold at once the long and ancient history of mankind with this plant, and the amazing notion that cloth that someone soon will wear is growing out of that piece of ground.

Martin Rickenbacker relaxes on the porch of a small country store in Vance.

Nothing has been as central as cotton to the history of South Carolina, from cotton plantations to cotton mills. Today, the state still struggles with its legacy of that history.

Cotton no longer dominates South Carolina's politics, economy, or agriculture. California and Texas, by far, produce more cotton. Still, South Carolina and three other states of the old Confederacy—Mississippi, Georgia, and Louisiana—remain among the top 10 cotton-producing states in the nation.

Patches of cotton are grown in most of the state, but the heart of what's left of the old cotton kingdom in South Carolina is in **Santee Cooper Country**. The region is a strip of the coastal plain along the northwesterly route of I-26 from north of Charleston to south of Columbia, including Orangeburg and Sumter counties, the state's top cotton producers.

Santee Cooper Country gets its name from a huge hydroelectricity project built by the U.S. Army Corps of Engineers. In 1939 the Corps of Engineers began building two dams about 20 miles from each other on two of South Carolina's historic rivers, the Santee and the Cooper, in a swampy region 50 miles inland from the Atlantic coast near the town of Moncks Corner.

The procedures of cotton production are illustrated in this newspaper article from 1862.
(South Caroliniana Library, Univ. of S.C.)

Santee Cooper, a state-owned electric utility, is the fourth-largest public power utility in the nation today. One of every three South Carolinians receives electricity either directly from Santee Cooper or from one of the 15 electric cooperatives that buy their power from the utility.

When the project was completed in 1941, it created two of the largest reservoirs in South Carolina. The southern one, **Lake Moultrie,** is at the headwaters of the Cooper River. The other, just north of Lake Moultrie and connected to it by a six-mile canal, is **Lake Marion,** on the Santee River.

The clear, olive-colored waters of the lakes, sometimes blending into swamps along their shores, are famous for freshwater fishing, annually producing world-record catches. Because neither lake bottom was fully cleared of stumps and trees before the floodgates were closed and the reservoirs filled, Moultrie and Marion are havens for species such as striped bass, crappie, bream, white and largemouth bass, and catfish.

Lakeside communities such as Rimini, Santee, Pineville, Cross, and Bonneau, and sprawling Santee State Park, specialize in supplying anglers.

Both lakes are relatively shallow, and neither ices over in winter, so, weather permitting, fishing is year-round. Moultrie, the smaller of the two at 60,400 acres, is also the more open, its waters 14 miles across at one point. The northern Lake Marion, 110,600 acres, narrows as it leads to the Wateree and Congaree rivers (which form the Santee River).

Experts say the best time for fishing the lakes' renowned striped bass is in spring when they head north from Moultrie through the diversion canal to Marion, then up the Wateree and Congaree rivers. Live herring is the recommended bait. There are scores of experts, guides, fish camps, restaurants, and lodgings all around the lakes. One of the prime fishing havens is **Santee State Park** on Lake Marion's western shore just north of the I-95 bridge. The park has 30 cabins, some on land, others on piers over the lake, 150 campsites, fishing and pedal boat rentals, a swimming lake, boat ramp, tackle shop, hiking trails, tennis courts, and a restaurant.

Across Lake Marion and just south of the I-95 bridge is **Santee National Wildlife Refuge.** The refuge, on the east bank of the lake, has a one-mile, self-guided wildlife trail, and from November through February is a vantage point from which to view wintering flocks of Canadian geese and 17 other species of migratory waterfowl.

■ SANTEE COTTON COUNTRY

Cotton and slavery raced inland from their former domains on the Sea Islands, where the silky, longer-fibered cotton was cultivated, and from the coastal rice river plantations. For more than a century before the dams were built and the lakes created, cotton spread though the region, on plantations along the Santee, Congaree, Wateree, Pocotaligo, Black, and Edisto rivers.

With the cotton also came communities and growth.

Branchville (at US 78 and US 21), in the southern tip of Orangeburg County, grew during the 1830s around what is the oldest railroad junction in America. The town of 1,000 has a railroad museum and festival held the last weekend in September to celebrate the nation's first scheduled railroad. It began running Christmas Day, 1830, between the cotton port of Charleston and the spreading cotton fields inland. The South Carolina Canal & Railroad Company's first locomotive, "The Best Friend of Charleston," blew up one year later when its fireman, annoyed with the hissing steam from the safety valve, closed it. He blew up with the engine.

Policeman David Ragin (above) also works as a bass-fishing guide on Lake Marion (left).

CAROLINA COTTON

In the springtime cotton is planted in rows, and by late summer the plants reach their mature height of about three feet. Then, swiftly and at varying times from field to field, one day the plant flowers in a creamy, yellow blossom. The next day the flowers turn pink, and before the end of the third day, they fall to the ground, leaving a tiny green boll, or seed pod, which will grow to the size of a hen's egg. When ripe, it bursts open, revealing white fibers.

Early in the fall, the plants are defoliated, leaving only the boll and stem for harvesters to pick. The boll is two-thirds seed and one third fiber (or lint), and the task is to separate the seeds of the boll from the fibers and spin the fibers into thread—a process that's been going on with various degrees of success since ancient times.

Cotton has been cultivated in southern Asia for 2,000 years, was known to the ancient Greeks, and by the time of Columbus's voyage to America, was well established among indigenous cultures from the West Indies to Mexico to Peru and Brazil. When a new spinning jenny and power loom came into use in England between 1767 and 1790 the Industrial Revolution was roaring to life, and a great maritime nation such as England had the ships to import raw cotton, process it quickly and efficiently, then market it around the world. This capability in turn created a huge new demand for raw cotton, a need happily filled by farmers from the American South.

It was in the South that another new invention made the cotton easier to process. Before downy white cotton fibers can be sold and spun into thread, they have to be cleaned, and as seeds comprise two-thirds of the cotton boll, this can be a time consuming process. In early days, large numbers of slaves were used to separate the fibers from the seeds by hand. Then in 1793, Eli Whitney invented his cotton gin—a revolving, toothed cylinder that caught the fibers and pulled them though a grate with openings too small for the seeds to pass through.

If this process has by now been further refined, you'll nevertheless find the country roads of South Carolina every fall, full of tall, wire-sided and -topped cages and flatbed trucks heading to the scores of cotton gins. There, the cleaned fibers are compressed into huge bales weighing 500 pounds, wrapped in coarse burlap, bound with steel strips, and shipped, eventually, to mills.

Modern cotton gins often allow casual visitors (just stop and ask) to watch the seeds and fibers being separated. Every pound of cotton ginned also results in two pounds of cotton seed, and this, too, is valuable. When squeezed under a hydraulic press at processing plants, the seed yields an oil which is refined and used in cooking, in making oleomargarine and lard, and in soaps. The husks also are used as a rich food for farm animals and as a fertilizer.

A cotton press squeezes oil from cotton seeds.
(South Caroliniana Library, Univ. of S.C.)

Orangeburg, settled during the 1730s by German immigrants from Pennsylvania, boomed as a cotton market and commercial center on the North Fork of the Edisto River; Orangeburg County today is the state's top cotton producer. Now a town of about 14,000, Orangeburg is home to the traditionally black Claflin College and South Carolina State University.

The latter was founded in 1896 as the Colored Normal, Agricultural, and Industrial College. Today, its campus includes the state's largest planetarium and an art museum featuring African and African-American works. The university is a bright spot in the otherwise dismal history of higher education involving African Americans in South Carolina.

Orangeburg is also home to one of the oldest and best September county fairs, and the **Edisto Memorial Gardens,** a testing ground in the All American Rose selection process, with masses of azaleas, camellias, wisteria, dogwood, crabapple, and roses.

Sumter (population 42,000), at the headwaters of the Pocotaligo River and halfway between the cotton plantations along the Black and Wateree rivers, also grew with cotton. Today, Sumter County is the state's number two cotton producer. The town's **Swan Lake Iris Gardens** are home to seven species of swans, and in spring its dark swamp-water lake is surrounded in the colors of Dutch and Japanese iris. Cotton fortunes built the 1845 Victorian mansion called the **Williams-Brice House,** now a museum and archives (122 North Washington Street), as well as the antebellum home of the late artist Elizabeth White. The palatial, clock-towered, 1890s stone **Sumter Opera House** is another landmark of the boom era.

Mary McLeod Bethune, who founded what became Bethune-Cookman College

Dogwoods and azaleas in full bloom at the Edisto Memorial Gardens.

Brig. Gen. Thomas Sumter, nicknamed the "Gamecock" for his harassment of British forces during the Revolution, was the namesake for the city of Sumter. (South Caroliniana Library, Univ. of S.C.)

in Daytona Beach, Florida, in 1904 and was its president for 38 years before becoming an advisor to President Franklin D. Roosevelt, was born and raised in the small (population 7,000 today) cotton farm town of Mayesville by the Black River in Sumter County.

Driving from one to another of these Santee Cooper Country towns, you'll occasionally see long-abandoned tenant farmers' shacks standing forlornly in fields, ghostly reminders of how freed slaves and poor whites lived for almost a century after the Civil War. These two- or three-room houses were primitive, without water, sewer, or electricity.

Some tenant farmers worked for a small salary, but most labored in exchange for their shack, a garden spot, and a small percentage of the profit on the crop they harvested—cotton. The tenant, also called a sharecropper, was dependent upon the landowner for a livelihood, and the landowner dependent upon the tenant for labor. The system began to collapse after World War II, when many tenants began moving to Northern cities in search of better-paying work.

■ SUMMERTON AND SCHOOL DESEGREGATION

During the 1950s, as new kinds of farm machinery spread through Santee Cooper Country's cotton farms, tens of thousands of African Americans still living in the region found themselves out of work. Their children's segregated schools were so inferior to white public schools that they barely functioned—meaning the children would have no jobs either. And yet from this dire predicament arose one of the least known but most historic legal rulings in the history of both South Carolina and the nation. A historic marker commemorates the site.

On the north side of Lake Marion near Summerton (take US 15 to St. Paul, then go north one mile on Road 373) in Clarendon County is the **Liberty Hill AME Church,** built in 1905. Parents began meeting and organizing there before finally contacting the South Carolina branch of the NAACP. Nineteen members of the Liberty Hill AME congregation, all of them parents, became plaintiffs in a suit first known as *Briggs et al. v. Elliot and the Summerton Public School System.* The parents contended that so long as the public schools were segregated by race, their children's education would suffer—that, in fact, separate schools would always be unequal, and must be declared unconstitutional.

The suit was heard in federal district court in Charleston in 1952. Their lawyer from the NAACP was Thurgood Marshall, who would go on in 1967 to become the first African American appointed to sit on the Supreme Court.

The Summerton/Clarendon County case was merged with similar appeals from other states to become *Brown v. Board of Education,* and in 1954, the Supreme Court outlawed segregated schools.

Thirty miles east of Liberty Hill AME, in the cotton and tobacco town of **Kingstree** on US 52 in Williamsburg County, granite monuments to Marshall and to Dr. Martin Luther King Jr. were dedicated on the county courthouse grounds on an August weekend in 1993. The county's population is 65 percent black, and in recent years its black residents gained political control, including offices such as county school superintendent. However, the desperately poor county's taxes are paid mostly by its white residents, who remain the largest employers and landowners, and who send their children to virtually all-white private schools. The county school district is almost 90 percent black and has little support from whites on matters such as bond issues to build new schools.

The Liberty Hill AME parents who brought suit in 1952 were grandparents by the time Clarendon County schools finally desegregated during the 1970s. When that did occur, whites abandoned the public school system in Clarendon, and by 1994 the historic school district had the state's lowest test scores, the highest number of students from impoverished families, and a 98 percent black enrollment.

The Clarendon, Williamsburg, Sumter, and Orangeburg counties of the Santee Cooper Country have among the highest unemployment rates (around 10 percent) in the state, and a high percentage of their citizens receive federal food stamps for the poor. The same story about jobs, food stamps, schools, and race relations exists all across the agricultural coastal plain.

African Americans hold elected and appointed offices throughout South Carolina, from mayors of small farm towns to a justice of the state supreme court, to members of the state legislature. South Carolina's first black congressman since Reconstruction was elected in 1992 from the Pee Dee. Yet in every small town across the coastal plain, small groups of young, middle-aged, and elderly black men spend their days idling, poorly educated and unemployed, in parking lots of crossroads country stores.

■ SWAMPS: A WET WILDERNESS

South Carolina encompasses more swampland than any state except Louisiana, and almost all of it is within the coastal plain. The Great Swamp which once spread across much of the Pee Dee was eventually drained for farming, and exists now in countless patches of smaller swampland throughout the area.

Of these hundreds of small swamps, some are barely noticed, such as Pudding Swamp in the Pee Dee along US 378 west of Turbeville. Yet each have their glories, such as the cathedral majesty of the bald cypress, kin to the redwood and sequoia, in the internationally renowned Congaree Swamp National Monument in Santee Cooper Country. Salkehatchie Swamp is where the Coosa Indians once lived (near Yemassee in the southern tip of the state); at Wambaw Swamp on the lower Santee River the early French Huguenots settled; and there's also Four Holes Swamp, Pee Dee Swamp, Wateree Swamp, and swamps no one knows the names of except the people who live nearby.

There are shallow water swamps of shrub-like willows, alder, oak, maple, and water hickory, and there are deep-water swamps of bald cypress, tupelo gum, and the epiphytic Spanish moss.

Francis Beidler Forest and Congaree Swamp National Monument are two of the most splendid and readily accessible parks preserving the subtle grandeur, and the sometimes simply spooky beauty, of a wet wilderness. Both parks are most comfortably visited from late fall to early spring, when insect populations are down.

■ FRANCIS BEIDLER FOREST
The **Four Holes Swamp,** fed by springs and rainfall, meanders for more than 60 miles, from Lake Marion near the village of **Cameron** (US 176 and SC 33) to the Edisto River near **Givhans Ferry State Park** (SC 27 and SC 61). Since Four Holes depends mostly upon rainfall, its water levels fluctuate with the seasons. In winter and spring, the swamp is a shallow river, and in summer and fall, it shrinks to a series of creeks and ponds.

Within this swampland, the 5,800 acres of the Francis Beidler Forest contain the largest remaining virgin stand of bald cypress and tupelo gum trees in the world. Many of the cypress sentinels are 1,000 years old or older.

A visitors center, staff naturalists, and a mile-and-a-half boardwalk are available to whomever comes along, 9 A.M. to 5 P.M., Tuesday through Sunday. There is no camping, or food facilities, and canoe trips, night walks, and other explorations of the preserve are available only by reservation and in season.

Kayaking in the Congaree Swamp (above). Pitcher plants thrive in the swamps and bays of coastal Carolina (right). (Photo by Robert C. Clark)

The National Audubon Society, the same outfit which tried to buy the golf course on Kiawah, in the Sea Islands, manages the Beidler Forest. The forest is named for the wealthy lumberman and conservationist who preserved it from logging. Unconventional for his time, Beidler allowed much of his timber in South Carolina to stand. After his death in 1924, his family continued to preserve the area, and during the late 1960s, with the liquidation of the estate, local conservationists and the Nature Conservancy acquired the land as a sanctuary.

Francis Beidler Forest is in Four Holes Swamp, just off I-26 near Harleyville, 40 miles northwest of Charleston.

■ C O N G A R E E   S W A M P   N A T I O N A L   M O N U M E N T
Congaree Swamp National Monument, 20 miles south of Columbia (on SC 48) and just north of Lake Marion on the Congaree River, is more a floodplain than a swamp, but its "redwoods of the East" include six bald cypress believed to be the largest of the species in the nation.

More than 90 species of trees have been identified in the Congaree's 22,000 acres, and half the preserve has never been logged. A boardwalk, five hiking trails ranging from one to 10 miles, and canoeing routes make the Congaree accessible to visitors, and more than 60,000 a year, including scientists from around the world, tour the unique ecosystem. In 1983, the United Nations designated the swamp an International Biosphere Reserve.

■ SAVANNAH RIVER CORRIDOR

South Carolina's diversity reveals itself most dramatically along the hundred miles paralleling the historic **Savannah River,** from the thick pine forests of Jasper County in the southern tip of the state, to the mansions and stables built by Vanderbilts, Astors, Whitneys, and Hitchcocks in the fall-line town of Aiken.

Sleepy railroad hamlets follow the rails in a straight line through the pines. Grocers sell less and less feed, seed, and groceries to a dwindling number of customers. Locals find work at the sawmill, and hope maybe a sock plant (yes, as in for your feet) will come along.

Inland and beyond the pine farms, one of the largest, most technologically and scientifically sophisticated industrial complexes ever built—producing the most lethal weapon on earth—took over and changed the towns and people around it more suddenly and thoroughly than pine trees ever did to row crops.

At the end of the corridor, **Aiken County**, perhaps after Charleston the most historic part of South Carolina, seems simply to line up and present one jarring contrast after another: cotton mill hands, the richest men in America, pit mines for kaolin clay, bucolic pastures for Kentucky Derby champions.

In the antebellum South of cotton and slavery, paddlewheel steamboats regularly navigated the Savannah River all along this corridor. There were a score or more steamboat landings they called upon, no more than riverine whistlestops. Not so much as a hamlet grew along the river between the paddlewheelers' two destinations, the seaport of Savannah and the inland port of Augusta, both in Georgia. Not then, not now.

Railroads, beginning with the oldest railroad in the nation, created almost every town in this corner of the state. They are not factory railroad towns, nor wheat and cattle railroad towns, but simply rural railroad towns that used the trains as truckers and tourists use the interstate highways of today.

From an airplane, it seems as though the entire corridor is a forest, interrupted only occasionally by plowed fields, orchards, and a few commercial blocks.

SUMMERS OUT ON THE PORCH

*T*hat was the summer it was so hot the katydids failed to sing and everyone spent their evenings out on the porch with large glasses of ice tea and damp hand towels to cool the back of the neck. Alma wouldn't even start cooking until after the sun had gone down. Twilight came on early, though, a long-drawn-out dimming of the heat and glare that made everything soft and magical, brought out the first fireflies, and added a cool enchantment to the metallic echoes of the slide guitar playing on Alma's kitchen radio. Granny would plant herself in the porch rocker, leaving Alma's girls to pick through snap beans, hope for a rainstorm, and tease her into telling stories.

I always positioned myself behind Granny, up against the wall next to the screen door, where I could listen to Kitty Wells and George Jones, the whine of that guitar and what talk there was in the kitchen, as well as the sound of Aunt Alma's twin boys thumping their feet against the porch steps and the girls' giggles as their fingers slipped through the cool, dusty beans.

—Dorothy Allison, *Bastard out of Carolina*, 1992

■ TREE FARMS

Timber and pulpwood stands—not so much forests as they are tree farms, planted in rows like cotton or tobacco plants—cover thousands of square miles of the entire coastal plain. Most of them are loblolly or longleaf pines. They grow, in tree terms, fast as weeds and are just as hardy.

The vast pine belt stretches naturally from Horry County in the tobacco country of the Pee Dee, through the cotton fields of Santee Cooper Country, to the Savannah River. Forests cover nearly 60 percent of the entire state, but unlike in western states, only five percent of South Carolina's forests are federal lands. About 22 percent of the forest is owned by forest industry corporations. Another 68 percent is owned by individuals, most of whom lease their land, or sell their tree crops, to corporate buyers.

In the Low Country counties of Jasper and Hampton, there is not much else to the economy but what comes out of the pine forests; and as a result, there often is not much to the local economy.

For two decades, at an increasing pace, the nation's major source of lumber for construction and pulpwood used in paper products has been shifting from the forests of the Pacific Northwest to the tree farms of the southeastern states. In South Carolina, harvesting tree farms is a multibillion-dollar industry, and most of that industry is within the coastal plain.

Most of that money, however, comes from selling the trees or products made from them, not from the value of local payrolls. Unless there is a sawmill, or a paper plant, the forest products industry creates few jobs in the forest, and most of the few it does create pay little.

Throughout the Low County, the family farms have disappeared, to be replaced not by corporate farming but by corporate tree farming. Not every old, rural railroad town can get a sock plant, and the few that do are lucky. Farmers throughout the nation are struggling; few in the Low Country can survive on lease payments or the once-a-decade crop payments of a tree farm.

What's left?

The stars whirl above a pine tree plantation in this time-exposure photograph.

■ HUNTING PLANTATIONS

For a growing number, what's left is another niche in the outdoor sports industry: hunting plantations.

Perhaps the densest deer-per-acre population in the nation is along the Savannah River Corridor of South Carolina, especially in the Low Country. The state also has the longest deer hunting season in the nation and liberal bag limits. A 1991 survey by Clemson University estimated that recreational hunting adds about $240 million a year to the state's economy. In some counties, such as Jasper, hunting income has surpassed agriculture in the local economy.

One of the first to convert his farm and forest into a hunting plantation was Joe Bostick, whose 5,000-acre plantation is near the Hampton County town of **Estill** (US 321 and SC 3). Bostick's forebears farmed the plantation from the time it was given to them by King George III in 1769. Falling livestock and crop prices during the 1970s led Bostick to consider other uses for his land, and a commercial hunting operation was the idea he settled upon.

Now, about 500 hunters a year pay to shoot deer, turkey, quail, and wild boar on Bostick's plantation. They pay about $400 a day to stay in the three-story plantation-style lodge he built in 1980, and they get not only hunting privileges but also servants and fine dining.

Hunting is an old, stylized, and almost formal tradition in South Carolina. Plantation families depended upon hunting for part of their food supply and made hunts into social gatherings. Before 1800, planters along the Santee and Cooper rivers had formed two of the oldest hunt clubs in the state—St. John's and St. Stephens. The St. John's by-laws required each member in turn to supply the seasonal or monthly club meeting with:

> A barbecued shoat or sheep, a ham or piece of salt beef, a turkey, two fowls or two ducks, two loaves of bread, and in the season, potatoes, a half bushel of rice, pepper, salt, mustard and vinegar, one bottle of rum, half gallon of brandy, and one dozen of good wine. Pipes and tobacco, or one hundred segars, one dozen tumblers and two dozen wine glasses.

The hunt clubs founded on old rice plantations during the 1910s and 1920s by wealthy northerners, as well as those established by South Carolinians, preserved their lands from development and saved thousands of acres of wildlife habitat. The ACE Basin project is an example.

■ SAVANNAH RIVER SITE

In the Savannah River Corridor of the coastal plain, the pine forest often seems to be all there is along any road going inland and north along I-95 from the small towns of Walterboro, Ridgeland, or Hardeeville. For long stretches of highway, pines, small farms, and fading old farm towns present a life of apparent somnambulism. There is one highway route through the corridor, however, that is scenic and fascinating at every mile, a literal drive through history and current events.

From **Estill**, in Hampton County, drive north on SC 3 for about 30 miles through **Allendale County**. The highway has little traffic and plenty of small, prosperous farms and pastures and bucolic churches. A few decades ago, most of the coastal plain farms still looked like these.

At the intersection of SC 3 and SC 125, turn left and follow 125 into and through the site of one of the most remarkable industrial facilities in the nation. This is the **Savannah River Site,** run by the U.S. Department of Energy, constructed in the early 1950s by the old Atomic Energy Commission, and covering more than 300 square miles in Barnwell and Aiken counties, from the Savannah River inland for 25 miles.

The "bomb plant," as it is known locally, produced tritium and plutonium for the nation's hydrogen bombs until the late 1980s when the end of the Cold War curbed the demand for those two "bang" ingredients.

When it was built, a dozen little farm towns and scores of farms were moved, or razed, and within months, the economy and pace of life changed thoroughly in towns all around the plant, including Aiken, Barnwell, North Augusta, and a dozen others, where thousands of technicians, engineers, and scientists from around the nation came to live. It became, and remains, with about 20,000 employees today, the single largest private employer in the state.

The plant's future is unsettled. Its five giant, weapons-grade nuclear reactors and other processing facilities are too old to safely operate again without costly repairs, and there no longer is a market for their products. Uncounted millions of gallons of radioactive waste remain on the site, some deadly on exposure, others merely hazardous. No other spot in the nation seems willing to accept these wastes in "permanent" storage, and it is possible the vast site will become a nuclear waste dump, requiring close monitoring for thousands of years.

■ AIKEN COUNTY HISTORY

As unusual as the presence and history of the bomb plant is, it is only another chapter in the unusual history of Aiken County.

A dark side of that history, and a beautiful place to visit, is about 10 miles north of the Savannah River Site near the community of Beech Island. Turn right off SC 125 onto US 278, and about two miles down that highway is **Redcliffe Plantation State Park.**

The antebellum plantation mansion, with many of its original furnishings still on display, was completed in 1859 by James Henry Hammond, for whom the term "scoundrel" may have been coined.

Elected to the U.S. House in 1835, then as governor in 1843, and in 1857 to the U.S. Senate, Hammond is best known for his 1858 Senate speech in which he warned the Northern states: "No, you dare not make war on cotton. No power on earth dares make war on it. Cotton is king." His lesser-known pronouncements included: "Slaves are the mudsills of society," and women were created "to breed . . . and serve as toys for the recreation of men."

Hammond made a name for himself after marrying a homely 16-year-old heiress to several plantations. Their marriage was rocky after Mrs. Hammond's four nieces returned home from a visit and told their father that Henry had fondled them to "all but the last degree." Mrs. Hammond again moved away to protest the presence of her husband's slave mistress, refusing to live at Redcliffe while the other woman was there. Hammond, like so many planters with a second, black family, was in effect passionate about the continuing enslavement of his own offspring.

Hammond's mansion, restored during the 1940s and 1950s by a descendant, John Shaw Billings, then editing director of Time, Inc., is often used for weddings and is rented by the state parks department for similar social events.

An even older part of South Carolina's history, the state's oldest Baptist Church, is about five miles from Hammond's old plantation. Founded by white settlers in 1750, it was turned over to slaves in 1773 and is still going strong. Through nearly 250 years, the congregation has been forced to move its church three times, spurring the start of other churches but retaining its history.

Silver Bluff Missionary Baptist Church is on the western (river) side of SC 125, in Beech Island, on US 278.

The first large-scale cotton mill and mill town in the South are about five miles further north in **Horse Creek Valley.** Most of the old cotton and textile mills

EXTREMELY STYLISH

[Dear Mother:]

I might almost have staid at Silverton, for anything that I saw of the Bride. We got to Redcliffe about half past ten o'c, and she came down stairs a few minutes before 1 o'c, after having been sent for repeatedly, to see some of the neighbors who had called to see her. When she finally appeared, she entered the room, led by the "Proud husband," gave us all a sweeping bow, and curtsy, said a very fashionable, clipped off "good morning," took her seat, next to Dr. Cook, and began with much manner, and emphasis to apologize for her delay in coming down, being at the moment when he called in the act of "disrobing." This form of expression, which I heard, without exaggeration, three times afterwards, seemed the only appropriate one, for the removal of such fine clothes as those she had on then, and as I heard had worn since she came. She was dressed in a white swiss muslin flounced, with a low neck and short sleeves, and a cape of the same, trimmed with the richest valenciennes three or four inches wide. She had on too the handsomest diamonds I think I ever saw and a belt which I am sure was solid gold with gold and enamelled knobs in front, added to this a crimson and gold net on her hair, and a crimson silk fan. She looked extremely stylish, but as you may suppose, utterly out of place and keeping with the time and place and people around her. She was perfectly easy and self-possessed, and has evidently lived in a certain gay fashionable watering-place society, in which they say she was a belle. I was agreeably surprised in her appearance, for except that she has bad teeth, I think she is decidedly fine looking. Gen. and Mrs. Hammond seem very much pleased with her, and Mrs. Paul [Loula Comer Hammond] is perfectly carried away. Catty is by no means so enthusiastic. For myself, she did not impress me as having the right style or finish. Indeed she seemed to me rather a "flash article." This opinion however is to be received with allowance, as Mr. Hammond intimates with a degree of earnestness which mortifies me not a little that I am envious of the notice and attention she received, and you know that I am unfortunately not superior to that weakness. I think tho' that I felt more, the superb indifference with which she treated me thro' the day. I am rather afraid, that she must have mistaken me for the Baby's nurse . . .

—Emily C. Hammond to her mother, Julia A. Cumming, 1861

which filled this valley between Aiken and Augusta, Georgia, closed during recent years. The only one in operation today is the one which began it all, historic **Graniteville Mills** in Graniteville (six miles west of Aiken, off US 1). The mill and its company-owned village were founded in 1845, and much of both remain in **Graniteville's National Historic District.**

This includes the 1846 canal; the original 1849 mill; 26 original mill-hand houses, their early Gothic Revival exteriors virtually unaltered; the 1847 academy built for mill children; and the 1849 St. Johns Methodist Church.

Graniteville was built by William Gregg, who came to South Carolina from Pennsylvania in 1824 at the age of 24 and quickly built a fortune as a jewelry craftsman and merchant in Charleston. Gregg was a pioneer in many ways, urging the development of cotton mills along the creeks and streams where the coastal plain meets the fall line (the swifter streams of the Piedmont region just to the north in time drew most of the mills).

Gregg saw mills as a place of employment for poor whites, and unlike most of his contemporaries, he refused to employ children under age 12. He also enforced compulsory school attendance for his employee's children in the academy he built.

Graniteville Mills thrives today—more than $500 million sales in 1993, for example—with more than 3,600 employees. Its principal product is indigo-dyed denim, used in blue jeans marketed under Levi, Lee, Guess, and other labels.

Gregg already was living nearby when he founded his mill and company town, and that is another chapter in Aiken County history. During the 1840s, Gregg owned about 5,000 acres on the large hill—**Kalmia Hill**—at what are now the western town limits of Aiken where US 1 enters the town.

■ A I K E N   C O L O N Y

When the Charleston merchants and cotton brokers built their railroad across the coastal plain in 1833, they used it not only to capture cotton trade from the river port of Augusta and seaport of Savannah, but also as a route of escape from Charleston's summers of malaria. **Aiken,** established during the 1830s and named for the railroad's president, became their summer resort, and a colony of regulars developed. Gregg was among the first.

The South's defeat in the Civil War left the Charleston merchants too poor to summer in Aiken anymore, but during the 1880s, the town began attracting a new winter colony of wealthy northerners.

It was pure serendipity.

The Highland Park Hotel in Aiken was one of the first grand resorts of the area when it was built in 1869. (South Carolina Historical Society, Charleston)

The short version is, a frail heiress with prominent relatives in New Orleans and New York began living in Aiken for health reasons and fell in love with the place. When she married a prominent and wealthy New York sportsman, she informed him they would be spending a lot of time in Aiken. The couple began bringing their crowd with them for the winters.

Vanderbilts, Whitneys, Mellons, Astors, and others followed Louise Eustis Hitchcock, the frail heiress, and her husband, Tommy, to Aiken every November, and left every March. The town began calling itself "the Newport of the South."

By 1935, the winter colony had built nearly 100 mansions, with horse stables, training tracks, polo fields, steeplechase courses, and a golf course. The colony's heyday passed after World War II, although the estates and stables remain, used by others.

During its height, there often were 80 private Pullman cars at a time sitting on the railroad siding in Aiken. A regular sleeper train made the overnight run from New York to Aiken daily during the season, sometimes adding as many as 50 extra cars and sometimes followed by a special freight of 60 cars carrying horses and tack.

Two of the nation's most famed horse-racing and breeding grounds flourish in Aiken and Camden.

The colony became so well known that no further explanation was necessary for a 1937 cartoon published by the *New Yorker,* portraying a smartly dressed matron stepping off a train and sighing, "Aiken, my Aiken."

Streets were left unpaved (and many are to this day) for the comfort of horses' hooves. Broughams and Victorias with their matched teams were a familiar sight throughout town during the season. One coach-and-four bearing Joseph Wilshire, heir to the Fleishmann yeast fortune, often rounded corners in the downtown shopping district with liveried footmen aboard sounding a flourish on trumpets: Look out, serfs, rich guy coming! And the serfs came out on the sidewalks to tell him how fine he was looking today, maybe while tugging a forelock and knuckling a brow.

Those without a mansion of their own made the **Willcox Inn** famous, including Franklin D. Roosevelt, Winston Churchill, John Barrymore, and Fred Astaire. Today the inn is open for lodging and meals and is a good spot to stop and get the flavor of the old colony.

The town still thrills to the old colony gossip. There was Sabrina, cook for the Grace family (Bethlehem Steel) who insisted her string beans all be the same

The Willcox Inn can count Franklin D. Roosevelt and Winston Churchill among its many famous guests.

length, naturally, not cut. It took **Fulmer's Market** three bushels to get one bushel she liked. There was Catherine, cook for the Iselin family (fine china) who insisted her leg of lamb orders be filled only with left legs. She said the right legs would be tough, since lambs would stand more of their weight on the right than the left.

The mansions, estates, and neighborhoods of the winter colony, 177 properties today, make up three National Historic Districts in Aiken. Their presence—even though nearly all the colony members themselves are long gone—gives the town its unique charm.

What equestrians such as the Hitchcocks and the colony also gave to Aiken, and through it to other parts of South Carolina, is an equine industry valued today at about $300 million. Some of the most famous thoroughbred racing champions in history have trained in Aiken during the late fall to early spring, racing the colors of the nation's most famed stables. They still do.

The horses, stables, trainers, jockeys, and owners, from Kelso to Pleasant Colony, are commemorated, with their photographs, racing silks, and trophies, at the **Thoroughbred Hall of Fame,** open afternoons in the heart of the winter colony district on the grounds of the old **Iselin Estate.**

The estate, donated to the town by the late Mrs. Iselin, includes 14 acres of gardens and ponds, including a "touch-and-scent" trail with plaques in Braille. Concerts and plays are given Monday evenings on the grounds during the summer. Next door, the **Carriage Museum** has a collection of vintage horse-drawn carriages.

Although horses are trained in Aiken throughout the year, the principal season for the major stables is the same as the old social season for the colony: November through March. There, you will find polo games most Sunday afternoons. Visitors are welcome to lean on the track railing early on weekday mornings and watch the training sprints and exercise rides.

A variety of equestrian events, from shows to drag hunts, enlivens **Hitchcock Woods,** the largest urban nature preserve in the nation, near downtown Aiken. The woods have miles of trails for hikes, strolls, or horseback riding for the public, and, on three weekends in March, the Aiken Triple Crown.

Dogwood Stable's Summer Squall won the 1990 Preakness, Rokeby Stable's Sea Hero won the 1993 Kentucky Derby, and R. J. Key Stable's American Winner won the Hambletonian in 1993.

■ MIDLANDS

In 1786, South Carolina's feuding factions of coastal planters and Charleston merchants vs. inland and upstate settlers chose a compromise site for relocating the state capital from Charleston. This was an unpopulated tract of two square miles at the confluence of the Broad and Saluda rivers, which together form the Congaree.

As a compromise, the location seems ideal: almost exactly in the geographic center of South Carolina. As often is the case with any compromise, however, the result was problematic. The old legislature picked a place hardly anyone wanted to visit.

■ C O L U M B I A

Until relatively recently, the primary entertainment in the capital city, christened Columbia, was the annual session of the legislature itself. Its antics and pratfalls remain high on the list, much like a scary, but essentially harmless, thrill ride at the beach or a county fair. With only the legislature, the state bureaucracy, and (since 1801) the University of South Carolina, Columbia became a ghost town every weekend as its residents left to find something to do.

The city's remarkable moments came in February 1865, when Gen. William T. Sherman's Union troops burned 80 blocks of its downtown to the ground and shot up what was left. Six bronze stars on the Classical (1855) blue granite State House at Main Street and Gervis mark where shells made direct hits. A tour of this building, offered weekdays, affords visitors an opportunity to view fine marble floors, balconies with brass railings, and mahogany woodwork, as well as a chance to hear about the building's history. (For information, call 734-2430.)

A view of Columbia looking down Main Street from the steps of the capitol, ca. 1870. (South Carolina Historical Society, Charleston)

Columbia and the Midlands lack the architectural history of Charleston, but there are a few antebellum houses in downtown Columbia typical of those in the capital city before Sherman's troops burned it. They are open to the public as house museums. (Call 252-1770 for days and hours.)

Two of the houses were designed by Robert Mills, the first architect trained in America, and during the 1830s the official architect of the U.S. government. Mills designed the Washington Monument in the nation's capital. His two Columbia houses are across the street from each other at 1615 and 1616 Blanding Street, between Henderson and Pickens streets. One, the **Hampton-Preston Mansion,** was home to both Gen. Wade Hampton of Revolutionary War fame and his grandson, Gen. Wade Hampton II of the Civil War. It later became a convent, then a fashionable private college for young women. The **Robert Mills House and Park** across the street at 1616 Blanding reflects Mills's neoclassical style.

The third house, the **Mann-Simons Cottage,** is devoted to the black history of the area. At 1403 Richland Street between Marion and Bull streets, the house was bought in 1850 by Celia Mann, a Charleston slave who purchased her freedom

An interior view of the historic Robert Mills House.

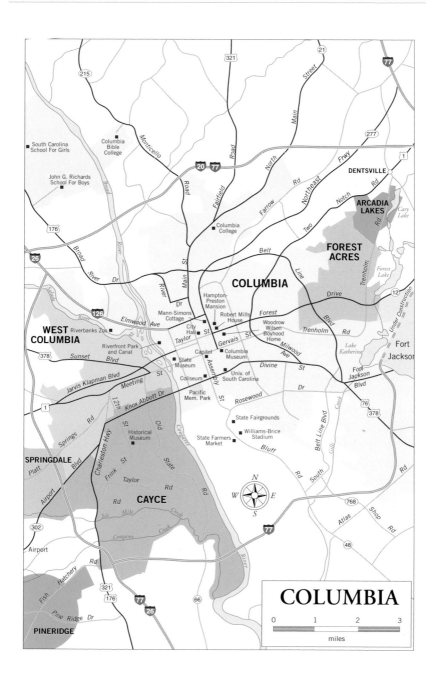

and walked to Columbia. Built in the early 1800s, the house is now a historical heritage house, open Tuesday through Sunday. A fourth house museum is **Woodrow Wilson's boyhood home** at 1705 Hampton Street. Wilson's father was a minister and this Victorian house is typical of a minister's home in the late nineteenth century.

There also is in Columbia one of the least publicized but most interesting places in the Midlands, the **State Farmers' Market.** Located south of downtown on Bluff Road (SC 48), across from the USC football stadium, the huge market, one of the largest in the southeast, offers year-round access to a dizzying array of fresh fruit, vegetables, and other produce.

Columbia is the site of several schools. The **University of South Carolina** was chartered in 1801 and opened with two professors and five students; today it has 23,000 students. Its historic area is the old "**Horseshoe**" of Georgian buildings set among magnolias and live oaks. Nearby Five Points neighborhood, five blocks east of campus at Harden and Green streets, is an eclectic mix of coffee shops, book and music stores, restaurants, and nightclubs frequented by the university community. **Columbia College,** a women's school affiliated with the Methodist church, and two private black schools—Allen University and Benedict College— add to the student life of the city.

Finley Park (named for mayor Kirkman Finley) gives downtown an aesthetic boost with its reflecting pools and walkways. **Columbia Art Museum** has the permanent Kress Collection paintings of the Italian Renaissance. The now-abandoned Central Correctional Institution where state prisoners were confined is expected to become a shopping and residential development on the banks of the Congaree River, just west of downtown. **Main Street Jazz** is a spring jazz festival held outdoors that has attracted much attention. For the first time in memory, visitors are traveling to Columbia for reasons other than to do business with the bureaucracy or visit students at the university.

■ NEAR COLUMBIA

The small towns, and even most of the farms in the two-county area known as the Midlands, are primarily bedroom communities for state government employees, who commute to and from Columbia, expanding the circle of suburbs and subdivisions every year. Columbia (population 103,000) and surrounding Richland and Lexington counties (population 454,000) seem destined to remain largely the domain of their principal industry: state government.

Fort Jackson, one of the U.S. Army's largest bases and an infantry training center, blocks the suburban sprawl east of Columbia. As a result, the population, subdivisions, shopping centers, and office complexes spread north and west, into Lexington County and toward Lake Murray.

This lake, impounded by an earthen hydroelectric dam a mile and a half long and 208 feet high, was filled in 1930. It covers 78 square miles, with 525 miles of shoreline, and is 14 miles across at its widest point and 41 miles long. Boating, sailing, fishing, picnicking, camping, and swimming attract thousands to the lake, especially during summers. For details and directions on public facilities, including **Dreher Island State Park** near the center of the lake, visit the Lake Murray Country Visitors Center near the dam (I-26 north from Columbia to the Irmo exit and SC 60 west to its intersection with SC 6).

Fly fishermen, canoeists, and kayakers also frequent the 10-mile stretch of the **Saluda River** below the dam, running to the Broad River. The rapids range from easy to dangerous, and outfitters and guided trips are available.

Riverbanks Zoo opened in 1974. After years of struggle, the zoo is renowned for its worldwide conservation work, and attracts more than a million visitors a year. The zoo's large animals are housed behind "psychological barriers," such as moats, water, and light, not in cages. Among the highlights at Riverbanks are the aquarium and reptile complex; the birdhouse; a working farm of domesticated animals; and, to open in 1995, a 70-acre botanical garden. The zoo is off I-126 at the Greystone Riverbanks exit near the confluence of the Saluda and Broad rivers.

Downstream from Riverbanks Zoo, on the historic old Columbia canal and the banks of the Broad River (Gervais Street at Huger Street just off US 1) the **South Carolina State Museum** opened in a unique setting in 1988.

This largest museum in the state is housed inside its own largest exhibit, a huge renovated textile mill, the first totally electric textile mill in the world. Bricks for the five-story mill came from the nearby **Guignard Brick Company,** the oldest continually operating brickworks in the nation. The Columbia Mills Company ran its textile plant inside the building from 1894 until 1981. Its 1915-era spinning room, with the original spinning machines, is one of the museum's exhibits. Other exhibits include the **Lipscomb Art Gallery,** featuring South Carolina artists; a full-scale replica of the "Best Friend of Charleston" locomotive used on the historic Charleston railroad of the 1830s; a replica of the Confederate submarine CSS *Hunley,* the first submarine to sink a ship in battle; a permanent exhibit on antebellum plantation slave life; and cultural displays from a variety of South Carolina regions.

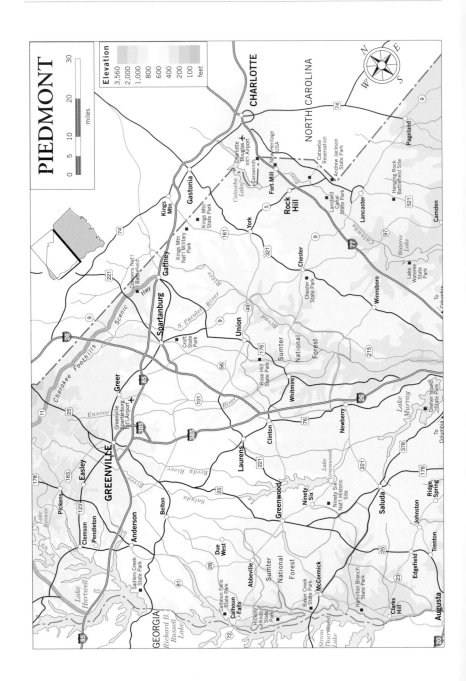

PIEDMONT

Elevation	
3,560	
2,000	
1,000	
800	
600	
400	
200	
100	
feet	

0 5 10 20 30
miles

NORTH CAROLINA

CHARLOTTE

Charlotte Douglas Int'l Airport
Carowinds
Paramount's Carowinds
Catawba Reservation
Andrew Jackson State Park
Fort Mill
Rock Hill
Lancaster
Hanging Rock Nat'l Heritage USA
Lansford Canal State Park
York
Kings Mtn
Kings Mtn State Park
Kings Mtn Nat'l Military Park
Gastonia
Gaffney
Cowpens Nat'l Battlefield
Spartanburg
Croft State Park
Union
Chester
Chester State Park
Winnsboro
Sumter National Forest
Whitmire
Rose Hill State Park
Greer
Greenville Spartanburg Int'l Airport
GREENVILLE
Easley
Pickens
Clemson
Pendleton
Anderson
Belton
Laurens
Clinton
Newberry
Lake Murray
Dreher Island State Park
To Columbia
Ninety Six
Ninety Six Nat'l Historic Site
Greenwood
Lake Greenwood
Saluda
Ridge Spring
Johnston
Due West
Abbeville
Sumter National Forest
McCormick
Trenton
Edgefield
Clarks Hill
Augusta
Baker Creek State Park
Hamilton Branch State Park
Sadlers Creek State Park
Calhoun Falls State Park
Calhoun Falls
Hickory Knob State Park
Lake Hartwell
Lake Keowee
GEORGIA
Richard B. Russell Lake
Strom Thurmond Lake
Cherokee Foothills
Scenic Hwy
Enoree
Reedy River
Saluda River
S. Pacolet River
Broad River
Catawba
Wateree Lake
Lake Wateree State Park
Lake Marion
To Columbia
Camden
Pageland

N W E S

THE PIEDMONT

A GREAT CRESCENT CURVES for hundreds of miles through the southeastern United States, from Virginia through the Carolinas and across northern Georgia and Alabama. The foothills of the Appalachians and the Blue Ridge mark its northwestern boundary. The fall line marks its southeastern boundary. The region in between is the Piedmont, almost a separate zone of geology, terrain, and of society.

In South Carolina, those two frontiers of geology—foothills and fall lines — mark social shorelines separating the old, agricultural, antebellum culture of the coastal plain and Sea Islands from a more hardscrabble, pioneering (and later, manufacturing) way of life.

The Piedmont's red clay soil was ill-suited to farming, but settlers persisted in tilling it for over 150 years. Then, a century ago, a manufacturing boom spread across the Piedmont—in the form of cotton mills and company-owned mill towns—which held the Piedmont in captivity just as cotton once held the coastal plain.

The people of this region never had the money or the time, or the inclination either, to be as casual, confident, and arrogant as the old guard on the coast, but in one sense the table is turned now, especially along South Carolina's 100-mile stretch of Interstate 85 as it runs past Gaffney, Spartanburg, Greenville, and Anderson. In this booming manufacturing area jobs pay wages that few residents of the old farm towns in the coastal plain can hope to match. The essence of the Piedmont lies in the fact that the people here make things: shock absorbers for cars in Anderson, silicon wafers in Spartanburg, roller bearings for cars and machinery in Gaffney. Yet there is more to the Piedmont than manufacturing. Historic towns such as Abbeville are worth any traveler's curiosity, as are four significant battle sites of the American Revolutionary War. Lush peach orchards line the byways of Edgefield County, and along the Savannah River, a series of dams and reservoirs form an inland "freshwater coast," fine for boating, camping, fishing, and swimming.

■ RED CLAY AND COTTON

In a sense, just as with the coastal plain, the history of this region is intertwined with geology and terrain. Merely by digging your fingers down into the soil anywhere in the Piedmont, you'll see you're in a region unlike the rocky foothills and mountains to the northwest, or the dark loam of the coastal plain to the southeast. Here is a red-yellow clay, a soil produced by millions of years of weathering rocks into a material called sapprolite. It often lies concentrated in deposits 100-feet thick and is mined for pottery. It was first utilized for this purpose by the Catawba tribe near the Piedmont town of Rock Hill; in the late eighteenth and early nineteenth centuries, pioneer settlers in the Edgefield area used the clay in the same manner. Today Edgefield and Catawba pottery are still highly valued.

Because of a warm, moist climate and relatively mild winters, bacteria thrive in the clay soil of the Piedmont, decomposing vegetation almost as fast as it falls to the ground. Very little humus accumulates, and without the acids produced by humus, iron oxides accumulate in the soil, making the land less fertile.

The region's hilly terrain also made farming on a large scale more difficult than on the flatlands of the coastal plain. Still, before and after the Civil War, farmers in the Piedmont persisted in planting cotton, overworking an already poor soil,

PLAIN FOLK

*M*y kinfolks did not live in magnolia groves with tall white columns to hold up the front porches. We did not care for magnolias—they were swampy; and as for the white columns, we considered them pretentious. We did not call our farms plantations in the Upcountry, and we did not call ourselves old Southern planters—we were old Southern farmers. We were plain people, intending to be plain. We believed in plain clothes, plain cooking, plain houses, plain churches to attend preaching in on Sunday. We were Southerners, native-born and of the heart of the South, but we preferred the ways of Salem, Massachusetts, to those of Charleston, South Carolina. Charleston was a symbol to us—it represented luxury and easy soft living and all the evils of Egypt. Charleston believed in a code that shocked us. It was Cavalier from the start; we were Puritan.

—Ben Robertson, *Red Hills and Cotton*, 1942

Mike Lake transports chicks, known as biddies, between hatchers and chicken farmers in the Ridge Springs area.

sometimes in hopes of cotton fortunes, often simply because they didn't know how to grow any other crop.

By the 1880s, the Piedmont's croplands were virtually exhausted, and eroding into huge gullies. (The exception to this is the peach-growing area along what is known as "The Ridge.") At the same time, South Carolina's economy, like that of all the former Confederate states, remained in ruins after the Civil War. The state's political and business leaders during the 1880s began to envision economic salvation in one aspect of the Piedmont which had never been put to such a use before: textile mills powered by the area's rushing rivers and waterfalls.

■ TEXTILE HISTORY

In scores of places all across the Piedmont, the region's major streams and rivers fall rapidly. The power of this falling water was ideal to power machinery, first with water wheels, later utilizing small dams and hydroelectric plants.

A campaign began to build cotton mills on those streams and rivers, and nearly every town in the Piedmont sought its own mill.

In 1880, there were 14 textile mills in South Carolina, employing about 2,000 persons. By 1910, there were 147 mills employing 45,000, and by 1931, the state had 239 mills with 73,000 workers and a mill village population of 190,000. Thousands of farm families across the Piedmont, and from the Blue Ridge foothills just northwest, left their small farms and entered the heat and noise of the mills, living in company-owned housing, buying groceries on credit at the company store. Soon the cotton mills dominated life in the Piedmont as much as cotton itself dominated life in the coastal plain.

Most of the mills were built by New England companies seeking cheap labor. In 1930, South Carolina textile workers were paid the lowest wages in the industry.

The mills, and later the apparel plants, virtually ran the Piedmont's economy and way of life until well into the 1970s. Through all those decades, mills and mill villages also remained the domain of white South Carolinians. In an unspoken, unofficial, and well-known agreement, mill hands regularly voted against allowing unions into their plants, and mill owners reciprocated by promising to keep the plants and company towns all-white.

Today, almost all the state's textile mills remain non-union, but the company town became obsolete during the 1970s, when most mills sold their houses and stores. The slow, general desegregation of schools, public accommodations, and the workplace beginning that same decade also opened mill jobs to African Americans.

Textile mill employment in South Carolina peaked in 1973 at about 160,000 workers, almost all of them in the Piedmont. Since then, the industry's work force in the state has dropped to about 90,000 and continues to fall as competition from overseas mills and automation within the state's own textile industry take their tolls.

Wages in the state's textile industry now are the highest within the Southern textile business, averaging about $9 an hour, but still relatively low when compared with wages in most other manufacturing jobs. Despite its declining status, textiles continue to dominate South Carolina's manufacturing economy, remaining the largest segment of industry in the state. About 22 percent of the state's manufacturing work force works in a textile mill, another 10 percent works in an apparel or fabric plant, and most of those jobs remain in the Piedmont.

What the cotton mills created in the Piedmont, beginning in the 1880s, was not only hundreds of mills and thousands of mill hands, but also an industrial and

National Guardsmen confront strikers at Greenville's Woodside Mill following a strike by textile workers in September 1934. (Underwood Photo Archives)

manufacturing point of view wholly different from the flavor of life in the rest of South Carolina.

■ THE RIDGE

There is a patch of rolling hills and tiny towns on the southwestern edge of the Piedmont, an area no more than five miles wide and 12 miles long in Edgefield County, which in a good year produces more peaches per acre than anywhere else in the nation. In April, when pink peach blossoms cover those hills, there are few roads anywhere in South Carolina with as stunning a display of color. (Drive US 121 between Trenton and Johnston or SC 23 from Johnston to Ridge Spring.)

South Carolina's peach harvest is second in size only to California's. Peaches are grown in most parts of South Carolina, but the Piedmont's crop dominates the commercial harvest.

Spartanburg County on the northern border of the Piedmont led the state in production until several years of unusually cold and long winters (as well as industrial development) cut the size of its orchards and put Edgefield County in the lead.

There are nearly a million peach trees in Edgefield County alone, all part of a strip of peach orchards along a district known as The Ridge, extending from Edgefield into Lexington County along US 25, SC 23, and US 1. Small towns along The Ridge put on street festivals celebrating the fruit—Johnston in April, Trenton in June, Gilbert in July.

From June to September, roadside peach stands pop up at every intersection in The Ridge. Thousands of migrant workers, from Mexico, Haiti, and other Central American or Caribbean countries pour into the district to harvest the crop. (They are among about 22,000 migrants who travel through South Carolina each year, harvesting peaches and apples in the Piedmont and Blue Ridge, tomatoes in the Sea Islands, tobacco in the Pee Dee, watermelons in the coastal plain, and planting pines on tree farms throughout the state.)

Edgefield County has been producing peaches commercially since shortly before the Civil War. It has been the home of South Carolina political leaders for just as long: 10 governors and five lieutenant governors of the state, including "Pitchfork" Ben Tillman and Strom Thurmond.

The entire small town of **Edgefield,** the county seat (on US 25), is listed on the National Register of Historic Places. Laid out around the courthouse square, the town has about 40 structures from the nineteenth century, mostly frame homes with center entrances and fan lights.

For longer than any of that history, Edgefield's thick deposits of clay have been a source of raw material for pottery. Archaeologists date Edgefield clay pottery found along the Savannah River to 2500 B.C., among the earliest pottery vessels known in North America.

Shortly after 1800, potters began establishing small businesses in Edgefield County to supply pioneers moving into the Piedmont with kitchen utensils such as storage jars, pitchers, pans, and bowls. By 1850, five potters employing about 35 persons were operating in the area. The invention of the Mason screwtop glass jar in 1858 closed most potteries in Edgefield and across the nation.

By then, however, Edgefield pottery had evolved to the production of pieces now collected by museums, such as "face vessels" made by slaves working in the region's potteries (with faces modeled into the jug) as well as other pieces with verses and scenes on them. The **Pottersville Antiques and Museum** on US 25 just north of Edgefield, and other Edgefield potters, are open to the public daily. For details and directions, see the Courtesy Center and Archives/Arts and Cultural Council at 104 Courthouse Square in Edgefield or call 637-4010.

Edgefield began supplying quality pottery to pioneers in 1800 and continues its tradition today utilizing the area's thick deposits of clay. (Photo by Robert C. Clark)

■ OLD NINETY-SIX DISTRICT

What happened to agriculture in much of the Piedmont as the cotton mills spread across the region, first during the 1880s, then in a second wave of expansion during the 1920s, is easy to see on the US 25 route north from Edgefield to Greenwood. For the entire 40 miles, there is not a hamlet, settlement, or farm left. There are dairy pastures and small cattle ranches here and there along the hillsides, and long stretches of thick forests as the highway passes through a section of Sumter National Forest, but nothing agricultural beyond the occasional patch of corn or pasture of grain. (An even more scenic, east-west route through this section of the Piedmont, one equally bare of farms, is US 378 from Columbia to McCormick, Strom Thurmond Lake and Hickory Knob State Resort Park, about a two-and-a-half-hour drive encountering only one town, Saluda.)

The demise of all those smalls farms has turned into at least one bonanza. It seems that most of the old furniture, furnishings, tools, and implements belonging to the farm families were put into storage, then during the past decade brought out again and put on sale. Consequently, antique shops and collectibles emporiums are thriving in the Piedmont today, especially in Abbeville, McCormick, and other towns in a four-county part of the western Piedmont just north of Edgefield and The Ridge.

The four counties—McCormick, Greenwood, Laurens, and Abbeville—were part of what was the "Old Ninety-Six District." The area takes its name from an eighteenth-century British fort which was 96 miles south of the old Cherokee capital, Keowee, in the Blue Ridge. At that time, this was the western frontier of the colony. When the colony became a state, with districts created by the legislature, the colonial fort and village around 96 became the district seat of government.

Today's town of **Ninety Six** is a small mill village 10 miles east of Greenwood on SC 34. Two miles south of town on SC 248 is the old fort, site of South Carolina's first battle of the Revolutionary War, a national historic site operated by the National Park Service, with a visitors center, interpretive trail, and restorations.

The towns of the Old Ninety-Six District, like those throughout the Piedmont, rarely display any antebellum or Old South architecture or aura. Most seem crisp, almost upright, with redbrick buildings and Victorian architecture. Irish, Scottish, and German pioneers established these towns during the early decades of the nineteenth century, and they had little in common with the Barbadian, English, and

Huguenot gentry who settled the coast of South Carolina. Examples of these towns are Clinton (population 8,000), home of Presbyterian College; Due West (population 1,200), home of Erskine College; and Greenwood (population 30,000), home of Lander College.

The famous mail-order seed catalog firm Park Seed Co., founded in 1868, and its test gardens, open to the public, is seven miles north of Greenwood on SC 254. The gardens are at their most brilliant during the summer months.

■ ABBEVILLE

Despite the fact that the Piedmont's architectural styles are decidedly different from those of the gentrified south, and that its manufacturing mode of life has created a different culture, some of the most significant moments of antebellum and Confederate history took place here, especially in the small town of Abbeville, on SC 72 about 15 miles west of Greenwood.

Abbeville may be the jewel of the Piedmont. It definitely is one of the best places in South Carolina to go strolling. The town's large historic district spreads for several blocks in all directions from Abbeville's restored town square, where the streets have been resurfaced with redbrick. A visitors center on the south side of the square provides brochures and maps for walking tours. (Call 459-4600.)

On the east side, in the old county courthouse, presently the **Abbeville Opera House,** restored in 1968 to Victorian elegance, stages professional productions year-round. When the ornate theater opened in the early 1900s, Abbeville was a railroad stopover for theater companies en route from New York to Atlanta, and one-night performances continued until the late 1940s. The Ziegfield Follies, Jimmy Durante, and Fanny Brice were among the performers. There are free tours daily, except during rehearsal times.

On the southeast corner of the square, renovated and refurbished in the same Victorian style as the opera house, is the **Belmont Inn,** with its elegant lobby, wide porches, and excellent French restaurant.

Restaurants, book stores, and antique and collectibles shops are on all four sides of the square, and along Trinity Street, at the northwest corner. One block down Trinity is **Trinity Episcopal Church,** built in 1859 and one of a score of structures in the historic district listed on the National Register of Historic Places.

Abbeville calls itself "the birthplace and deathbed of the Confederacy." In the middle of the square, a monument to the Confederacy explains, "The first mass meeting for secession was held at Abbeville, November 22, 1860. The last cabinet

Freedom Weekend Aloft sends balloonists into a gray sky in the Greenville area. (Photo by David Crosby)

meeting (of the Confederate government) held at Abbeville, May 2, 1865." John C. Calhoun, the South's leading antebellum politician, was born near Abbeville in 1782, had his law offices on the town square from 1807 through 1817, and was first elected to Congress from Abbeville.

■ INLAND COAST

Ice Age glaciers never reached as far south as South Carolina, and as a result, there are no large natural lakes in the state. Along the Savannah River, on the western border of the Piedmont, however, is a string of huge, Army Corps of Engineers dams and reservoirs. They turn the river into an almost continuous lake, from near the fall line just above Edgefield County all the way into the Blue Ridge foothills.

Campsites, marinas, and state parks—including an almost elegant Hickory Knob State Resort Park near McCormick—draw millions of visitors to the Savannah River reservoirs each year. From south to north on the river, there is Thurmond Lake (also called Clarks Hill), Russell Lake, and Hartwell Lake.

Hartwell Lake, on the Savannah River at I-85 in the heart of the Piedmont's industrial and manufacturing boom, is in fact a troubled reservoir.

PCBs (poly-chlorinated biphenyls, shown to cause cancer in laboratory animals) traced to a capacitor manufacturer's discharges from the mid-1950s until 1977 contaminate an upper branch of Hartwell known as the Twelve Mile River arm. The only significant health risk to humans so far identified would come from eating fish caught in this upper branch of the reservoir.

State and federal agencies believe containing the PCBs in that upper branch may be the only way to manage the pollution. Visitors to the area might conclude, on the other hand, that with so many other nearby reservoirs available, why bother with Hartwell at all.

Downriver from Hartwell is the smallest of the three Savannah River reservoirs, Richard B. Russell Lake, named for the late, powerful, longtime senator from Georgia. It also is the least used, and in part because of that, is popular with bass fishermen and smallboat sailors. The old mill town of Calhoun Falls, 30 miles west of Abbeville at SC 72 and 81, is the base camp for supplies. Relatively new

Portman Marina on Hartwell Lake serves boaters on
South Carolina's "inland coast." (Photo by David Crosby)

Calhoun Falls State Park, off SC 81 two miles north of town and on the lakeside, has campsites, RV hookups, and a small marina—the only one on the lake—with a store.

Downriver from Russell is the largest and most popular Army Corps of Engineers reservoir east of the Mississippi River. Its name is yet another wonderful story of southern politics and southern roots.

■ THURMOND LAKE (A.K.A. CLARKS HILL LAKE)

During the early 1950s, when the reservoir was filled, it was **Clarks Hill Dam and Lake,** named for a small South Carolina town nearby. During the 1980s, after having schools, roads, office buildings and monuments named for and erected to him in virtually every part of South Carolina, either he or his fawners decided if a reservoir was named for Senator Russell, then one should be named for Sen. J. Strom Thurmond, the "Energizer bunny" of Southern politics. The Corps of Engineers, ever alert to where its budget comes from, had no objections, and bingo, what had been Clarks Hill became **Thurmond Lake.**

The locals in Clarks Hill, Modoc, Plum Branch, and other hamlets on the South Carolina side of the reservoir, most of whom always vote for Thurmond, are outraged to this day. Billboards protesting what happened years ago continue to appear, saying, "Keep Clarks Hill." (As they say: It is unwise to mess around with a South Carolinian's dog, pickup, or the names he's used to.) How Thurmond, probably the most savvy politician in modern times when it comes to taking care of the home folks, ever got roped into this is unclear.

In neighboring Georgia, everyone still calls the lake Clarks Hill. State highway maps printed in Georgia also call the lake "Clarks Hill," while maps published in South Carolina call it "J. Strom Thurmond Lake."

The lake itself, with 1,200 miles of shoreline and 70,000 acres of water, is big enough that a boat can get caught in a squall at one part while others are becalmed in another part.

Nearly all the South Carolina shoreline of Thurmond Lake is either within Sumter National Forest or in one of three state parks.

Hamilton Branch (US 221 and SC 28) and **Baker Creek** (US 378) state parks, both near McCormick, have campsites, water and electrical hookups, hot showers, and rest rooms. Hickory Knob is more of a self-contained resort than a state park.

Hickory Knob (six miles west of McCormick on US 378) has an 18-hole championship golf course and clubhouse on the lake, rental boats, a skeet shooting range, a swimming pool, tennis, basketball, and volleyball courts, nature trails and programs, guided bus tours to nearby attractions such as Abbeville, a boat ramp and docks, a restaurant, convention facilities, campsites, and fully furnished cabins and motel rooms with cable TV and phones.

Along with Abbeville's Belmont Inn, Hickory Knob Resort State Park offers the premier accommodations in the western Piedmont.

■ REVOLUTIONARY WAR SITES

From one month after the Revolutionary War battle at Bunker Hill in 1775 until the British surrender at Yorktown, Virginia, in 1781, virtually the entire state of South Carolina became a battleground. The state was the site of the key battles of the southern campaign of the war and of one battle most historians consider the turning point leading to the American victory.

There are roadside historical markers at many of the 137 battlefields and skirmish sites in South Carolina, and four of them, all in the Piedmont, are national historic sites. These are Ninety Six, Camden, Kings Mountain, and Cowpens.

■ NINETY SIX

The first significant battle of the Revolution in South Carolina began November 19, 1775. About 560 rebel Patriots behind a crude stockade of straw bales, fence rails, and animal hides at the old colonial fort of Ninety Six were attacked and defeated by a Tory force three times larger than that of the Patriots. There was not a British officer on the field of battle.

Ninety Six became a key British stronghold in the Piedmont, where Tory sympathy was widespread. (See "Olde English District," following.) In May 1781, Loyalist Col. John Harris Cruger and his forces defended the Tory stronghold against Gen. Nathanael Greene and 1,000 Patriots. Greene's losses were twice those suffered by Cruger, but the Patriots managed to cut off the Tory water supply and cause a great deal of damage with fire arrows. The assault led to the British abandonment of their last backcountry fort.

Located on Route 248, the Ninety Six National Historic Site is open daily. (Call 543-4068.)

■ C A M D E N

By 1778, the war in the North was a stalemate, and the British turned to a southern campaign, hoping to control the Southern colonies before sweeping north to victory. The strategy began well. Savannah, Georgia, fell to the British in 1778. In 1780, nearly 11,000 British troops laid siege to Charleston, which surrendered May 12 of that year.

On June 1, 1780, Lord Cornwallis took Camden, the oldest inland city in the state, established in 1732 near the Wateree River on the southern rim of the Piedmont (US 1 and US 521 two miles north of I-20 and 32 miles northeast of Columbia). For 11 months, Camden was the principal supply post for British operations in the South. The town was heavily fortified and surrounded with a stockade and redoubts. The old fort and village, partially restored, is part of the 92-acre Historic Camden Revolutionary War Park, affiliated with the National Park Service, on US 521 just south of the city.

Then, in October 1780, the British southern strategy began to crumble.

Cornwallis had headed into North Carolina, leaving a force of 1,100 to scour the South Carolina Piedmont. Instead, that force found itself beset by backwoods Patriots.

BATTLE OF CAMDEN — DEATH OF DE KALB.

From the original painting by Chappel, in the possession of the Publishers.

■ REVOLUTIONARY WAR IN SOUTH CAROLINA ■

South Carolina experienced some of the fiercest fighting of the Revolutionary War. One hundred and thirty-seven battles were fought there, 103 of them without help from other colonies.

1775   April 19, Revolutionary War begins at Lexington and Concord.

November 19, about 560 Patriots at the old fort of Ninety Six are attacked and defeated by Loyalists.

1776   In June, British fleet of 11 warships under Admiral Parker is repulsed at Charles Town by Colonel Moultrie from fort at Sullivan's Island.

On July 4, Declaration of Independence signed in Philadelphia by delegates of the last Revolutionary convention.

1778   British turn to a southern campaign. Savannah, Georgia, falls.

France recognizes the United States of America.

1780   April 14, British victorious in battle at old Moncks Corner.

Nearly 11,000 British troops lay siege to Charles Town, which surrenders on May 12.

June 1, Lord Cornwallis takes Camden, the oldest inland city in the state.

Americans win two battles at Hanging Rock, July 30 and August 6.

October 7, Americans defeat 225 British soldiers in a one-hour battle at Kings Mountain. Considered the turning point in the war.

Huguenot planter Francis Marion becomes known as "the Swamp Fox" for his brilliant guerrilla raids and ability to hide his forces in the swamps.

1781   January 17, Americans defeat British at a cattle drover's shelter called "The Cowpens."

April 25, British win at Hobkirk's Hill near Camden.

May 12, Americans capture the British "Post at Motte's."

September, Battle of Eutaw Springs (now Eutawville) ends in a draw.

1781   October 19, Lord Cornwallis surrenders British army to Gen. George Washington at Yorktown, Virginia.

1782   In December, British forces withdraw from Charles Town.

1783   Peace of Paris; Britain recognizes the United States of America.

(left) The Battle of Camden. (South Caroliniana Library, Univ. of S.C.)

■ KINGS MOUNTAIN AND COWPENS

A Tory militia force of over 1,000 men led by Maj. Patrick Ferguson took a defensive stance at Kings Mountain on October 7, 1780, surrounded by about 900 Patriots. In a one-hour battle, 225 British were killed and the remainder wounded or captured.

The Kings Mountain battle is considered the turning point in the war because Cornwallis was forced to split his forces, leaving some in South Carolina. On January 17, 1781, much of that force was defeated by Patriot militia in another key battle at a cattle drover's pasture called "The Cowpens."

The meadow's terrain, gradually sloping up to a rise 70 feet above the surrounding forest, was effectively used by Gen. Daniel Morgan to defeat Gen. Banastre Tarleton and his Loyalist troops. Carefully positioned lines of riflemen at different elevations on the slope shot at advancing Loyalists, who charged into the firing until reserve cavalrymen refused to follow. The battle was an important victory for the American Patriots after their defeat at Camden the previous summer.

Today, **Cowpens National Battlefield,** about 30 miles west of **Kings Mountain National Military Park** on SC 11 at SC 110, has a visitors center with exhibits, picnic areas, a walking trail, and marked road tour. The Kings Mountain National Military Park offers similar facilities (16 miles northwest of York on SC 161, just off I-85 near the North Carolina border). Nearby is **Kings Mountain State Park,** with campsites and a lake for fishing and swimming.

■ "OLDE ENGLISH DISTRICT"

When the Revolutionary War began, the eastern Piedmont, from Camden north to Rock Hill, was a hotbed of Tory sympathizers. In part, this was due to the settlers' feeling that if they had a real enemy, it was the planter-merchant gentry of Charleston and the coastal rivers and islands who refused to share political power with the Up Country.

A nearly cohesive wave of pioneers from the Pennsylvania colony settled most of the region during the early and mid-eighteenth century. They named their settlements, such as York, Lancaster, and Chester, after towns left behind in Pennsylvania, which had in turn been named after towns in England.

As a result, in a bit of a stretch, South Carolina tourism promoters call the eastern Piedmont the "Olde English District," complete with the cute "e."

It might as easily be called "southern Pennsylvania."

Those early pioneers were as much interested in cottage industry as they were in cotton farming. They manufactured things—tools, farm implements—much as the earlier pioneers in the region, the Catawbas, manufactured and sold to other tribes their pottery.

When the "New South" industrialism of the 1880s began, the eastern Piedmont, already used to things mechanical, was one of the first areas to build cotton mills. Today, it remains dominated by textile and chemical fiber plants. DuPont's huge fiber plant at Camden and the largest textile mill under one roof in the South—Springs Industries' Lancaster plant—are examples.

Camden (population 6,700) is better known to most South Carolinians not for its Revolutionary War history but for its "Carolina Cup"—a day of steeplechase and flat racing, held each spring around Easter, and hailed as "the world's largest outdoor cocktail party." Crowds of 55,000 or more, most of the women in spring finery and apparently required to wear "Easter bonnets," jam Springdale Race Course. Tailgate picnics may include china, silver, crystal, and linen. Couples often get married during the annual Saturday event, which also is one of the

A portrait of Andrew Jackson hangs in a parlor room of
the Kershaw-Cornwallis House near Camden. (Photo by Lyle Lawson)

South's most prestigious steeplechases. In late fall, another prestigious steeplechase, the "Colonial Cup," is held here.

Camden does not have the mansions, estates, and winter colony historic districts which South Carolina's other "horse town," Aiken, has. But nearly 300 thoroughbred jumpers and 300 thoroughbred flat racers train from fall through spring at its Springdale and nearby Wrenfield courses and stable complexes. The Jell-O magnate, Ernest L. Woodward, and his friend, Harry D. Kirkover, began Camden's winter colony steeplechase fraternity during the 1920s. Mrs. Marion du Pont Scott expanded it during the 1930s, and upon her death donated the Springdale course to the state.

The WPA's 1941 guide to South Carolina observes that Camden was once known for its duels, and gentlemen flocked to the city seeking instruction in the code of honor. The state's last legal duel occurred in 1880, when Col. William S. Shannon and Col. E. B. C. Cash fought (apparently in an inheritance dispute). Colonel Shannon was mortally wounded, and his death resulted in the adoption of the state's anti-dueling law.

Even for those who don't follow the horses, Camden remains a charming town to visit, with some fine homes and beautiful old gardens.

■ EASTERN PIEDMONT

For the Catawbas, the usual route through the eastern Piedmont was via the Catawba-Wateree river system. For modern motorists, especially truckers, the usual route today is I-77, the busy connection between Charlotte and Columbia.

For the curious, slow-paced traveler, however, there is a less-traveled route: SC 97, which branches off US 601 just north of Camden. This scenic backroad passes by Wateree Lake, a Duke Power Company reservoir popular with smallboat sailors, waterskiers, and fishermen. Several marinas are on the highway. The route crosses the Catawba River at the mill town of Great Falls, and six miles west is I-77.

An alternate route north is US 21 from Columbia to Charlotte, along the river and leading to the Catawba Reservation, then Rock Hill. Along that way is **Landsford Canal State Park,** one of the most scenic picnic spots in the eastern Piedmont.

The architect Robert Mills designed a series of four canals on the Catawba-Wateree system during the 1820s to ship goods from the Piedmont to Charleston and the Atlantic coast via the Santee and Cooper rivers. The canals never quite worked properly, and railroads quickly made them obsolete. But Landsford State Park includes the best preserved section of the old canals, as well as a museum and interpretive center. The park's 222 acres also offer a nature trail along the canal and leading to shoals in the river where one of the world's largest populations of rocky shoals spider lilies bloom in May, and where striped bass and bream regularly draw fishermen.

The Catawba Reservation, and Catawba pottery exhibits and sales, are at the intersection of US 21 and SC 5, a few miles south of Rock Hill. (For more on the Catawbas, see the essay "Native Americans" in the "BLUE RIDGE" chapter.)

In an entirely different style, north of Rock Hill, are two huge, water-oriented theme parks. **Carowinds,** straddling the state line 13 miles north of Rock Hill on I-77, is a roller-coaster, water-ride complex that opened during the 1970s. The other theme park, at Fort Mill just north of Rock Hill (exit 90 off I-77 on US 21 Business), is the once infamous, now reopened-under-new-management, **New Heritage** USA. This 2,200-acre retreat, with its horseback riding, boating, tennis, camping, and hotel, was the downfall of its founder, the Rev. Jim Bakker, who was sent to federal prison for defrauding 116,000 lifetime partners who paid $1,000 each for an annual, three-day stay at the resort. The resort closed after the televangelist was convicted. Its new owners, a Malaysian corporation, reopened the park in 1992, still with a Christian theme.

■ I-85 CORRIDOR

The economic engine behind the booming Piedmont economy is visible—in some places—to anyone unfortunate or foolish enough to be driving I-85 as it crosses the northwestern corner of South Carolina during commuter hours. The 100 miles from the North Carolina to Georgia state lines often is plant-to-plant in industrial development, the majority relatively new and owned by foreign corporations.

It wasn't always like this. In the 1950s, when I-85 was being built, there were only two major stories newspapers in the area dealt with each year: whether the textile mills would permit summer vacations, and how the peach crop was doing.

By the 1970s, towns and cities along I-85 (which is almost the northwestern limit of the Piedmont) were facing economic hardship. Spartanburg County's famous peach crop, once the state's biggest with 40 peach-packing plants, was dwindling. An unusual series of harsh winters contributed to the decline, but so did the prices being offered for peach grove real estate by industrial, commercial, and residential developers.

The area's textile plants were virtually its only major employers, and they were cutting back, closing, or moving overseas. Greenville especially was an economic basket case.

Things began to improve with the arrival of foreign-based companies. The first foreign firm to arrive in Spartanburg County was Rieter, a Swiss manufacturer of textile machinery, which built its plant in 1962. Now, there are so many foreign corporations with plants in the county, and about 12,000 foreign citizens, most of them Germans, that little Cowpens National Battlefield, 17 miles north of Spartanburg, provides brochures in English and German. French and Spanish versions are coming soon.

In Spartanburg County alone, 19 German, Swiss, or Austrian companies can be seen just from I-85. A mammoth new BMW plant, the German auto maker's first outside Germany, recently began production in the county, and it is the twentieth visible from the Interstate.

Ground-breaking ceremony at the new BMW plant near Spartanburg (above). Foreign corporations have opened many factories along the I-85 corridor in recent years; one of the resulting highway landmarks is this peachoid water tower (right). (Photo by Robert C. Clark)

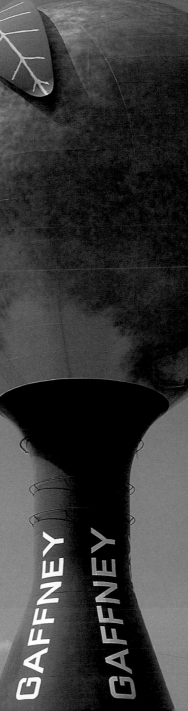

Just over the horizon from I-85 in the county are another 60 or so foreign-owned plants. There are 40 German-owned plants in Spartanburg County, which has had the highest rate of foreign investment per capita in the nation for a decade.

All that is just Spartanburg County. The boom envelops, to a lesser degree, all of I-85, from Gaffney to Anderson. In 1996, the BMW plant is expected to be in full production with 2,000 workers, and the same year, a big new regional shopping mall employing 2,000 (plus drawing thousands more customers) opens on I-85 not far from the BMW plant. Everyone, even state highway officials, predicts gridlock soon will set in on I-85 between Spartanburg and Greenville as I-85 is only a four-lane highway. It will be at least a decade before it can be widened to six lanes, which by then might not be enough either. About 60,000 vehicles use the route daily now, and by 2020, that is expected to double.

Unless you live, work, or have business to do along I-85, or don't mind driving it between 10 P.M. and 6 A.M., find another route—perhaps SC 11, a longer but more scenic route not subject to gridlock.

The BMW plant and its higher wages and multibillion-dollar investment is the prize catch in South Carolina's recent industrial development, and not just for itself. A slew of BMW suppliers and their new plants and payrolls came with it.

It is not just BMW in the boom. There are nearly 500 foreign-based companies employing about 85,000 persons in South Carolina, from the Swiss-based Hoffmann-LaRoche pharmaceuticals plant at Florence to the Japanese-owned Fuji Photo film plant in Greenwood to the Italian-based Union Switch & Signal plants in Columbia and Batesburg.

Industrial development observers usually point to two main reasons for the state's appeal to new industry, especially foreign-based industry. Beginning in 1961, South Carolina opened 16 technical education campuses across the state, promising new industry it would train new employees specifically for their plants. The program has been so successful it is a model, and pacesetter, for other states.

The second reason is South Carolina's traditional anti-union population and laws. It is a "right-to-work" state, meaning no worker can be openly compelled to join a union—even if the union represents the majority of workers in a plant. The state has less than three percent of its workplace union-organized, the second-lowest percentage in the nation. BMW opposes organizing efforts by the United Auto Workers, just as the state's textile industry long has opposed unions—almost always successfully.

For all the foreign-owned plants and industrial diversification in the Piedmont, especially the I-85 corridor, textile and textile-related employment remained dominant. It dropped from about 100,000 to about 86,000. But in 1990, the textile industry still employed twice as many workers in the I-85 corridor as all other manufacturing combined. The same is true statewide.

■ PENDLETON

Fifteen miles north of the I-85 corridor, on US 76, is the small town of Pendleton, a welcome relief after the manufacturing plants and commute traffic along the interstate. The entire town and a nearby area are listed on the National Register of Historic Places, one of the largest historic districts in the nation. More than 45 buildings here are worth seeing and some are open to the public. Among them are the **Farmers Hall,** the oldest such meeting hall in continuous use in the nation; **St. Paul's Episcopal Church,** built in 1822; and **Hunter's Store** on the town green, also the tour center for the historic district, where you can buy cassettes and maps.

RIDING HOME

I rode my bicycle home from school. All looked normal. I sniffed: high spring, Carolina, health and prosperity. People were shopping like crazy in stores along the highway. Plants were growing in the median, big sturdy weeds that looked a lot like carrots and celery, with thick stalks and ferny leaves dense enough to hide the underlying road trash. Traffic was a carefree stream of cars. The afternoon was average and happy, to the eye of a casual observer...

Out in the developments, some of the new roads curved back upon themselves, and I sometimes lost my sense of direction trying to get somewhere; or I might be riding along and all of a sudden the smooth asphalt turns to soft dirt and I'm in the country, with wooden houses balanced on concrete blocks, and the tragic crowing of roosters...

It was as if new places had been slapped down over the old ones, but some of the old was still showing through. I tried not to lose myself in those pockets. It could sometimes be too much for me, a house at the edge of a field, the rim of pines, and the smoke. It wrenched my heart. There was too much emotion for me in the country.

—Josephine Humphreys, *Rich in Love,* 1987

B L U E   R I D G E

IN THE WONDROUS WAY the natural world works, the tiny reproductive spores of the Tunbridge fern growing in the rainforest of South America were carried by wind and water north across the equator, across the Caribbean Sea, and into the Gulf Stream. The great current transported the tiny cells further north along the Atlantic Ocean coast of the southeastern United States. Somewhere off that coast, perhaps in winter when northeasterly storms sweep across the ocean, over the coast, and all the way to the mountains of South Carolina, the Tunbridge fern spores were swept from the surface of the Gulf Stream and carried far inland.

They landed in the mists of Eastatoe Gorge, at the end of a long valley near Sassafras Mountain, at 3,560 feet the highest point in the state. There, the Tunbridge fern thrives. It seems improbable, but so far as is known, that fern grows nowhere else on earth but in the South American rainforest and in Eastatoe Gorge.

The fern, Eastatoe Gorge, and the valley are among the subtle, remote charms of South Carolina's Blue Ridge, the southern end of the mountain chain which begins in Virginia and is the "front range" of the southern Appalachians.

Soc'em Dog, Screaming Left Turn, and Jawbone—fearsome rapids on one of the nation's most famous whitewater rivers, the Chattooga, the *Deliverance* movie river—are among the Blue Ridge's wilder wonders.

Remote streams for fly fishing; deep, clear lakes renowned for trout; an 85-mile, eight-day mountain hiking trail; amateur Saturday night bluegrass music jams at country stores; hillsides thick with apple orchards; and six of South Carolina's best state parks all within 45 miles of each other make this old homeland of the Cherokee Nation one of South Carolina's most splendid corners.

The Blue Ridge covers only the northern sections of Oconee, Pickens, and Greenville counties in South Carolina. Its boundaries are set by the state's borders with Georgia and North Carolina on one side, and on the other by the Cherokee Foothills Scenic Highway, SC 11, from the foothills town of Walhalla northeast to the intersection of SC 11 and US 25 north of Greenville.

Within this small area is the greatest annual rainfall in the eastern United States. Six rivers drain from its low mountains: the Chattooga, Eastatoe, Thompson, Horsepasture, Middle Saluda, and Toxaway. Actually, the deep, cold, clear waters of Lake Jocassee, created by a hydroelectric dam in 1973, inundated the Toxaway

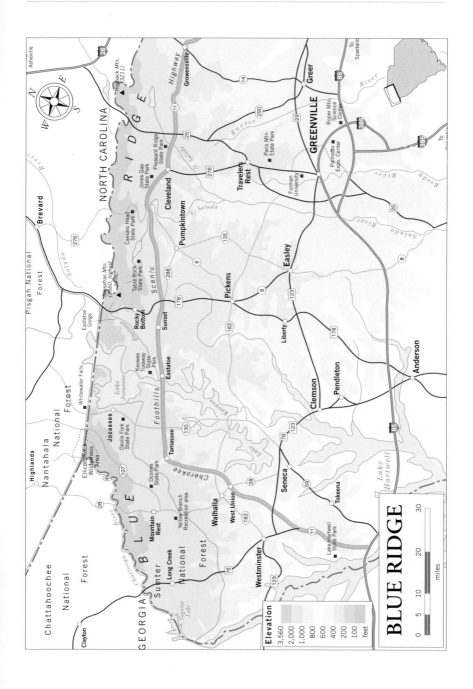

BLUE RIDGE

and Horsepasture rivers within South Carolina, as well as portions of the Thompson and Whitewater.

Just up the Whitewater River from Lake Jocassee, and straddling the border of North and South Carolina, the highest series of falls in eastern North America, Whitewater Falls, drop a total of about 900 feet.

Most of the Blue Ridge is within **Sumter National Forest**. Oaks dominate the mountain and ridge tops, pines the lower and the southern slopes. Carolina laurel, kalmia, rhododendron, large hemlocks, tulip poplars, hickory, black gum, beech, white ash, and sweet gum trees make this a varied forest.

Chestnut trees once grew here too, but a blight in the 1900s wiped out most of them. Another blight is attacking dogwoods with a fungus that has spread south from forests of the northeast.

The Blue Ridge of South Carolina, like mountain forests almost everywhere in the nation, suffers from extensive use.

■ MOUNTAIN FOLKS

South Carolina's Blue Ridge once was home for the Lower Cherokee Nation, which established a town and capital on the banks of the Keowee River. Neither the river, the capital town, nor the Cherokees are here anymore. The Cherokees began retreating deeper into the Appalachian Mountains to the northwest during the 1780s, as broken treaties and constant warfare with invading white settlers and their armies forced the Native Americans to flee their homeland. By the 1820s, only the names the Cherokee gave to rivers and places were left—Keowee, Toxaway, Jocassee, Seneca, Tokeena, Tamassee, and Eastatoe.

The Cherokee capital, also named Keowee, was just south of what today is Keowee Toxaway State Park, on SC 11. The town and the entire Keowee River are submerged in Lake Keowee, a reservoir filled in the late 1960s to provide cooling water for Duke Power Company's Oconee Power Plant.

As the Cherokees left, the Scotch-Irish arrived, and their descendants remain in the Blue Ridge today, fighting a losing battle of their own against another wave of invaders—wealthy resort developers and retirees seeking Blue Ridge beauty while driving up property taxes.

The Scotch-Irish came to America by the hundreds of thousands throughout the eighteenth century. They came from northern Ireland's Ulster Province, fleeing drought and war. When they arrived at ports such as Philadelphia, they kept on going, through more populous Pennsylvania, Maryland, Virginia, and most of North Carolina, until reaching the dark mountain hollows and river bottoms of the Blue Ridge.

For a bit less than two centuries, the Scotch-Irish and their descendant generations lived almost in isolation, and liked it. They survived by hunting, raising livestock, and growing corn, cabbage, and apples. There was a time, and it's almost gone now, when they also made applejack and "white lightning," or moonshine — illegal, untaxed whiskey.

Cultural changes across the Blue Ridge didn't begin to occur until the twentieth century, and even then the changes were few and far between. First, during the 1900s and 1910s, came the timber and lumber industry. Roads were built, sawmills constructed, towns established, railroads laid down. Forests which had stood for centuries were leveled, and where the ridge of mountainside was clearcut, erosion soon

This 1937 photograph from the files of the WPA shows an Appalachian mother of 14 children and 56 grandchildren. (South Caroliniana Library, Univ. of S.C.)

NATIVE AMERICANS

Beyond archaeological remnants and the small tribe of Catawbas near Rock Hill in the northeastern Piedmont, there is little left of the estimated 15,000 Native Americans living in South Carolina in 1600.

There is evidence of an aboriginal presence going back at least 12,000 years. By the early 1600s, there were 46 separate tribes in the state, the largest being the Cherokee and Catawba. Along the coastal rivers and on the Sea Islands were a dozen or more small tribes, each existing separately. European, mostly English, translations of their tribal names remain in the place names of the region today: Edisto Island, Kiawah Island, the Stono River, the Ashepoo and Combahee rivers, the town of Yemassee.

Traveling primarily by canoe, these small tribes summered on the coastal islands, catching fish, harvesting oysters, growing corn, peas, and beans. They wintered as far as 80 miles inland on the coastal plain, gathering nuts and wild fruit, and hunting game, especially deer.

Up the rivers of the eastern coastal plain, along the Pee Dee, Waccamaw, Lynches, Black, Sampit, Pocotaligo, and Wateree rivers, lived a dozen or more tribes of Siouan heritage, known as hunters and warriors. Along the Savannah River were a half dozen more bands, including the Apalachee, Yuchi, and fierce Yemassee. In the Midlands and western Piedmont were the powerful Cherokee, and along the Catawba River in the eastern Piedmont were the Catawbas.

All these tribes were village dwellers with diversified crops as their primary source of food and hunting as their second. They lived in huts of cypress or cedar bark, often inside log palisades. The Cherokees built houses, sometimes two stories high, of post and clay, and roofed with narrow boards. There, the similarity ended, according to one seventeenth-century English frontier trader, John Lawson: "I have never felt any ill, unsavory smell in their cabins, whereas, should we live in our houses as they do, we should be poisoned with our own nastiness, which confirms these Indians to be, as they really are, some of the sweetest people in the world."

The Native Americans also were susceptible to diseases brought by Europeans, especially smallpox. An epidemic of smallpox in 1738 killed half the Catawbas as well as half the Cherokees, and in the end killed more Native Americans than did all their wars combined.

By the 1670s, most of the coastal tribes had retreated inland. In 1684, they signed a treaty surrendering claim to the lands—all except the Yemassee.

This tribe, known among the other tribes as fiercely independent, lived mostly in the swamps and forests inland from Beaufort. After years of being swindled, en-slaved, and killed by white traders financed by Charleston merchants, the Yemassees attacked with devastating suddenness on Good Friday, April 15, 1715. They hit plantations and settlements in the Beaufort region, killing about 100 whites, then moved rapidly north to attack plantations on the Combahee, Edisto, and Stono rivers, coming within a few miles of Charleston, and raiding plantations along the Ashley, Cooper, and Santee rivers.

White refugees and their African slaves streamed into Charleston seeking protec-tion. The war did not end until early in 1716, when the Cherokees agreed to attack from the north (the Yemassees, a Creek tribe, were traditional enemies of the Chero-kee). This relieved pressure on Charleston, and a militia force attacked the Yemassees from there. The Yemassees retreated across the Savannah River into Georgia, and eventually into Spanish Florida, where they became extinct as a tribe, assimilated with remnants of another Creek tribe, the Miccosukee, and eventually were called the Seminole Indians of Florida.

continues

Benjamin Hawkins and the Creek Indians, *painted by an unidentified artist,* *depicts the early settler bartering for foodstuffs in the eighteenth century.* *(Greenville County Museum of Art)*

The war almost broke the South Carolina colony. Buildings and fences were burned, livestock killed or stolen, and crops went unplanted for years.

The Cherokees, whose southern capital was at Keowee on the Keowee River near what today is Clemson, never occupied the western Piedmont, but held sway over it. Accommodating the steady advance of white settlers, in 1755 they ceded to the British colony all but the northwestern tip of South Carolina, reserving for themselves their Keowee capital and today's Anderson, Oconee, Pickens, and Greenville counties, as well as land in Georgia and North Carolina. In return, the British were allowed to build forts in the Piedmont, such as the fort at Ninety Six.

The peace ended, the treaty broken, and the Cherokee War was launched in November 1757, after four Cherokees were murdered by whites near Saluda. Cherokee reprisals and raids continued until 1760, when an army of 1,200 Highlander and Royal Scots arrived from Canada, marched north from Charleston to Keowee, and routed what had been the Lower Cherokee Nation. In 1761, another force of 2,600 British troops, colonial militia, and warriors from both the Chickasaw and Catawba, enemies of the Cherokee, drove them into the mountains of the Blue Ridge. In 1761 the Cherokee Nation sued for peace, and the long war ended.

Hardly had the treaty been signed, however, when white settlers began moving into Cherokee lands, even as the Cherokees signed treaty after treaty ceding vast tracts in hopes of preserving a homeland for themselves. Warfare again broke out in the Blue Ridge and Appalachian Mountains, from Georgia through the Carolinas into Virginia, Kentucky, and Tennessee. Overwhelming colonial armies scoured the entire Cherokee Nation during 1776, and in 1777, the Cherokees surrendered all their lands in South Carolina, and all their lands east of the Blue Ridge in all the southern colonies.

In 1838, most of the Cherokee Nation left in the southern Appalachians was forcibly marched west to Indian Territory on the arid Oklahoma plains. Thousands died en route in the infamous tragedy known as the "Trail of Tears."

As a recognizable tribe, only the Catawbas remained in South Carolina, and by the time the Cherokees left, they too were rapidly dwindling and had lost their status with the government as an independent tribe.

Today, the Catawbas have regained federal status as a tribe, and have reestablished a reservation near Rock Hill. The reservation operates a community and cultural center where Catawba pottery is sold, and an annual tribal festival is held in November.

followed. During the 1930s, another transformation arrived—electricity from the Rural Electrification Administration.

Then, beginning in the 1970s, two centuries after the Cherokees were forced out, other people and other people's money arrived. Vacation homes, resort developments, dams, and reservoirs—pleasant as they are—where mountain rivers once ran.

■ CHEROKEE FOOTHILLS HIGHWAY

The Cherokee Foothills Scenic Highway (SC 11) is the only road connecting one part of the Blue Ridge to the other. Despite its "scenic" title, don't expect the valley and mountain vistas of scenic routes such as the Blue Ridge Parkway of North Carolina and Virginia. Autumn leaves and spring blossoms make sections of SC 11 a beautiful drive, while other sections of the route offer vistas of mobile homes, small factories, and convenience stores. The 130-mile two-lane road, as state tourism brochures put it, is "beautiful but still utilitarian."

■ SHOOTING THE CHATTOOGA

The first time I ran rapids on the river the Cherokee Indians named "Pouring White Rocks" was in an open, tough plastic canoe stuffed to the gunnels amidships with blocks of Styrofoam for flotation. I had the bow paddle. I did not have enough respect for the river.

We glided downstream over deep, quiet pools, steep ridges of what seemed to be impenetrable forest rising on both sides, the only sound the river's murmurs and gurgles, the only sign of human life just us, a writer and an architect, living in Atlanta then.

Sometimes I wonder if Mother Nature and a throne room of giggling Nature-ettes are lounging around somewhere waiting for yet another pair of fools to amuse them, just as my friend and I were about to, though mostly, I suspect nature is indifferent to such human endeavors.

The Chattooga got busy in a hurry. We rounded a bend and found ourselves in the middle of the river, caught in a powerful current which allowed no stopping, and headed straight for "the Ledge," a six-foot, sheer drop onto boulders we knew were below. We realized our only chance to avoid capsizing and injury, or death,

was to turn that canoe into a stunt car, paddling it faster than the swift current in hopes of flying off the Ledge as though it were a ramp, hoping to land upright and beyond the boulders.

Metaphorically speaking, Joe Meisel and I for two minutes (that seemed like hours) became the Emerson Fittipaldi and Mario Andretti speed kings of canoeing. We made it.

Canoeing, kayaking, or rafting the wild sections of the Chattooga in the early 1970s, the careless, ill-equipped, unprepared, or unlucky died at the average rate of four a year. Most of them were strangers to the river, drawn by the enormously popular movie, *Deliverance,* based upon the novel by poet James Dickey, who today is the poet laureate of South Carolina.

The movie was released in 1972. The year before, the U.S. Forest Service estimates about 800 river-runners visited the Chattooga. The year after *Deliverance,* 21,000 persons came, some to shoot the Chattooga, some to watch others try. The Scotch-Irish locals, already offended by what they considered an insulting portrayal in *Deliverance,* were angered at having their baptisms, picnics, and fishing trips disrupted by the exuberance of outdoor junketeers. (Joe and I made our run in 1970.)

Congress solved some of this in 1974, when it named the Chattooga one of the nation's rivers protected by the Wild and Scenic Rivers Act. The Forest Service was given jurisdiction over the quarter-mile of land on both sides of the Chattooga and regulation of river use.

Under federal protection, the Chattooga corridor is divided into sections: 68 percent classified "wild," with only foot or boat travel allowed, five percent "scenic," with vehicles allowed to cross only by bridges, and 27 percent classified "recreational," and accessible by car on only five roads. Hiking trails and primitive campsites are on both sides of the "wild and scenic" corridor. Fishing (brook, brown, and rainbow trout and redeye bass) and hunting in season (deer, wild turkey, quail, and grouse) is also allowed.

The Chattooga is much more than wild water. The 50-mile river originates as a trickle of runoff in the mountains between Highlands and Cashiers in North Carolina, and 10 miles later becomes the border between Georgia and South Carolina for 40 miles to Tugaloo Lake and River, which then becomes the border for a

Along the wild and beautiful rivers of the Blue Ridge Mountains are many waterfalls, including Little Whitewater Falls which empties into Lake Jocassee.

short stretch to Hartwell Lake and the Savannah River. From 3,360 feet in North Carolina to 891 feet at Tugaloo reservoir, the river drops almost a half mile. That's an average of almost 50 feet per mile, a sharper drop than the average mile on the Colorado River. It crashes through rock plumes and over boulders, a challenge many kayakers, canoeists, and rafters cannot resist. Its rapids run the entire "class" list, from I to VI, and the final seven miles below Earl's Ford—where Jawbone, Decapitation Rock, and more lie in wait—are restricted to professional raft guides and the most skilled kayakers.

The Chattooga is also pristine, its mountain climate heady in forest aromas of pine, in short, paradise for retirement and vacation homes and resorts. A mere quarter mile on either side cannot entirely protect the Chattooga corridor. As a result, the Forest Service, urged by the Wilderness Society and other environmental and conservation groups, continues to buy, bit by bit, parcels of prime real estate beyond the corridor, from landowners threatened by development and willing to sell.

The best road to the river from the South Carolina side passes through Westminster on US 76 through the heart of Blue Ridge apple orchard country. Roadside stands sell apple juice, cider, and butter, and of course, apples, all along the way. The small town of Long Creek is the "apple capital" of South Carolina, host of the South Carolina Apple Festival in mid-September. The orchards bloom in early April, and harvesting begins in September.

This route leads to the US 76 bridge over the Chattooga. On the right, just before the bridge, is a

Apples and honey for sale along a Blue Ridge highway.
(Photo by Robert C. Clark)

large parking area. An easy, 15-minute walk leads to picnic sites overlooking one of the most spectacular and dangerous of the river's rapids, Bull Sluice Falls, a 14-foot, three-level drop rarely ventured in a canoe but a favorite of kayakers. Bring a camera for action shots.

Kayak aficionados can visit Perception, Inc., the world's largest manufacturer of whitewater and touring kayaks, just below the Blue Ridge in the Piedmont town of Easley, 15 miles west of Greenville on SC 8 and US 123.

■ THE FOREST

One day in 1990, a fed-up Blue Ridge native of the little town of Long Creek, Hunter Sams, shinnied up a towering white pine in the Sumter National Forest and perched there for five days. Sams, of an environmental frame of mind (and no slouch at tree-climbing either, or media-luring, for that matter) was protesting a Forest Service timber sale in the Chattooga River basin.

Sams's theatrics struck a sympathetic chord among politicians and led to a three-state alliance, the Chattooga River Coalition, with supporters in both Carolinas and

Spectacular autumn colors paint the forests of Appalachia.

Georgia. The coalition in turn persuaded the Forest Service to embark on an unprecedented step in forest management history that could, if successfully completed by the end of this decade, change how all of us, from loggers to developers to hunters, campers, and canoeists use the nation's national forests.

In short form, the Forest Service and its research arm hopes to define just what are the complex ecological relationships inside the forest. The project—defining an ecosystem—covers portions of three national forests in the Chattooga Basin: the Chattahoochee in Georgia, the Nantahala in North Carolina, and the Sumter in South Carolina's Blue Ridge. It requires the enormously complex task of completing an ecological classification system for inventorying national forest resources. Hundreds of forest users are taking part, from the Forest Service, state and county agencies, Trout Unlimited, the Chattooga River Coalition, outfitters and guides, local businesses, private landowners, and lumber and timber interests.

The testing grounds of the Chattooga watershed cover 122,000 acres of national forests and the convergence of two rich and different ecosystems, the Piedmont and the southeastern escarpment of the Blue Ridge Mountains. Although the region was heavily logged earlier in this century, the forests have recovered enough to be classified again as maturing forest well on the way to their pristine condition.

Although the Forest Service still manages the Sumter and other national forests with an emphasis on timber production (which by law it is mandated to do), travel and tourism produce the most jobs. A Wilderness Society study (unchallenged by the Forest Service) in 1994 found that service-related jobs in the southern Appalachians, including the Blue Ridge, grew from 43 percent of all jobs in 1970 to 55 percent of all jobs in 1990. Timber employment in the area, meanwhile, accounted for less than 5 percent of all jobs—less than one percent within the national forests.

Blue Ridge locals such as Hunter Sams didn't need a study to figure out that much.

The pleasures and wonders of Sams's homeland, the Sumter National Forest, can be enjoyed and seen perhaps best with a stay at **Oconee State Park**, in the heart of Blue Ridge nature and Blue Ridge culture. Oconee was one of South Carolina's first state parks, built during the 1930s by young men lucky to find food, shelter, and a few dollars with jobs in the Depression-era Civilian Conservation Corps (CCC).

Their handiwork remains today in the park's 19 rental cabins; each has a fireplace and is fully furnished, heated, air-conditioned, and supplied with linens and necessary cooking and eating utensils. The CCC's bathhouse, stone picnic shelter, log picnic shelter, and a waterwheel built to provide electricity are other examples of the use of native materials and local resources at the park.

Visitors enjoy a 20-acre lake, rental fishing boats and canoes, lake swimming, and picnic areas. Many use Oconee State Park as a base camp for trips on the Chattooga River or setting out on the 85-mile foothills trail, which winds along the Blue Ridge border with North Carolina and ends at Table Rock State Park. Take note: "Foothills" is a misnomer. This is rugged, steep, mountain country in a forest wilderness.

Crossing through icy mountain streams and forests of hemlock, some four feet thick, the trail passes Whitewater Falls and some eighty primitive campsites. Hikers can join the trail from four other roadheads or two boat access points on Lake Jocassee.

Stumphouse Mountain Tunnel and **Issaqueena Falls** are about six miles northwest of Walhalla, on the right side of SC 28. A short, steep path leads from the parking area and campground to the bottom of the 100-foot falls, named for a legendary Indian maiden. No locomotive ever passed through the 1,600-foot tunnel, built in hopes of linking the port of Charleston and the cities of the Midwest. Its builders went bankrupt in the 1850s. A half-mile further up SC 28, in the Yellow Branch recreation area, **Yellow Branch Falls** cascade 60 feet over a series of ledges.

For suppliers, yarns, local yore, and, beginning about 9 P.M. every Saturday night, bluegrass mountain music, stop at Cuzzin's Country Store on SC 28 near the town of Mountain Rest. Every July 4th holiday, "Hillbilly Days" is held in Mountain Rest, a festival with local food, crafts, and music.

■ LAKE JOCASSEE

When Duke Power Company dammed the Keowee River just north of SC 11 near Salem in the 1960s, it created South Carolina's most beautiful reservoir, Lake Jocassee, then built a park on the lake, **Devils Fork**, with villas—*villas,* not cabins —unlike any in the state.

The setting, backed by the Blue Ridge Mountains, includes several waterfalls pouring directly into the lake, which is remarkably clear and as much as 440 feet deep in places. Brown and rainbow trout raised in Walhalla National Fish Hatchery (on SC 107 north of Oconee State Park and open to the public) are stocked in the lake annually.

Duke Power built the park and the state manages it. There are 59 campsites on the 620 acres of the park, each equipped with the usual water and electricity for RVs, plus picnic tables and outdoor grills, and another area for walk-in tent camping, as well as picnic areas, swimming, and a public access boat ramp.

The prize accommodations, rhapsodized in travel magazines and newspapers so much that reservations are necessary a year or more in advance, are the 20 mountain villas. With a lake like Jocassee, and villas like these, no wonder Duke Power kept title to the park.

The villas overlook the lake from a stand of mixed evergreens and hardwoods, and are luxurious. They come in one- or two-story, two- or three-bedroom flavors. All have cathedral ceilings, stone fireplaces, central heat and air, color TV, screened porches, and the kitchens come with microwave ovens and countertop blenders — catch a fish, make a soufflé.

A little bluegrass music livens up Cuzzin's Country Store. (Photo by Robert C. Clark)

Jocassee has become famous for its trout and white bass. A 17 $\frac{1}{2}$-pound brown trout, a two-pound-five-ounce brook trout, and a four-pound, 13-ounce white bass are among its record catches.

At 385 feet the second highest in the eastern United States, Jocassee Dam backs the reservoir into gorges and coves in the Blue Ridge. Fish grow at phenomenal rates in the cold, oxygen-rich depths. Nine-inch rainbow trout stocked in January average 17 inches about 10 months later.

Keowee Toxaway State Park is just across the valley from Jocassee and Devils Fork, also on SC 11. It protects the headwaters of Duke Power's other reservoir, Lake Keowee, just downstream from Jocassee. The park has one three-bedroom cabin for rent, 10 RV sites, and 14 tent camping sites, as well as picnic areas.

A few miles before SC 11 reaches Jocassee and Keowee, turn north on SC 130, and in about 10 miles (watch for the sign at the state line) is Whitewater Falls. The highest waterfall in the eastern United States, it descends over six sets of cascades. The South Carolina border runs through the middle of the 900-foot drop.

A misty mountain morning frames two horses and Lake Jocassee.

■ EASTERN BLUE RIDGE PARKS

The Blue Ridge range reaches its southern end at an abrupt precipice 20 miles, as the hawk flies, northwest of Greenville in the Mountain Bridge Wilderness and Recreation Area. The drop of about 2,000 feet from the mountains to the Piedmont foothills along this escarpment creates scenic vistas of far horizons.

The state's tallest mountain, Sassafras (3,560 feet), rises just west of the wilderness preserve. Its most famous natural landmark, Caesar's Head (3,266 feet), looms within the preserve, as does what many consider to be the state's most spectacular waterfall, 400-foot Raven Cliff Falls. A network of hiking trails, ranging in challenge levels and including portions of the National Trails System, traverses the mountains.

The lair of the Tunbridge fern is within one of South Carolina's most undeveloped, unspoiled, and least-known valleys, the **Eastatoe**. The valley extends west from US 178 along the first creek north of Rocky Bottom, and there are no road signs marking it. A one-and-a-half-lane paved road parallels Eastatoe River (more accurately a large creek) down the middle of the valley, past a few houses and vegetable gardens, to **Eastatoe Gorge**. Fly fishermen often prowl the seven miles of creek before the gorge, hoping for rainbow trout. At the end of the paved road, a strenuous hike through places where the gorge walls come within a few feet of each other leads to a whitewater mist, the Tunbridge fern, and 11 species of moss, including one found nowhere else on earth.

Sassafras Mountain is visible farther north and to the east of US 178. There are no access roads nor parks at the mountain.

Three state parks in this eastern part of the Blue Ridge offer a mountain experience of wilderness, waterfalls, primitive trailside camping, and climbs to the summits of two Blue Ridge mountains.

Table Rock State Park (on SC 11 about four miles east of US 178) is the oldest and most popular state park in the Blue Ridge. Built in the 1930s by the Civilian Conservation Corps, it was placed on the National Register of Historic Places in 1989. Table Rock has 14 rustic cabins with fireplaces, 100 campsites, a restaurant with dining patio, a 36-acre lake for swimming (with rental canoes, pedal boats, and fishing boats), and a 10-mile network of hiking trails. One trail leads to the 3,425-foot summit of Pinnacle Mountain, and is an access to the Foothills Trail. Another leads to the 3,157-foot summit of Table Rock.

Mountain Bridge Recreation and Wilderness Area is just east of Table Rock, and includes Caesar's Head and Jones Gap state parks, two of South Carolina's best fly-fishing streams, Raven Cliff Falls, and a challenging network of mountain trails.

Caesar's Head State Park, with its rocky promontories and lookout tower, is popular among birders who—for a change—can look down upon hawks, ravens, and turkey vultures flying in the valley. From mid to late September, great numbers of migrating broad-winged hawks pass by, drawing hundreds of binocular and camera-toting visitors. The migratory period continues into November as osprey, sharp-shinned hawks, red-tailed hawks, peregrine falcons, and other species pass by Caesar's Head.

The same overlooks drawing birders also attract amateur and professional photographers. Visibility, however, is sometimes obscured by fog or haze. Caesar's Head is a day-use park, although trailside camping is permitted. One of the park's trails is a moderately strenuous, 2.2-mile hike to an overlook at Raven Cliff Falls.

Jones Gap State Park, six miles east of Caesar's Head on SC 11 and US 276, is within a pristine Blue Ridge valley known for its diverse plant life, hiking trails, and the Middle Saluda River, the state's first Scenic River. More than 400 species of plants have been found in the valley, including rare or endangered species and state-record-size trees.

Primitive trailside camping is permitted along the five-mile Jones Gap Trail, which threads its way along the Middle Saluda, connecting with the three-mile Cold Spring Branch Trail, which in turn leads to Caesar's Head. Both the Middle Saluda and Cold Spring Branch are noted for rainbow, brook, and brown trout.

The network of trails across South Carolina's Blue Ridge is much like the labyrinth of tidal creeks and rivers across the marshes of the state's Sea Island coast—inspiring, at times humbling; two kinds of wilderness no more than an hour from centers of population.

(following pages) Table Rock State Park is near Sassafras Mountain, the state's highest point at 3,560 feet.

PRACTICAL INFORMATION

Note: Compass American Guides makes every effort to ensure the accuracy of its information; however, as conditions and prices change frequently, we recommend that readers also contact the regional chambers of commerce for the most up-to-date information. See "Tourist Information" beginning on page 313.

■ AREA CODE

The area code for all South Carolina numbers is **803**.

■ METRIC CONVERSIONS

1 foot = .305 meters
1 mile = 1.6 kilometers
Centigrade = Fahrenheit temp. minus 32, divided by 1.8

■ CLIMATE

In winter, temperatures generally average in the low 40s inland, in the 60s by the shore. Summer temperatures, modified by mountains in some areas, by water in others, range from the high 70s to the mid-80s, now and then the low 90s.

Spring is probably the most attractive season in this part of the United States. Peach blossoms are followed throughout the season by blooming azaleas, dogwood, and camellias from April into May, and by apple blossoms in May. Folk, craft, art, and music festivals tend to take place in summer, as do sports events.

State and local fairs are held mainly in August and September, though there are a few in early July and into October.

CITY	FAHRENHEIT TEMPERATURE			ANNUAL PRECIPITATION	
	Jan. Avg. High/Low	July Avg. High/Low	Record High/Low	Average Rain	Average Snow
Charleston	57 41	88 75	104 6	47"	1"
Columbia	56 33	92 70	107 -2	42"	2"
Greenville	51 31	88 68	104 -6	51"	7"
Myrtle Beach	56 37	87 72	104 9	49"	0
Caesar's Head	47 30	80 63	99 -19	81"	8"

■ ACCOMMODATIONS

South Carolina offers accommodations of every sort, ranging from quaint bed and breakfasts to lavish seaside resorts. The list below consists primarily of bed and breakfasts and inns, and is merely a sample of what is available in the major towns. Another option, for those desiring a more personal experience or planning to stay a week or longer, is to rent a house or cottage. Contact the Hospitality Association of South Carolina, Suite 505, 1338 Main St., Columbia 29201; 765-9000.

America's major hotel and motel chains are well-represented in South Carolina. To find out what is available, where, and for what price, it's best to use the following toll-free numbers:

MAJOR HOTEL CHAINS

Best Western International. (800) 528-1234
Days Inn. (800) 329-7466
Hilton Hotels. (800) HILTONS
Holiday Inn. (800) HOLIDAY

Hyatt Hotels & Resorts. (800) 233-1234
Marriott Hotels. (800) 228-9290
Ramada Inn. (800) 2RAMADA
Westin Hotels & Resorts.(800) 228-3000

INNS AND BED AND BREAKFASTS

Prices
$ = Up to $45 $$ = $45 to $90 $$$ = $90 and above

■ A B B E V I L L E
Abbewood B & B. 509 Main St.; 459-5822
   Built in the mid-1800s and recently restored, serving a continental breakfast.
   Three rooms. $$
The Belmont Inn. 106 E. Pickens St.; 459-9625, ext. 131
   Combine a night at this three-story hotel with an evening at the Opera House.
   The best room in the house is the John C. Calhoun Room. $$
The Hitching Post B & B. 503 N. Main St.; 459-2959
   Two rooms with private baths. Continental breakfast. $$
The Painted Lady. 307 N. Main St.; 459-8171
   An 1870 Steamboat Gothic. Julia Roberts spent a night here in the film
   Sleeping With the Enemy. Continental breakfast. $$
The Vintage Inn. 909 North Main St.; 459-4784
   Three rooms with a breakfast of quiche and muffins. $$

■ A I K E N
Annie's Inn. Hwy. 78 E., Montmorenci; 649-6836
   A two-story 200-year-old farmhouse just outside of Aiken. Originally three floors until
   a cannonball hit it during the Civil War. Full breakfast. $
The Briar Patch. 544 Magnolia Lane; 649-2010
   With only two double rooms, this tiny B&B provides a true Aiken experience. $
The Brodie Residence. 422 York St.; 648-1445
   Featured in *Southern Living* and run by an Aiken native. Pool and hot tub. $
The Constantine House. 3406 Richmond Ave.; 642-8911
   A formal and elegant B&B on six and a half acres. $$
The Willcox Inn. 100 Colleton Ave.; 649-1377
   A classic three-story inn with a history of famous guests including Winston Churchill,
   Franklin Roosevelt, and Elizabeth Arden. The lobby features two stone fireplaces and
   original pegged oak floors. $$$

■ A N D E R S O N
Evergreen Inn. 1103 Main St.; 225-1109
   An historic bed and breakfast. $$
Centennial Plantation. 1308 Old Williamston Rd.; 225-4448
   Ten acres, farm animals, and pastures. Three units. $$

River Inn. 612 E. River St.; 226-1431

Three units with private baths. Full breakfast with the likes of grits, biscuits, and red-eyed gravy. $-$$

■ BEAUFORT

Bay Street Inn. 601 Bay St.; 522-0050

Eight rooms on the intercoastal waterway. Used as a hospital in the Civil War. $$$

The Cuthbert House. 1203 Bay St.; 521-1315 or (800) 327-9275

A 200-year-old mansion offering two suites. Sherman stayed here on his march from Savannah to Columbia as the guest of General Saxton. $$$

Old Point Inn. 212 New St.; 524-3177

Four rooms in the historic district. Full breakfast. $$

Rhett House Inn. 1009 Craven St.; 524-9030

A lavish Greek Revival mansion with a live oak in front, Spanish moss, and double decker verandas. Used for filming *The Prince of Tides.* Continental breakfast; candlelight dinners by reservation. $$$

Two Suns Inn. 1705 Bay St.; 522-1122 or (800) 532-4244. A Neoclassical building that looks over the river. "Tea and toddy hour" and a full breakfast. Large rooms. $$$

■ CAMDEN

The Carriage House. 1413 Lyttleton St.; 432-2430

Built in the 1840s with two rooms. $$

Greenleaf Inn. 1308 N. Broad St.; 425-1806

Near downtown, built in 1840. Four-poster beds, and private baths. $-$$

■ CHARLESTON

For information on Charleston area resort islands, call 853-8000.

Anchorage Inn. 26 Vendue Range; 723-8300 or (800) 421-2952

An antebellum warehouse by the harbor. $$$

Ansonborough Inn. 21 Hasell St.; 723-1655 or (800) 522-2073

What used to be a stationer's warehouse has been turned into an all-suite inn. $$$

Barksdale House Inn. 27 George St.; 577-4800

Very elegant with bay windows, fireplaces, and whirlpool baths. Located in the heart of the district. Continental breakfast. $$

Belvedere. 40 Rutledge Ave.; 722-0973

Breakfast is served looking out over the Ashley River and Colonial Lake. The interior features woodwork from an 18th-century plantation. Continental breakfast. $$$

Brasington House Bed and Breakfast. 328 E. Bay St.; 722-1274

Rooms furnished with antiques. Private baths. $$-$$$

Cannonboro Inn. 184 Ashley Ave.; 723-8572

Elegantly decorated with period furnishings. Full English breakfast. $$-$$$

1837 Tearoom and Bed and Breakfast. 126 Wentworth; 723-7166. $$

Elliot House Inn. 78 Queen St.; 723-1855

Take a jacuzzi beneath wisteria in the courtyard of this lovely stucco inn. Canopied four-poster beds. $$$

John Rutledge House Inn. 116 Broad St.; 723-7999 or (800) 476-9741

George Washington ate breakfast here in 1791. Beautiful marble fireplaces and iron-work. Evenings include wine and sherry in the ballroom. $$$

King's Courtyard Inn. 198 King St.; 723-7000

Near boutique and antique shopping and furnished with 18th-century replicas. Private and accommodating. $$$

Maison DuPre. 317 E. Bay St.; 723-8691 or 662-4667

Built in 1801. Daily Low Country tea and fresh flowers. Complimentary tickets to the Nathaniel Russell House museum. $$$

Two Meeting Street. 2 Meeting St.; 723-7322

A Queen Anne Victorian with oriental carpets, four-poster beds, oak paneling, stained glass windows, and landscaped gardens. Afternoon sherry; continental breakfast. $$$

■ C O L U M B I A

Chestnut Cottage. 1718 Hampton St.; 256-1718

Four luxurious rooms in a Federal-style cottage, where Mary Chestnut wrote her famous Civil War diary and Jefferson Davis delivered a speech. The hosts run your bath water, turn down your bed, and treat you to afternoon beverages, brownies and milk at bedtime, and a full breakfast in bed upon request. $$$

Claussen's Inn. 2003 Greene St.; 765-0440 or (800) 622-3382

A converted bakery warehouse in the attractive Five Points neighborhood. There are eight loft suites, with downstairs sitting rooms and spiral staircases leading to sleeping areas furnished with period reproductions and four-poster beds. Private baths. $$$

Town House. 1615 Gervais St.; 771-8711 or (800) 277-8711

The meeting spot for a shag club. Artists and government types lodge here. $-$$

The Whitney Hotel. 700 Woodrow St.; 252-0845

Formerly condominiums, the building is now an all-suite hotel. $$$

■ D A R L I N G T O N

Croft Magnolia Inn. 306 Cashua St.; 393-1908

A four-room B&B done English-style. Homemade breakfast. $$

■ E D G E F I E L D

Carnoosie Inn. 407 Columbia Rd.; 637-5544 or (800) 622-7124
   An antebellum house with four rooms and private baths. $
The Inn on Main. 303 Main St.; 637-3678
   In the heart of Old Edgefield Village. $

■ E D I S T O   I S L A N D

Accommodations are limited on the island, and many families return to the same houses
year after year, so reservations should be made a year in advance. Weekly rentals on the
beach run from $750 up; houses a block or two from the beach are $450-$550. Three
Edisto Beach house rental agencies are Edisto Sales and Rentals Realty, (800) 868-5398,
Sea Islands Rentals, 869-3163, and Lachicotte and Harbour Realty, (800) 962-1930. In
addition, cabins can be rented at Edisto Beach State Park for $45 per night, or $282 per
week.

Bay Creek Villas. 3701 Dock Site Rd.; (800) 533-7145
   Overlooking the marina at the south end of Edisto Beach. Fully furnished 2- and
   3-bedroom apartments. $-$$$
Cassina Point Plantation. 1642 Clark Rd.; 869-2535
   A restored plantation house where the fields were once white with cotton. Full break-
   fast. $$$
Fairfield Ocean Ridge Resort. 1 King Cotton Rd.; 869-2561 or (800) 845-8500
   Contemporary-style villas with full recreational facilities. $$-$$$

■ F L O R E N C E

See phone numbers for chain hotels listed at the beginning of "Accommodations."

■ F R I P P   I S L A N D

Resort reservations: (800) 845-4100. Private island; focus on tennis and golf.

■ G E O R G E T O W N

Ashfield Manor. 3030 S. Island Rd.; 546-0464
   Comfortable screened porch overlooks a little lake that's home to alligators. $$
530 Prince Street Bed and Breakfast. 530 Prince St.; 527-1114
   A colorful and eclectic 1920's house in the heart of the historic district; homemade
   breakfasts. $$
Guest Quarters, Riverfront Apartments. 707 Front St.; 527-6944
   Contemporary apartments on the waterfront. $$
The Shaw House. 8 Cypress Ct.; 546-9663
   A bed and breakfast that epitomizes Southern hospitality. $

■ G R E E N V I L L E

Pettigru Place Bed & Breakfast. 302 Pettigru St.; 242-4529
　Built in the 1920s. Friendly service and a gourmet breakfast. $$-$$$

■ G R E E N W O O D

The Inn on the Square. 104 Court St.; 223-4488
　A European-style hotel. Local social events happen here. $$

■ H I L T O N   H E A D   I S L A N D

As most of the island is private, it's best to call ahead to rent a house or villa for a week or more.

Hilton Head Central Reservations. (800) 845-7081

■ K I A W A H   I S L A N D

Private island; this is a place to make reservations by the week and in advance.

Beachwalker Rentals. (800) 334-6308.
Kiawah Island Resort (Inn). P.O. Box 12357, Charleston 29422; 768-2121
　Three golf courses; 150 units.

■ M A R I O N

Montgomery's Grove. 408 Harlee St.; 423-5220
　Five acres of wooded property to stroll along. Full breakfast and private baths. $$
Rosewood Manor. 900 N. Main St.; 423-5407
　Covers an entire city block with four rooms rented out. Private baths; continental breakfast. $$

■ McC L E L L A N V I L L E

Laurel Hill Plantation. 8913 N. US 17; 887-3708
　Thirty miles north of Charleston with views of Cape Romain and the ocean. Reconstructed after Hurricane Hugo in 1989. Comforts of the 20th century with the nostalgia of the past.
McClellan's Bed and Breakfast. 915 Kit Hall Rd.; 887-3371
　Three bedrooms on three acres with very reasonable rates. Full breakfast. $

■ M O N C K S   C O R N E R

Rice Hope Plantation. 206 Rice Hope Dr.; 761-4832 or (800) 569-4038
　An old Southern rice plantation on Cooper River. Formal gardens and swaying oak trees. Continental-plus breakfast. $$

■ MT. PLEASANT
Guilds Inn. 101 Pitt St.; 881-0510

An 1888 Victorian with a grocery store, restaurant, and inn. $$-$$$

■ MULLINS
Webster's Manor Guest House. 115 E. James St.; 464-9632

Fifty minutes from Myrtle Beach with eight rooms. Uptown. Small fee for breakfast. $

■ MYRTLE BEACH AND GRAND STRAND
One of the most popular resorts on the Atlantic seaboard, Myrtle Beach is lined with high-rise hotels. For a complete list call the South Carolina Division of Tourism at 734-0122 and ask for their booklet. For chain hotels, see the list at the beginning of "Accommodations." Following are small, private lodgings.

Brustman House. 400 25th Ave., Myrtle Beach; 448-7699

A bed and breakfast with goosedown comforters and homemade breakfasts. $$

Chesterfield Inn. 700 N. Ocean Blvd., Myrtle Beach; 448-3177

Built half a century ago, this inn offers verandas and ocean views. Simple, old-fashioned rooms with private baths. $$-$$$

Sea Island. 6000 N. Ocean Blvd., Myrtle Beach; (800) 548-0767

Contemporary and luxurious. Rooms have balconies with ocean views. $-$$$

Serendipity. 407 71st Ave., North Myrtle Beach; 449-5268

Rooms decorated according to different historical periods. $$

■ PAWLEYS ISLAND
Manor House/Litchfield Plantation. 237-9322 or (800) 869-1410

Built in 1750 with a quarter-mile of live oaks lining the driveway. $$$

Sea View Inn. 414 Myrtle Ave.; 237-4253

A boardinghouse on the beach serving three meals a day. Low Country food, family-style. No TV, no phones. $460-$490 a week.

■ PENDLETON
195 E. Main. 195 E. Main St.; 646-5673

Two private suites with private baths and entrances. Ten minutes to Clemson University. $

Liberty Hall Inn. 621 Mechanic St.; 646-7500

An old summer home, with rooms decorated with antiques and family heirlooms. Great dinners served in the dining room. Continental breakfast included. $$

■ RIDGE SPRING
Southwood Manor. 100 E. Main St.; 685-5100

An antebellum house with four rooms, a pool, a tennis court, and horseback riding. There's even a 200-foot airstrip for those jetting in. $$

■ ROCK HILL

The Book & The Spindle 626 Oakland Ave.; 328-1913
A four-bedroom brick Georgian home. Breakfast served. $$

East Main Guest House. 600 E. Main St.; 366-1161
All the rooms have private baths. Jacuzzi and fireplace in the honeymoon suite.
Continental breakfast. $$

Park Avenue Inn. 347 Park Ave.; 325-1764
Built in 1916, it has only changed hands once. Breakfast included. $

■ SIMPSONVILLE

Hunter House. 201 E. College; 967-2827
Built in 1906, this two-story house has two lovely bedrooms. Located in the quaint
downtown, serving a full breakfast. $$

■ SPARTANBURG

Refer to numbers for chain hotels at the beginning of "Accommodations."

■ SUMMERVILLE

Bed and Breakfast of Summerville. 304 S. Hampton St.; 871-5275
Only one room that can accommodate up to four people. Located in restored servants'
quarters with a queen-sized bed. Pool. $

Linwood. 200 S. Palmetto; 871-2620
Three rooms with private baths. Within walking distance of antique shops and restau-
rants. Continental-plus breakfast. $$

■ SUMTER

Magnolia House. 230 Church St.; 775-6694
A Greek Revival house with gracious hosts. Five rooms decorated with antiques of
different eras. Full breakfast. Private baths. $-$$

■ TABLE ROCK

The Schell House. 4913 Scenic Hwy. 11; 878-0078
Recently built on eleven private acres. Views of the Blue Ridge foothills. Across from
Table Rock State Park. Full gourmet breakfast. $$-$$$

■ UNION

The Inn at Merridun.
Three blocks from downtown Union; 427-7052
A *Gone With the Wind* type of antebellum house. Thirty pillars and nine acres. $$

CAROLINA CUISINE

South Carolina . . . Ain't we got food! It comes from our forests and rivers, our gardens and ponds. It comes from three centuries of taming those forests and rivers, and balancing a fine European civility with a keen respect for the outdoors. We're proud of our land and we're proud of our sea, and we're proud of the signature dishes that so reflect our roots—steaming Beaufort stew, hot cornbread and collards, thick chicken bog, chunky catfish stew, ocean-fresh shrimp, and grits. Just when you think there's nothing better than barbecue and slaw, you remember how good that fish fry was, or how much fun you had at that oyster roast, or how that venison tenderloin made your mouth water and tremble.

Get any group of Sandlappers together and you're bound to find one of those favorites, and plenty of laughter. Of course, there are rules. For barbecue and chicken bog, the bread must be white, the tea must be sweet. For Beaufort stew—a coastal celebration of steamed shrimp, corn, and sausage—you need nothing but paper towels, and plenty of them. Catfish stew requires only a spoon. Make it big. You'll want every drop. That's because, simply put, South Carolina food is wonderful.

First to secede from the Union, first to invite you to supper, South Carolina remains stubborn but gracious. We believe in our traditions, but we've long since started experimenting with other trends. Our city restaurants are serving Mediterranean-style cooking, French bistro fare, and every ethnic variety across the globe. Small-town matrons pointedly say South Carolina's best cooking is in the home. And it's in the home that you'll find the South Carolina of novels—heirloom silver pulled out and polished, family linens pressed and laid out. Likewise, guests and hosts wear their best behavior, and it's not a chore, because we love to entertain and be entertained. Look for flat homemade biscuits and sliced ham, fresh vegetables, and rice, lots of rice. That's a holdover from the days when South Carolina's coastal rice plantations made us one of the colonies.

Years ago, the Carolina sun came up on breakfasts of salmon cakes and grits and went down on biscuits, molasses, and butter. Families in the country put cornbread in their buttermilk, plops of mayonnaise on sliced tomatoes and pears, butchered their own hogs and were grateful for what they had. You don't see that as much anymore, although now and then, you might run across an old man in a farmhouse kitchen slicing pats of butter and forking them into a plate of sorghum, molasses, or fig syrup. For him, there's no finer dessert.

continues

The diversity of South Carolina people—the strong and frugal Scotch-Irish, the resilient and ebullient Africans, the proper French Huguenots—have left their spirit and recipes behind. Today you can go to any barbecue and see all colors and creeds mixing—and no doubt debating over whose hash or sauce is the best. But rarely is a plate left unempty.

In South Carolina, barbecue is almost as important as religion. But all our food is wonderful. And we love to share.

—Aïda Rogers, restaurant columnist, *Sandlapper* magazine

■ RESTAURANTS

Prices
(not including tax, tip, or drinks)
$ = under $10 $$ = $10-$20 $$$ = $20 and above

Restaurants marked with an asterisk in the list below represent the recommendations of Aïda Rogers, who writes a restaurant column for *Sandlapper* magazine. See her essay "Carolina Cuisine," above, for more on South Carolina food.

■ ABBEVILLE
The Belmont Inn. 106 E. Pickens St.; 459-9625
  Built in 1903 and recently restored, it houses a restaurant too. $$
Dutch Oven. 112 N. Main; 459-5513
  Mennonite restaurant. Homemade breads and desserts typical of the Pennsylvania Dutch served cafeteria-style. Open for breakfast and lunch. Located in downtown. $
Yoder's Dutch Kitchen. US 72 E.; 459-5556
  Choices from traditional Pennsylvania Dutch home cooking. Shoo-fly pie, stuffed cabbage, meat loaf, and fried chicken. $

■ AIKEN
Malia's. 120 Laurens St.; 643-3086
  Gourmet and ethnic fare; pasta, soup, and salad—all served in tiny restaurant in back of The Gazebo, a downtown dress shop. Favorites are crabmeat bisque, corn chowder, black bean soup, steak salad. Signature dessert: Bananas Foster. $-$$*
No. 10 Downing St. 241 Laurens St.; 642-9062
  Restaurant, bakery, and shop. Upscale dining. $-$$

Pheasant Room of the Willcox Inn. 100 Colleton Ave.; 649-1377 or (800) 368-1047
A nice Sunday brunch, good steak and trout. Closed Sunday and Monday dinner. $-$$$
Up Your Alley. 222 In the Alley; 649-2603
Healthy selections along with steak and seafood. $-$$
The West Side Bowery. 151 Bee Lane; 648-2900
Casual and popular with a terrace. $-$$

■ A N D E R S O N
1109 South Main Restaurant. 1109 S. Main; 225-1109
Located in a Greek Revival-style mansion. Seafood and fresh fish daily. $$

■ B E A U F O R T
The Anchorage. 1103 Bay St.; 524-9392
Seafood gumbo, shrimp étouffée and the likes. Seasonal Sunday. $-$$
Banana's. 910 Bay St.; 522-0910
Wide range of foods; casual and on the waterfront. $-$$
Blackstone's. 915 Bay St.; 524-4330
This large marina store includes a sophisticated deli and live entertainment on the
weekends. Soups, sandwiches, smoked salmon, beer. Casual. $*
Gatsby's. 822 Bay St.; 525-1800
Overlooking the river, Gatsby's specializes in seafood and steak. Everything from their
own swordfish Bloody Mary to fettucine alfredo. $$
Steamer Oyster & Steakhouse. Rte. 6, P.O. Box 70-A, Lady's Island Parkway; 522-0210
This casual seafood and steak place is famous across the country. Known for Frogmore
Stew, steamed shellfish platters, Black Angus beef, and its hamburger. Serves lunch and
supper. $$*

■ B E N N E T T S V I L L E
Southern Oaks. 509 Beauty Spot Rd. West; 479-3964
Farmhouse serves homemade, buffet-style country cooking. Famous for barbecue
chicken and ribs and a dessert bar that includes banana pudding, pound cakes, pies,
and cheesecakes. $*

■ B L A C K V I L L E
Miller's Bread Basket. Main St.; 284-3117
Mennonite buffet. Fresh meats and vegetables, homemade breads and desserts. The
shoo-fly pie and coconut cream pie are delicious, as is the honey oat bread. Breakfast
served also. $*

■ BOYKIN

The Mill Pond Restaurant. Hwy. 261 between Camden and Stateburg; 424-0261.
Innovative, gourmet food in the middle of the woods. Fish, lamb, beef, and duck,
served in a restored, three-part restaurant—an old country store, old post office, and a
new dining room made from an old barn. $$*

■ CHARLESTON/MT. PLEASANT/ISLE OF PALMS

A.W. Shucks Seafood Restaurant & Oyster Bar. 70 State St., Charleston; 723-1151
Traditional Low Country seafood. Try the stuffed shrimp, seafood casserole, and she-
crab soup. $$*

Binh Minh. 7685 Northwoods, North Charleston; 569-2844
Vietnamese cuisine, authentic and delicious. $-$$

Bocci's. 158 Church St., Charleston; 720-2121
A favorite of locals who love good Italian food. $-$$

Bookstore Cafe. Corner of King and Hutson St., Charleston; 720-8843
Breakfast and lunch; on weekends you can get breakfast all day. Espresso drinks for
those with addictions. $

California Dreaming Restaurant and Bar. One Ashley Point Dr., Charleston; 766-1644.
Housed in a stone fort overlooking the Ashley River and its harbor. Good ribs and
seafood. $-$$

Carolina's. 10 Exchange St., Charleston; 724-3800
Offers quail with sun-dried tomatoes, goat cheese and chutney, and similar fare. $-$$

The Colony House. 35 Prioleau St., Charleston; 723-3424
Traditional Low Country fare in pleasant, airy, arty surroundings. One of the oldest
restaurants in Charleston. Crabcakes, shrimp and grits, lamb stew, she-crab soup. $$*

East Bay Trading Co. 161 East Bay St., Charleston; 722-0722
Fresh seafood, beef, and pasta served in three-story, restored 19th-century warehouse.
Desserts made in-house. $$*

82 Queen. 82 Queen St., Charleston; 723-7591
Classic Low Country cuisine. Seafood, beef, fowl, lamb, veal. Noted for its courtyard
raw bar, oysters and shrimp. $$*

Fulton Five. 5 Fulton St., Charleston; 853-5555
Elegant Italian restaurant serving a wide variety of pasta, salads, appetizers, entrees,
wines, and liqueurs. Late-night cappuccino and desserts. $$*

Garibaldi's. 49 S. Market St., Charleston; 723-7153
Italian cuisine, fresh seafood, pasta. Famous for veal parmigiana. Casual elegance in a
historic building. $$*

Hyman's Seafood. 215 Meeting St., Charleston; 723-0233
This favorite of the locals is noted for its daily list of 15 or so varieties of fish—cooked
any way the customer wants. Casual setting in restored warehouse. $$*

The Last Catch. Coleman Blvd., Mt. Pleasant; 884-2780
 Here, the fried seafood won't weigh you down because it's so lightly battered. Broiled
 seafood also available. Locals love this casual spot. $$ *
Le Midi. 337 King St., Charleston; 577-5571
 Authentic French food in an unpretentious environment. Rabbit, duck, and steak are
 some of their specialties. $$
Louis's Charleston Grill. 130 Market St. at the Omni Hotel, Charleston; 577-4572
 A gourmet version of Low Country food. Expect to try things like scallops pan-seared
 with corn sauce and littleneck clams on green onion pasta. $$$
Magnolias Uptown/Down South. 185 E. Bay St., Charleston; 577-7771
 A circular bar overlooks the dining room housed in an 1823 warehouse. Steak with
 wild mushrooms, black-eyed peas, and Madeira sauce. Salt and pepper fried shrimp
 with honey-mustard and horseradish dip. $$
Marianne's. 235 Meeting St., Charleston; 722-7196
 Elegant French restaurant famous for Eggs Benedict, seafood, and late-night hours.
 Dinner only. $$
Marina Variety Store. City Marina, Lockwood Dr., Charleston; 723-6325
 This favorite of the locals overlooks city marina. Serves breakfast, lunch, and dinner. $*
Middleton Place Restaurant. Ashley River Rd. (SC 61); 556-6020
 Plantation-style luncheons served 11 A.M. to 3 P.M. Charleston specialties—red rice,
 13-bean soup, she-crab soup, fried chicken. $$*
Noelle's. 83 Cumberland, Charleston; 723-2843
 Caribbean fare served in the oldest brick building in Charleston. Try their Caribbean
 pepper pot, and West Indian specialties. Shrimp and fried cabbage is also popular. $$
Old Towne. 229 King St., Charleston; 723-8170
 Good Greek food. $$
One Eyed Parrot. 1130 Ocean Blvd., Isle of Palms; 886-4360
 Casual, Caribbean-style specialties served beachfront. Famous for chicken and rice,
 conch fritters, Jimmy Buffet-chilled lobster, stone crab claws. Burgers and ribs also
 available. $$*
Pinckney Cafe and Espresso. 18 Pinckney St., Charleston; 577-0961
 Popular with artsy types. The menu changes each day with a Tex-Mex influence. The
 black bean burrito is a great deal. $-$$
Poogan's Porch. 68 Queen St., Charleston; 577-2337
 This is Paul Newman and Joanne Woodward's favorite restaurant. The cajun and Low
 Country food is why. Famous for red beans and rice, okra gumbo, fresh seafood. $$*
Primerose House. 332 East Bay St., Charleston; 723-2954
 Fresh and innovative cuisine. Weekly menus. $$-$$$

R.B.'s. 97 Church St., Mt. Pleasant; 881-0466
   Eat local seafood and beef while watching the shrimp boats bring in their daily catch.
   Famous for crab dip, seafood steampot, and prime rib. $$*
Restaurant Million. 2 Unity Alley, Charleston; 577-7472
   French nouvelle cuisine for a special evening. Reservations necessary. Jacket and tie
   required. $$$
Robert's of Charleston. Corner of Market and Meeting Sts. in Planters Inn, Charleston;
   577-7565 or (800) 729-0094
   Continental-style prix-fixe menu with six courses. Jacket and tie suggested. $$$
Sea Biscuit Cafe. 21 J.C. Long Blvd., Isle of Palms; 886-4079
   Famous for breakfast, but serves lunch too. Casual dining inside and on screened
   porches. Recommended: Eggs Benedict, hash browns, biscuits, fried fish, pancakes
   with fruit. Breakfast Tuesday through Sunday; lunch is Tuesday through Friday. $*

❖ BBQ SHRIMP WITH GRITS ❖
serves 12

Shrimp
Sauté or poach 3 lbs. shrimp in 3 tablespoons butter.
Place in Southern Comfort BBQ Sauce and simmer for one minute.

Southern Comfort BBQ Sauce

$1/_4$ lb. bacon, diced
$1/_2$ cup red onion, finely diced
$1/_2$ red bell pepper, diced
$1/_2$ green bell pepper, diced

two 14 oz. bottles ketchup
$1/_2$ cup brown sugar
1.7 oz. Southern Comfort
salt and pepper to taste

Cook bacon until 3/4 done. Add onions and peppers, sauté until done.
Flame with Southern Comfort. Add remaining ingredients and season.
Simmer 10 minutes then cool. Serve over grits.

Grits

1 cup heavy cream
$1/_4$ cup butter
1 qt. water

2 cups instant grits
salt and pepper to taste

Heat cream and water to boil. Add butter, salt, and pepper.
Slowly add grits, lower heat, and cook 20 minutes, being careful not to scorch.

—This recipe compliments of 82 Queens restaurant in Charleston

Shem Creek Bar and Grill. 508 Mill St., Charleston; 884-8102
Sit on the docks and have a drink. Popular for its late-night fare with good seafood and an oyster bar. $-$$

Slightly North of Broad. 192 E. Bay St., Charleston; 723-3424
"Maverick Southern cooking" serving everything from grits to shrimp pilaf to pasta. Two sizes of entrees make it nice for smaller stomachs. $-$$

Tommy Condon's. 160 Church St., Charleston; 577-3818
Irish pub and eatery, serving Shepherd's Pie and sing-alongs. $$*

Village Cafe. Coleman Blvd., Mt. Pleasant; 881-0466
French restaurant famous for crabcakes, black beans, salads, and innovative cooking. $$*

■ C H E S T E R F I E L D
Shiloh Fish House. SC 102, 5 miles from Chesterfield; 623-7204
Casual seafood, all fried. An area favorite. Thursday through Saturday only, evening meal. $*

■ C L E M S O N
Pixie and Bill's. Hwy. 123 Bypass; 654-1210
Fine dining in comfortable, elegant surroundings. Prime rib a house specialty; also seafood platters, beef kabobs. $$*

■ C O L U M B I A   A R E A
A.J.'s. 2864 Devine St.; 254-0699
A variety of food including salads, pasta, grilled meats, and fish. $$

Al's Upstairs Italian. 304 Meeting St., West Columbia; 794-7404
Fine dining overlooking the city of Columbia and Saluda River. Italian and seafood dishes; famous for lemon sole stuffed with Alaskan snow crab meat. $$*

Amadeus. 1531 Richland St.; 799-2704
Austrian chef serves innovative food in artistic, unusual setting. Varied menu at lunch; fixed menu, seated dinner in evenings. Great desserts. $-$$*

Ava D's. Ashland Park Shopping Center; St. Andrews Rd., between Columbia and Irmo; 772-0093
Lively European-style bistro serving gourmet food—fish, pasta, pizzas, mixed grills—and fine wines. $-$$*

Basil Pot. 928 Main St.; 799-0928
New Age/vegetarian choices in casual, university atmosphere. Loved for its interesting pizzas at lunch and supper and whole-wheat blueberry and strawberry pancakes weekend mornings. $*

Camon Japanese. 1332 Assembly St.; 254-5400
An intimate setting with authentic Japanese food. Call for reservations. $-$$

Elite Epicurean. 1736 Main St.; 765-2325
Friendly place to see old-time locals. Try moussaka and squid stuffed with shrimp. $-$$
The Fountain Room. Basement of Tapp's department store, 1644 Main St.; 765-2411
This old-fashioned, bustling lunch spot is a Columbia institution. Sandwiches, salads, plate lunches. Famous for vegetable soup and homemade cornsticks. $*
Goatfeathers Coffee Bar & Restaurant. 2017 Devine St.; 256-3325
Popular with arty types, this bohemian restaurant/bar is famous for unusual desserts, interesting drinks, and New Yorkish waitresses. The surprise is that it has really great food—tasty pizzas, smoked oyster pate, chicken satay. $-$$*
Gourmet Shop. 724 Saluda; 799-3705
A good place for a croissant sandwich. $
Hennessy's. 1649 Main St.; 799-8280
Appropriate for a special occasion. Maryland crabcakes, and "Grouper Hennessy" are popular. Lunch and dinner. $-$$
Immaculate Consumption. 933 S. Main St.; 799-9053
Sandwiches and salads. House-roasted coffee beans sold by the pound and used for espresso drinks. $
India Pavilion. 2011 Devine St.; 252-4355
Northern Indian food. $
Motor Supply Co. Bistro. 920 Gervais St.; 256-6687
A small menu that changes daily. Good food. The likes of porter house pork chops, grilled chicken with cantaloupe salsa. $$
One*Two*Three. 7001 St. Andrews Rd.; 781-0118
Upscale dining in sophisticated atmosphere. Pasta, seafood, salads, prime rib, pork. $-$$*
100 State Street. 100 State St., West Columbia; 791-0136
Fancy menu in formal setting. Serves dinner Monday through Saturday. $$*
Oriental Garden. 1710 Main St.; 765-9393
Good Korean and Chinese food. $
Parthenon. 734 Hardin St.; 799-7754
Run by Greeks who make a wonderful eggplant parmesan sandwich. $
Piggie Park. 1600 Charleston Hwy.; 796-0220
Famous mustard-based barbeque, pork hash, and sweet tea. $
Restaurant at Cinnamon Hill. 808 S. Lake Dr.; 957-8297
An old Victorian houses this restaurant. Pasta, seafood, lamb, beef, and chicken. $-$$
Richard's. 936 Gervais St.; 799-3071
Wonderful Southern cuisine. Bourbon BBQ and curried lobster. $$
Sesame Inn. 280 Harbison Blvd.; 732-7867
Mandarin-style Chinese food in elegant atmosphere. $-$$*

Touch of India. 14 Diamond Lane; 731-5960
Tiny mom-and-pop restaurant serves traditional South India dishes. Chicken, lamb, beef, seafood—some very spicy. Vegetarian buffet for Sunday lunch. Great coffee and mango shake; delicious ice creams and desserts. $-$$*

Villa Tronco. 1213 Blanding St.; 256-7677
A well-known local family has been serving traditional Italian fare at this restaurant for decades. Carmella's cheesecakes are many-flavored and famous. $-$$*

Yesterday's Restaurant and Tavern. 2030 Devine St.; 799-0196
American country-style food. $

■ EDISTO ISLAND

Bay House Restaurant at Edisto Marina. 3702 Dock Site Rd., Edisto Beach; 869-1589
A casual restaurant specializing in seafood, but you can still get a good steak or hamburger. Lunch and dinner. $$

Dockside Restaurant. 3730 Dock Site Rd., Edisto Beach; 869-2695
Overlooking Big Bay Creek on the marsh side of Edisto Beach, serving shrimp, dolphin, crab, hush puppies, and more. Dinner only. $$

The Old Post Office. US 174, Edisto Island; 869-2339
Menu includes shrimp, broiled with a mousseline sauce, on whole-grain grits. Also available are filet mignon, quail, flounder. Reservations are recommended. $$

The Pavilion. 102 Palmetto Blvd., Edisto Beach; 869-3061
A casual restaurant specializing in seafood. Lunch and dinner. $$

■ FLORENCE

Bonneau's. 231 Irby St.; 665-2409
Restored 18th-century mansion. Try the prime rib, quail, and chicken cordon bleu. $$-$$$

The Grotto. 1749 S. Irby St.; 667-8651
Modern Italian food in casually elegant atmosphere. Fish, eggplant, veal parmigiana, desserts are famous. $-$$*

P.A.'s Restaurant. 1534 S. Irby St.; 665-0846
Recommended by the locals. $$-$$$

Roney's Cafe. 112 N. Gaillard St.; 669-9803. Old-fashioned diner serves inexpensive country cooking and grill orders. $*

■ GEORGETOWN

Alfano's. US 17 Bypass; 651-0330
Italian dishes ranging from veal to pizza and pasta. Reservations advised. $-$$

Daniel's Waterfront Eatery. 713 Front St.; 546-4377
Locals love the innovative cooking and casual atmosphere overlooking the Sampit River. Seafood, pasta, quail. $-$$*

Rice Paddy. 408 Duke St.; 546-2021

This cozy establishment serves fresh salads, and sandwiches for lunch. Dinner is more formal with crabcakes, fresh fish, quail, and veal. Reservations advised. $$

River Room. 801 Front St.; 527-4110

Overlooking the Sampit River, an evening here is especially romantic. Try sandwiches, grits, or shrimp for lunch. Blackened tuna, grilled dolphinfish, and other fish served at dinner. $-$$

The Seafood Kitchen. 1923 Highmarket St.; 527-2145

Seafood served the traditional way—fried. Affordable, casual, generous. $-$$*

■ G R E E N V I L L E

Cottage Cuisine. 615 S. Main St.; 370-9070

Imaginative light lunches served in a picturesque setting—a restored cottage overlooking waterfalls and city park. Choices include grilled spinach and eggplant sandwiches, gazpacho and sweets. Menu changes seasonally; weekday lunch only. $-$$*

Damon's. 261 Congaree Rd.; 288-7427

Ribs, onion ring loaves, and casual attire. $$

Never on Sunday. 210 Coffee St.; 232-2252

This small Greek mom-and-pop is an Up Country institution. Well-seasoned, traditional Greek offerings available for lunch and supper. Homemade desserts and Greek wine. $*

Seven Oaks Restaurant. 104 Broadus Ave.; 232-1895

Located in a 19th-century mansion. Try their rack of lamb. $-$$

■ H A M P T O N

Yesterday's. 1201 W. Elm St.; 943-4123

European chef serves fine food in this small Southern town. Lamb, seafood, veal, beef, and chicken in casual/elegant, relaxed setting. $-$$*

■ H I L T O N   H E A D

The Barony Grill. The Westin Resort, 135 S. Port Royal Dr.; 681-4000

The hickory-smoked prime rib is excellent, as is the lobster. $$-$$$

Cafe Europa. At the Lighthouse in Harbour Town; 671-3399

Casual with a view of the harbor. $-$$

Charlie's L'Etoile Verte. 1000 Plantation Center; 785-9277

French bistro, casual atmosphere, plentiful portions. Variety of fish, veal, lamb, and pate specials; Cobb salad at lunch is famous. Plenty of wine and delicious homemade desserts. Dinner reservations recommended. $$*

Crazy Crab. US 278; 681-5021 and Harbour Town Yacht Basin; 363-2722

Famous for fresh seafood. Try their Crazy Crab boil and seafood pot. $$

Harbour Town Grill. Lighthouse Lane in Harbour Town; 671-3119
Part of the Harbour Town Golf Links clubhouse. Jackets for dinner, and reservations recommended. $$-$$$
Hudson's. The Landing; 681-2773
Family-owned, this restaurant has its own fleet of fishing boats. Overlooks the coastal waterway. Quick and friendly service. $$
Old Fort Pub. Hilton Head Plantation; 681-2386
This informal restaurant overlooks Skull Creek and offers such dishes as Savannah chicken-fried steak and oyster pie. $$-$$$
Truffles Cafe. Sea Pines Center on Lighthouse Rd.; 671-6136
Soups, salads, sandwiches, pizzas, as well as prime rib and seafood. $-$$

■ **K E R S H A W**
Cromer's Cafeteria. S. Hampton St.; 475-6912
Country cooking buffet in casual surroundings. Fried chicken, country fried steak, variety of vegetables available. $*

■ **K I N G S T R E E**
Piccolo's. 121 N. Long St.; 354-7555
Local favorite. Italian food and a variety of dishes in comfortable surroundings. $-$$*
The Station House. 134 E. Main St.; 354-5042
Fairly fine dining in restored train station. Beef, seafood, prime rib, pasta, fowl, various mixed grill entrees. $$*

■ **L A U R E N S**
The Graystone. 1100 S. Harper St.; 984-5521
Elegant dining in resplendent old home. Rack of lamb, prime rib, Alaskan king crab, seafood, calves' liver. Famous for its salad bar and peppermint ice cream. $$*
The Sweet Shoppe. S. Harper St.; 984-3113
Casual lunch spot. Try the Gorgeous George, a tropical burger, or the Crabby John, a crab salad-tomato-mozzarella combo. Cookie Fantastic is a favorite hot fudge/chocolate chip dessert. $*

■ **L E E S V I L L E**
The Pine Cupboard. Rear of The Attic gift shop on Main St.; 532-3016
Great Americana lunch—homemade vegetable soup and creamy chicken salad on fresh sourdough bread. Fruit salads and desserts. Open every weekday except Wednesday; lunch only. $*
Shealy's Bar-B-Que House. 340 Church St.; 532-8135
They come from miles around to feast at this barbecue/country cooking buffet. Famous for hash, mustard-style pork barbecue, fried chicken, and creamed corn. Salad bar available for light eaters. $*

■ **LEXINGTON**

Hite's. 105 Columbia Ave.; 359-2589

A landmark famous for its country cooking buffet, barbecue, dairy bar, and pies. $*

Lexington Arms. 314-A W. Main St.; 359-2700 or 329-2226

German and French dishes along with steaks, seafood, veal, pasta, and poultry. Comfortable atmosphere somewhere between casual and dressy. A local favorite. Evenings only. $$*

Restaurant at Cinnamon Hill. 808 S. Lake Dr.; 957-8297

Elegant dining in restored Victorian home. Fish, beef, chicken, pasta, seafood, homemade desserts. Sunday brunch, lunch, and supper. Patio dining and live jazz. $-$$*

■ **LITCHFIELD BEACH**

Robby's on the Beach. Second floor of Litchfield Inn, US 17; 237-8888

Fresh seafood, gourmet-style. Ocean view. Famous for crabcakes, shad roe, softshell crab, baked crab Emogene, and wines. $$*

■ **MANNING**

Central Coffee Shop. 8 N. Brooks; 435-4289

This is the oldest family-owned restaurant in the state and the favorite place of author/poet James Dickey. Old-style diner famous for pies, plate lunches, and suppers. A few Greek offerings available. $*

■ **MONCKS CORNER**

The Dock. 761-8080

Casual, large, family seafood restaurant overlooking the Tail Race Canal, which connects Lake Moultrie to the Cooper River. Fried catfish is house specialty. Peanut butter pie is house dessert. $-$$*

■ **MURRELLS INLET AREA**

Anchovy's. US 17; 651-0664

Casual, fun spot serving pizza and other Italian favorites. Refreshing because it *doesn't* serve seafood in this regionally famous fishing village. $-$$*

The Gulfstream Cafe. 350 S. Waccamaw Dr., Garden City; 651-8808

Fresh seafood, waterfront view. $$-$$$*

Lee's Inlet Kitchen. US 17; 651-288

Homemade clam chowder, fresh baked pies, and hamburgers. Dinner only. $$

Oliver's Lodge. US 17; 651-2963

This is the granddaddy of them all, the oldest seafood restaurant in Murrells Inlet. Besides typical fried seafood platters, the Lodge serves more modern, sophisticated fare. $-$$*

Sunnyside. US 17; 651-9105

Old family recipes and new innovations at this favorite, casual seafood spot. $$*

■ M Y R T L E   B E A C H

Gullyfield Restaurant. US 17 N.; 449-3111

An established seafood restaurant with a casual atmosphere, Gullyfield features fresh king mackerel, and lobster pie. $$-$$$

Marina Raw Bar. US 17 N.; 249-3972

Specializing in fresh and steamed oysters and clams. $$-$$$

Outrigger Seafood. 1434 US 17 S.; 272-8032

This is a version of a Southern "fish camp" gone wild. A rambling restaurant with everything from grouper bearnaise to fried dishes, with diners in shorts as well as suits. All-you-can-eat. $$

Peaches. 900 N. Ocean Blvd.; 448-7424

Cheap eats. The best burger on the beach and foot-long hot dogs as well. $

Rice Planter's Restaurant. 6707 N. Kings Hwy.; 449-3456 or 449-3457

Seafood specialties as well as a plethora of other dishes. Low Country decor and candle-light. $-$$

Ristorante Villa Romana. 707 S. Kings Hwy.; 448-4990

Nouveau Italian cuisine, including freshly made bread, and pasta. Real Italian accents. You may catch some live music as well. $$

Rock Burger. 1107 N. Ocean Blvd. 448-7731

Casual burger joint with rock 'n' roll motif; famous for long fries and late-night hours. $*

The Sea Captain's House. 3002 N. Ocean Blvd.; 448-8082

A former bed and breakfast overlooking the ocean. Best seafood on the Grand Strand. $$

Toby's Restaurant and Raw Bar. 1407 US 17; 249-2624

For gourmet eating, Toby's offers scallops and oysters wrapped in bacon, crabcakes, and steak au poivre. Dress is casual. $$

Villa Mare. 7819 Kings Hwy.; 449-8654

A simple restaurant serving hoagies, pizza, pasta, and calzone. $-$$

■ P A W L E Y S   I S L A N D

Frank's Restaurant. US 17 N.; 237-1581

Serving a variety of dishes, including steak, veal chops, rack of lamb, and seafood. Reservations are recommended. $$-$$$*

Plantation House. US 17 between Pawleys Island and Georgetown; 237-4205

Landmark seafood restaurant that also serves steaks. $-$$*

Tyler's Cove. The Hammock Shops, US 17; 237-4848

Blackened tuna, shrimp parmesan, chicken kabobs, pasta, and T-bone steak. $$

■ P E N D L E T O N

Farmer's Hall Restaurant and Tea Room. Town Square; 646-7024

Desserts and sour cream drop biscuits. Open Tuesday through Saturday. $-$$

The Lazy Islander. Town Square; 646-7672

Seafood, stir fry, varied menu in casual, tropical, party-time atmosphere. $-$$*

Liberty Hall Inn. 621 S. Mechanic St.; 646-7500

Small restaurant in a historic bed and breakfast. Beef tenderloin recommended; veal, chicken, and fish dishes vary nightly. $$*

■ P L U M   B R A N C H

The Plum. US 221; 443-2201

This tiny McCormick County surprise serves French countryside appeal in an old post office. Eclectic atmosphere, plenty of wine. Lamb, veal, seafood, escargot. Superb. $$*

■ P R O S P E R I T Y

Perry's Back Porch. Main St.; 364-3556

Country cooking buffet in charmingly restored post office and grocery store. Bakery sells old-fashioned treats. Pure American South. $*

■ R E M B E R T

Lilfred's. Hwy. 521 between Sumter and Camden or 11 Main St.; 432-7063

Exquisite gourmet dining in the heart of the country. Established restaurant and former getaway for Columbia lawmakers. Mussels, quail, seafood, pheasant, steaks. $$*

■ R I C H B U R G

The Front Porch. Exit 65 off US 77 onto SC 9; 789-5029

Country cooking in restored farmhouse. Baked chicken, squash casserole, and apple cobbler are specialties. $*

■ R O C K   H I L L   A N D   Y O R K   C O U N T Y

Alexandrew's. One N. Roosevelt, York; 684-6735

Deli sandwiches, stuffed potatoes, hot dogs, soups and salads, homemade desserts. $

The Fish Hook. 4000 Mt. Gallant Rd.; 366-3001

Seafood, chicken, steak. $*

Hungry Fisherman. Hwy. 49, Lake Wylie; 831-2846

Seafood buffet and salad bar. Lake view. $-$$

Jackson Brother's Deli. 304 N. Main St., Clover; 222-7767 $

Roma's Bakery. 1164 Cherry Rd., Rock Hill; 327-3090

Deli sandwiches and baked goods. $

Shelley's Seafood. Hwy. 161 between Rock Hill and Tirzah, near Lake Wylie; 684-9485

Casual seafood, famous for all-you-can-eat crab legs. $-$$*

Tam's Tavern. Corner of Cherry Rd. and Oakland Ave.; 329-2226

Fresh seafood, chicken, beef, veal, and pasta served at lunch and supper. Comfortable casual elegance. $-$$*

■ S P A R T A N B U R G

Harry's on Morgan Square. 583-8121
  Busy, old-city atmosphere in elegantly restored barbershop and pool hall. Pasta, pork, seafood, Greek specialties. $-$$*

Spice of Life Gourmet Market and Restaurant. 100 Wood Row; 585-3737
  "California-style" cuisine with an excellent wine selection. $-$$$

■ S U M M E R T O N

The Summerton Diner. Exit 108 from I-95 on US 15; 485-6835
  Country cooking and hunter's breakfast at landmark roadstop between New York and Florida. Famous and very well loved for fried chicken, mashed potatoes, apple salad, and coconut cream pie. $*

■ S U M T E R

Sambino's. US 378, across from Shaw AFB; 494-9494
  Italian standards and seafood, from plain to fancy, in comfortable atmosphere. People love the bread, pizza, and fresh fish. $-$$ *

■ MUSEUMS

■ A B B E V I L L E

Abbeville County Museum. Poplar and Cherry Sts.; 459-2696. Early Abbeville District memorabilia is housed in this three-story 1850 jail. Prisoners' graffiti is still visible on the third-floor walls.

■ A I K E N

Aiken County Historical Museum. 433 Newberry St.; 642-2015. Displays artifacts from Indian times and early settlement and features a complete drugstore of the early 1900s. The grounds also house Frederick Ergle's 1808 log cabin, and the one-room China Springs Schoolhouse built in the 1890s.

Carriage Museum at Rye Patch. 100 Berrie Rd.; 642-7630. A collection of restored horse-drawn carriages.

Thoroughbred Hall of Fame. Hopeland Gardens. Whiskey Rd. and Dupree Place; 642-7630. Horse-racing memorabilia commemorating local horses.

■ B E A U F O R T

Beaufort Museum. 713 Craven St.; 525-7017. Highlighting the history and culture of Beaufort County, with relics of war, nature, and early industry. The museum is housed in an arsenal building constructed in 1798.

■ BENNETTSVILLE

Marlboro County Historical Museum. 479-5624. Tracing county history back 300 years, this one-block museum complex holds one of only a few known copies of the South Carolina Ordinance of Secession.

■ CAMDEN

Camden Archives and Museum. 1314 Broad St.; 425-6050. History exhibits, early records, books, Kershaw County memorabilia. 1825 town clockworks are one feature.

■ CHARLESTON

Avery Research Center for African-American History and Culture. 125 Bull St.; 727-2009. Showcases the history of slavery and of African-American life in Charleston.

Charleston Museum. 360 Meeting St.; 722-2996. Founded in 1773, first museum in the nation. Exhibits on plantation life, natural history, slavery, rice culture, and the Civil War.

The Citadel Museum. 25 Elmwood Ave.; 792-6846. Exhibits uniforms and weaponry dating back to the school's origin.

Confederate Museum. 188 Meeting St., in Market Hall; 723-1541 or 588-2291. Founded in 1898 and still maintained by the Daughters of the Confederacy, the museum displays uniforms, weapons, and other Confederate memorabilia.

Gibbes Museum of Art. 135 Meeting St.; 722-2706. Notable collection of American paintings, Japanese wood-block prints, engravings, and sculptures. Traveling exhibits, concerts, lectures presented throughout the year.

The Old Exchange and Provost Dungeon. East Bay at Broad; 727-2165. State delegates to the First Continental Congress were elected at the Old Exchange between 1767 and 1771. Beneath the Exchange, the Provost Dungeon served as a prison during the Revolution. Wax figures help to recreate the grim history.

Patriots Point Naval and Maritime Museum. Two miles east of Charleston on US 17; 844-2727 or (800) 327-5723. Featuring the USS *Yorktown,* a decommissioned aircraft carrier that served in World War II and in the Korean and Vietnam wars. Other vessels open for tours include a nuclear-powered merchant ship, destroyer, and submarine.

Studio-Museum of Elizabeth O'Neill Verner. 38 Tradd St.; 722-4246. A native Charlestonian, Elizabeth O'Neill Verner (1883–1979) painted the city's houses, churches, and landscape. Her studio is in the oldest surviving house in the city.

■ COLUMBIA AREA

The Cayce Historical Museum. 1800 12th St. Extension; 795-9022. The original setting for two Revolutionary battles. The building is a replica of a mid-1700s trading post.

Columbia Museum of Art and Gibbes Planetarium. Senate and Bull Sts.; 799-2810. Contemporary paintings hang beside Baroque and Renaissance works. Also features a children's gallery, weekend planetarium programs, and changing exhibits.

The Fort Jackson Museum. Fort Jackson, Jackson Blvd.; 751-7419. Built in 1917 and named after President Andrew Jackson, the museum houses collections relating to the history of the fort.

John Mark Verdier House Museum. 801 Bay St.; 524-6334. A fine example of Federal-style architecture and particularly impressive interior design.

Mann-Simons Cottage/Museum of African-American Culture. 1403 Richland St.; 257-1450. Collections include personal items that belonged to Celia Mann, the freed slave who bought the house in 1850.

The State House. Gervais St. between Assembly and Sumter Sts., 734-2430. The building was shelled by General Sherman's Union troops in 1865.

South Carolina Confederate Relic Room and Museum. 920 Sumter St.; 734-9813. Exhibits focus on the period of the Confederacy, with firearms, sabers, flags, currency, newspapers, photographs, and uniforms from the colonial period to the present.

South Carolina State Museum. 301 Gervais St.; 737-4921. This renovated textile mill features a wide range of exhibits: art, history, natural history, science, and technology. Hands-on exhibits.

■ DARLINGTON

Stock Car Hall of Fame/Joe Weatherly Museum. SC 34; 393-2103. Displays racing memorabilia, stock cars, trophies, and illegal parts removed from cars before races.

■ EDGEFIELD

Pottersville Museum. Just north of Edgefield on Rte. 25; 637-3333. Housed in 1810 kitchen building is a rare collection of late-18th- to mid-19th-century local stoneware pottery.

■ FLORENCE

Florence Air and Missile Museum. US 301 North; 665-5118. Check out a 98-foot Titan Intercontinental Ballistic Missile, a moon rock, memorabilia from World War II, and Frank Borman's Mercury pressure suit.

War Between the States Museum. Off US 52 and Irby St.; 662-1471. Relics from the war.

■ GREENVILLE

Bob Jones University Art Gallery and Museum. 1700 Wade Hampton Blvd.; 242-5100. Houses an important international collection of religious art, from the 13th to the 19th century, from Spain, Italy, France, Germany, and Holland. Features works by Dolci, Rembrandt, Rubens, Titian, and Van Dyck.

Greenville County Museum of Art. 271-7570. With a wonderful permanent collection of American art from colonial to contemporary, includes works by Georgia O'Keeffe, Helen Turner, John Ross Key, Andy Warhol, Jasper Johns, and others. Houses the world's largest collections of Andrew Wyeth paintings outside of his own holdings. Its regional art collection is recognized as one of the best in the United States.

■ HARTSVILLE
Hartsville Museum. 114 S. Fourth St.; 383-3005. Housed in a restored 1908 passenger train station, the museum focuses on the history, arts, and crafts of the region. Permanent collections of silverware and iron household implements, antique clothing and photographs, and a railroad caboose are well worth viewing.

■ LEXINGTON
Lexington County Museum. Rte. 378 and Fox St.; 359-8369. Several 18th- and 19th-century structures comprise this museum complex, including a one-room log cabin built by a Revolutionary War soldier, Lawrence Corley, in 1772. Other buildings include an 1832 former dormitory and classroom of a Lutheran seminary, a schoolhouse (ca. 1850), a cotton gin house and barn (ca. 1820), and other reconstructed outbuildings.

■ MT. PLEASANT
Herbie's Antique & Classic Car Museum. 176 L. O. "Bud" Darby Blvd.; 884-9700. Over 100 classic, custom, antique, and race cars.
Museum on the Common. 217 Lucas St., Shem Creek Village; 849-9000. Multisensory exhibits include "Hurricane Hugo Revisited."

■ MYRTLE BEACH AND THE GRAND STRAND
Brookgreen Gardens. A few miles north from Hobcaw on US 17; 237-4218 or (800) 849-1931. Built in the 1930s on the grounds of an old plantation, this sculpture garden displays over 400 works by 19th- and 20th-century artists. Frederic Remington, Augustus Saint-Gaudens, and Marshall Fredericks are all represented here.
Horry County Museum. 438 Main St., Conway; 248-6489. Archaeological and historic exhibits, all inside an old post office building.
Old Town Museum. 14 W. Main St., Andrews; 264-3715. Town memorabilia from the 19th century.
The Rice Museum. Front and Screven St., Georgetown; 546-7423. Inside the Old Market Building, it tells the story of rice and indigo.
South Carolina Hall of Fame. 710 21st Ave. North; 448-4021. Second floor of Myrtle Beach Convention Center. A tribute to outstanding South Carolinians and their achievements.

■ PARRIS ISLAND
Parris Island Museum. Rte. 281; 525-2951. Exhibits on the history of Parris Island, the Port Royal area, and the Marine Corps presence on the island, with uniforms, weapons, and historic photographs.

■ P I C K E N S

Irma Morris Museum of Fine Arts. 104 N. Lewis St. A collection of paintings and furniture housed in the Hagood Mauldin House, one of the city's historic buildings.

Pickens County Art Museum. Johnson and Pendleton Sts.; 878-7847. On the second floor of the restored 1903 Gothic Revival Pickens County Gaol, the museum features exhibitions of the works of contemporary upstate South Carolina artists.

Pickens County Historical Museum. Also housed in the Gaol, this museum exhibits memorabilia and artifacts of the county's history.

■ S E A   I S L A N D S

Hampton County Museum. 943-5484. A collection of historical items, county memorabilia and artworks, housed in a 100-year-old jail.

Penn Center. Land's End Rd., Frogmore, St. Helena Island; 838-2432. Preserves the language, culture, and history of the Sea Island's Gullah community. Bailey Museum is devoted to the history of black Sea Islanders.

Pratt Memorial Library/Webel Museum. 123-A and 123-B Wilson St., Ridgeland; 726-7744. The library contains 250 rare books on the history of the Low Country area, as well as several hundred portraits and maps. Webel Museum displays Indian artifacts, rice culture dioramas, and other historical materials.

■ HISTORIC SITES

South Carolina has lovingly preserved many historic homes and gardens, but many period homes are private residences. The list below includes only those sites open for public viewing. Call ahead for hours.

■ A B B E V I L L E

Abbeville Historic District. 14 miles west of Greenwood on SC 72. Settled in 1785 by French Huguenots. The historic district includes many 19th-century houses, in architectural styles from Greek Revival to Victorian. Jefferson Davis came through the town on his flight from Richmond at the end of the Civil War.

Abbeville Opera House. On Court Square; 459-2157. One of the few opera houses remaining in the state. Fanny Brice, Jimmy Durante, and Groucho Marx played here during the great traveling road show era. Now fully restored, with live theater presentations held regularly.

Burt-Stark House. N. Main and Greenville Sts.; 459-4297 or 459-2181. The site of the final meeting of the Confederate Council of War on May 2, 1865.

■ AIKEN AREA

Historic Aiken. Site of a battle between Confederates under Gen. Joseph Wheeler and Gen. Hugh Kilpatrick's cavalry during Sherman's march through the state. Aiken was a favorite wintering spot for the wealthy at the turn of the century, and still is home to the enormous "cottages" of that period.

Redcliffe Plantation. 181 Redcliffe Rd.; 827-1473. Home to former U.S. Senator James Henry Hammond. Authentically furnished with period furniture.

■ BEAUFORT

Beaufort Historic District. Includes more than 170 public and private buildings. Information is available at the chamber of commerce (1006 Bay St.; 524-3163).

George Parsons Elliot House Museum. 1001 Bay St.; 524-8450. Greek Revival house furnished with priceless period antiques. The house served as a Federal hospital during the Civil War.

John Mark Verdier House Museum. 801 Bay St.; 524-6334. Built in 1790 by a wealthy young merchant, the mansion is an excellent example of the Federal style. The Marquis de Lafayette stayed here in 1825 and addressed the townspeople from the portico.

Saint Helena's Episcopal Church. 501 Church St. Founded in 1712, the church is surrounded by several colorful legends. According to one, during the Civil War, the church's tombstones were used as operating tables.

■ CAMDEN

Historic Camden. The oldest inland city in South Carolina (founded in 1733), Camden was the site of two important Revolutionary War battles: The Battle of Camden (August 1780), and the Battle of Hobkirk's Hill (April 1781). George Washington passed through the city on his presidential tour in 1791, and the Marquis de Lafayette visited in 1825.

■ CHARLESTON

Aiken-Rhett House. 48 Elizabeth St.; 723-1159. Jefferson Davis, among other notables, was a houseguest at this remarkably preserved 19th-century mansion.

The Battery and White Point Gardens. East Bay and Murray Blvd. Stede Bonnet and other pirates were hanged here in 1718. During the Revolution and Civil War, this harborside park was fortified with artillery to defend against sea invasions.

Beth Elohim Synagogue. 90 Hasell St. The second oldest synagogue in the country was built on the site in 1792. When the original was destroyed by fire, this Greek Revival building was erected in 1840. A small museum is on the premises.

Boone Hall. Eight miles north on US 17; 884-4371. Built in 1935 in a Georgian style similar to the original plantation house, which fell into ruin. Nine original slave cabins remain, dating to 1743. Other original structures include the gin house, circular smokehouse, and commissary. Only the main floor is open for tours.

Calhoun Mansion. 16 Meeting St.; 722-8205. Patrick Calhoun, grandson of John C. Calhoun, inherited this ornate 35-room house from his father-in-law. The house is one of only a few demonstrating Charleston grandeur post–Civil War.

Charles Towne Landing. Off SC 171 about 3 miles northwest of Charleston; 556-4450. This park is located on the site of the first permanent English settlement in South Carolina. Guided tours of a 17th-century trading ketch, and several English gardens.

Dock Street Theater. 135 Church St.; 723-5648. Built ca. 1736. The first building in the nation designed solely to house theatrical performances has been reconstructed to reflect the style of an early Georgian playhouse.

Drayton Hall. SC Scenic Hwy. 61, 8 miles past US 17; 766-0188. Considered the best example of Georgian-Palladian architecture in the nation.

Edmondston-Alston House. 21 E. Battery St.; 722-7171. Beautiful views of the harbor from this Greek Revival mansion. The family's furnishings displayed throughout the house include their silver and porcelain collection, portraits, and engravings. Open daily.

Fort Sumter. At the entrance to Charleston Harbor, accessible via boat (722-1691), departing from Patriot's Point and the City Marina. The first shots of the Civil War were fired on this man-made island.

Heyward-Washington House. 87 Church St.; 722-0354. Built in 1772 by a prominent rice planter for his son, Thomas Heyward Jr., a signer of the Declaration of Independence. The mansion is full of period furnishings; the 18th-century kitchen is the only one in Charleston open to visitors.

Huguenot Church. 136 Church St.; 722-4385. Gothic architecture. One of the last functional Huguenot churches in the country.

Joseph Manigualt House. 350 Meeting St., 723-2926. Built in 1803. Fine Federal-style examples of French, English, and Charleston-made furniture. Hidden stairway.

Magnolia Plantation and Gardens. Adjoining the Drayton Plantation at SC Scenic Hwy. 61, about 10 miles past US 17; 571-1266. 300-year-old plantation with the oldest colonial estate garden in the state. Features include petting zoo, rental bikes and canoes, and a 500-acre wildlife refuge.

Middleton Place. SC Scenic Hwy. 61; 556-6020. Built ca. 1755, the present-day museum, located in the family's renovated guesthouse, exhibits Middleton family silver, china, furniture, and artwork. Particularly nice lawn and gardens.

Nathaniel Russell House. 51 Meeting St.; 724-8481. Federal architecture, ornate interior detailing, and period furnishings. The spacious garden alone draws most visitors.

St. Michael's Episcopal Church. Broad and Meeting Sts.; 723-0603. The Palladian Doric portico and storied steeple are considered a notable architectural achievement. The clocktower has marked the time since 1764. Old-fashioned pews and original pulpit.

■ C L E M S O N

Fort Hill. Clemson University campus; 656-2475 or 656-2061. The antebellum mansion-home of John C. Calhoun, vice president under Andrew Jackson and John Quincy Adams, a U.S. senator, and one of the South's most notable statesmen. Filled with family mementos and furnishings.

■ C O L U M B I A

Hampton-Preston Mansion. 1615 Blanding St.; 252-7742. Built by Robert Mills for well-known Hampton family. Became a convent, then a private women's college. The house is furnished with family pieces from three plantations of the Hamptons and Prestons.

Mann-Simons Cottage/Museum of African-American Culture. 1403 Richland St.; 252-7742. Bought in 1850 by Celia Mann, a former Charleston slave who purchased her freedom and walked to Columbia. The house is restored to its 1880 appearance.

Robert Mills Historic House and Park. 1616 Blanding St.; 252-1770. Designed by Robert Mills, the first federal architect of the nation and designer of the Washington Monument, this neoclassical structure holds Regency-style furnishings. Outside are formal English gardens.

Seibels House. 1601 Richland St.; 252-7742. The oldest home in Columbia, built in the late 1700s and renovated in the 1920s. It is now headquarters for the Historic Columbia Foundation.

●**Woodrow Wilson Boyhood Home.** 1705 Hampton St.; 252-1770. This Tuscan-villa-style house was home to Thomas Woodrow Wilson from the age of 14 to 17. The house, with gas lighting fixtures, Wilson family photos, period pieces, and some original furnishings, is an example of a Reconstruction-era Victorian middle-class Presbyterian home.

■ G E O R G E T O W N   A R E A

Hampton Plantation. Eight miles north of McClellanville off US 17; 546-9361. Once the home of Archibald Rutledge, poet laureate of South Carolina.

Hopsewee Plantation. US 17, 12 miles south of Georgetown; 546-7891. The 1740 home of Continental Congressman Thomas Lynch and birthplace of his son Thomas Jr., signer of the Declaration of Independence.

Prince George Winyah Episcopal Church. 232 Broad St. Established in 1721 by the Church of England to serve colonists, the building dates to 1750.

■ N I N E T Y   S I X

Ninety Six National Historic Site. On Rte. 248; 543-4068. The site in 1775 of the first Revolutionary War land battle fought in the South and the site of the longest Patriot army siege of the war. The well-preserved site includes a visitors center with exhibits and information.

■ PENDLETON AREA

Ashtabula. Rte. 88; 646-3847. Built in the mid-1820s, the house is an excellent example of Low Country plantation architecture transplanted by settlers from Charleston. It is now restored and open as a museum, with antique period furnishings.

Pendleton Historical District. North of I-85 on US 76. An area of more than 50 public and private 18th- and 19th-century buildings, notable structures including the 1826 Farmers' Society Hall and the 1802 Old Stone Church.

Woodburn. Rte. 76 west of Pendleton; 646-3655. Call ahead. An early-19th-century Greek Revival plantation house built ca. 1830 by Charles Cotesworth Pinckney, son of the state's governor, Thomas Pinckney. The house has been restored, with 18 rooms on four floors open to the public.

■ ST. HELENA ISLAND

Penn Center Historic District. Rte. 37, Land's End Rd.; 838-2432. Founded in 1862 by Philadelphia Quakers to educate blacks, lessons were first held in the Brick Church.

■ SPARTANBURG

Walnut Grove Plantation. Eight miles southeast of Spartanburg near intersection of I-26 and Rte. 221; 576-6546. The Moore family's 18th-century plantation furnished with pre-1830 antiques. The complex also has a number of outbuildings, including a 1777 kitchen, barn, smokehouse, and well house.

■ YORK

York Historic District. Sixteen miles northwest of Rock Hill on SC 5. Settled by Scotch-Irish, Scots, English, and Germans in the mid-1700s, the town of York was established as the county seat in 1785. The town's historic district, one of the largest in the state, includes more than 70 structures.

■ FESTIVALS AND EVENTS

South Carolina is host to all kinds of festivals and seasonal events, too numerous to list in entirety here. For more extensive listings, call the Division of Tourism at 734-0135.

■ JANUARY

Cowpens: Battle of Cowpens Reenactment. Living history encampments and tactical demonstrations mark this Revolutionary War reenactment at the Cowpens National Battlefield.

■ FEBRUARY

Charleston: Oyster Festival. Steamed oysters are the main attraction, but visitors can also enjoy live music, an oyster-shucking contest, children's events, and more.

■ MARCH

Aiken: Aiken Triple Crown. Three weekends in March showcase fine horse racing, as young thoroughbreds trained in Aiken race for the first time.

Barnwell: Possum Creep Festival. Eat real possum and coon and enjoy carnival rides, a horse show, and other attractions.

Beaufort: Spring Tour of Homes. Mansion and garden tours are given. A candlelight walk through the historic district is one highlight.

Camden: Civil War Days Encampment and Candlelight Tour. Features living history demonstrations, cavalry maneuvers, military tactics, and social skills of the Civil War era in Historic Camden.

Charleston: Charleston Blues Festival. A ten-day concert devoted to one of America's oldest and greatest art forms.

Charleston: Festival of Houses and Gardens. Tour of treasured homes and gardens, which are especially beautiful during this season.

Darlington: International Race of Champions. The best NASCAR, Indy, and road racing drivers compete for a coveted championship.

Myrtle Beach: Canadian-American Days Festival. A celebration welcoming Canadians on spring break with sporting events, concerts, a St. Patrick's Day parade, and more.

■ APRIL

Camden: Carolina Cup. Thoroughbred steeplechases and flat racing are featured. Held at the Springdale Race Course.

Charleston: Low Country Cajun Festival. Spicy Louisiana and Low Country cooking are the main attraction. Also features crawfish races, crawfish-eating contest, Cajun and Zydeco music.

Columbia: Culturalfest. An African-American cultural festival with food, dance, music, and other festivities.

Johnston: Peach Blossom Festival. Traditional festivities include crafts, food, rides, entertainment.

Manning: Striped Bass Festival. Celebrating spring and the legendary striped bass with a parade, crafts, car show, catfish wrestling, a boat poker run, and more.

St. George: World Grits Festival. Features the "Miss Grits" beauty pageant, a carnival, and grits-eating contests.

Walterboro: Colleton County Rice Festival. A parade, fireworks, rice cooking contests, and the "world's largest pot of rice" are a few of the attractions.

■ MAY

Beaufort: Gullah Festival. Highlights the fine arts, customs, language, and dress of Low Country blacks.

Charleston: Spoleto Festival USA. One of the world's biggest arts festivals; Piccolo Spoleto, running concurrently, showcases local and regional talent.

Columbia: Mayfest. The capital city's largest arts and entertainment festival, with a Southern food plaza, children's fun fair, and more.

Edgefield: Ten Governor's Pig Pickin'. Chefs come to town for a barbecue cookoff. Visitors can also enjoy live entertainment, an antique car show, and more.

Lancaster: Carolina Legends: A Musical Celebration. A bluegrass, old-time country, and gospel music festival with legendary figures from the Carolinas, food, and children's activities.

Little River: Blue Crab Arts & Crafts Festival. One of the largest arts and crafts festivals on the coast. Also offers great seafood!

■ JUNE

Greenville: Juneteenth Festival. Commemorates the end of slavery on June 19, 1865, with a black tie affair, block party, parade, and other weekend activities.

Hampton: Hampton County Watermelon Festival. A week-long festival offering free watermelon, food, parades, dances, races, and more.

Myrtle Beach: Sun Fun Festival. Summer gets under way on the Grand Strand with contests, live television shows, and a record-breaking sandcastle-building contest.

Trenton: Ridge Peach Festival. Enjoy arts and crafts, a softball tournament, and peach desserts at this festival.

■ JULY

Gaffney: South Carolina Peach Festival. A ten-day event celebrating the peach with concerts, sporting events, a parade, and, of course, delicious peach desserts.

Greenville: Freedom Weekend Aloft. The second-largest balloon rally in the country, also featuring amusement rides, a crafts show, and a fireworks finale.

McConnells: Revolutionary War Battle Reenactment. Watch a reenactment of the 1780 Battle of Huck's Defeat near Historic Brattonsville.

Mountain Rest: Hillbilly Days. Held every July 4th with local food, crafts, and music.

Pageland: Pageland Watermelon Festival. Features clogging, arts and crafts, watermelon eating and seed-spitting contests, a rodeo, and more.

■ AUGUST

Blacksburg: Ed Brown Rodeo. A full-scale rodeo, with bareback riding, saddle bronc riding, calf roping, steer wrestling, women's barrel racing, and more.

Charleston: Hispanic Festival. Spanish, Puerto Rican, and Mexican cultures are celebrated in music, dance, food, and other events at the Palmetto Islands County Park.

Pelion: County Peanut Party. Nearly 4.5 tons of peanuts are boiled in two days. Activities include the annual blessing of the peanut pots.

■ SEPTEMBER

Aiken: Aiken's Makin'. The downtown parkways of Aiken are the setting for this arts and crafts fair, with all-day entertainment and the Tastin'-Aiken food fair.

Charleston: Scottish Games and Highland Gathering. A gathering of Scottish clans featuring medieval games, bagpipe performances, Scottish dances, and other traditional activities.

Charleston: Moja Arts Festival. The African-American and Caribbean cultures of the Low Country are showcased with lectures, art exhibits, performances, tours, jazz concerts, and more.

Charleston: Boc Challenge. A single-handed yacht race starting in Charleston and going around the world before ending up there again.

Kingstree: Williamsburg County Black Heritage Festival. Enjoy traditional music and dance, homemade ice cream, other foods, and arts and crafts.

Mullins: Golden Leaf Festival. Celebrating the tobacco industry with live entertainment, a husband-hollering contest, a Party after Dark, and other events.

■ OCTOBER

Clemson: Idlewilde. A fall festival celebrating the area's Appalachian heritage with music, dance, and art at the South Carolina State Botanical Gardens.

Edisto Island: Edisto's Golden Age Tour. The historic plantations and churches of the island are the focus of a self-guided tour.

Georgetown: Ghost Tour. A self-guided tour sponsored by the "Ghost Capital of the World," also offering carnivals, contests, and other festivities.

McConnells: Red Hills Heritage Festival. Demonstrations from pioneer days include molasses making, candledripping, and storytelling. In Historic Brattonsville.

Myrtle Beach, Walhalla, Spartanburg: Oktoberfest. Oom-pah music, bratwurst, beer, and much more.

Troy: Battle of Long Cane Reenactment. A weekend bringing to life the Revolutionary War.

■ NOVEMBER

Camden: Colonial Cup. A championship steeplechase marked by tailgating and social picnics to end the steeplechase season.

Charleston: Plantation Days. Demonstrations of 18th- and 19th-century lifestyle skills: cider and syrup making, wool dyeing, spinning, basketmaking, and more.

Charleston: Worldfest-Charleston. A renowned international film festival, showcasing 50 of the world's newest feature films, offering film seminars and gala events.

Salley: Chitlin' Strut. Featuring deep-fried pig intestines. Also includes hog-calling contests, country music, and arts and crafts.

Society Hill: The Catfish Festival. Enjoy fried catfish and catfish stew, as well as children's games, fishing tournaments, and all-day entertainment.

St. Helena Island: Penn Center Heritage Celebration. Sea Island history and culture are the focus, with crafts, educational exhibits, traditional spirituals, and food.

■ DECEMBER

Christmas in South Carolina is a season of holiday festivals and tours. Many cities and towns offer events not listed here; to inquire, call the tourist office or chamber of commerce in the area of your interest. Below are a few choices.

Camden: Candlelight Tour of Homes. Historic homes and buildings decorated for a traditional Southern Christmas are featured on this evening tour.

Charleston: Christmas at Middleton Place. A plantation Christmas with tours of the Middleton Place House Museum, decorated with traditional holiday greenery. A family yuletide in the stableyards and other events also offered.

Columbia: The Lights Before Christmas. Riverbanks Zoo is transformed into a winter wonderland when more than 200,000 holiday lights illuminate the park.

Greenville: Holiday Fair. The state's largest holiday arts and crafts show, featuring clothing, jewelry, woodcraft, dolls, furniture, ceramics, and more.

■ TOURS

In addition to the tours listed below, visitors should call local chambers of commerce for additional tours and those offered in smaller towns.

■ AIKEN

Aiken Chamber of Commerce (641-1111) runs a 90-minute tour of the historic district and will customize tours to suit individual interests.

■ BEAUFORT

Carriage Tours of Beaufort. 521-1651. Narrated history of Beaufort during a mule-drawn carriage excursion through the town's historic district.

Fall Tour of Homes. 524-6334. Evening and afternoon tours through this port city.

Spring Tour of Homes. 524-0363. Mansion and garden tours. A candlelight walk through the historic district is one highlight.

■ CAMDEN

Candlelight Tour of Homes. Historic homes and buildings decorated for a traditional Southern Christmas are featured on this evening tour.

■ CHARLESTON

Personal guides can be obtained by contacting the Associated Guides of Historic Charleston at 724-6419.

Agricultural Walking Tours of Charleston. 893-2327. Guided walking tours of private homes and gardens, churches, and public buildings throughout the historic district. Tours leave from the Planters Inn at Market and Meeting Sts., and from the Hawthorne Suites Hotel at 181 Church St.

Charleston Strolls. 766-2080. Offers two guided walking tours of the historic distict. The Battery tour leaves from the Mills House Hotel Courtyard, 115 Meeting St., and the Omni Hotel at 130 Market St. The Market Street tour leaves from the Charleston Visitor Center and features the 18th-century suburb of Ansonborough, Beth Elohim Synagogue, St. Mary's Church, and the Market.

Charleston Tea Party Walking Tour. 577-5896 or 722-1779. A two-hour tour with tea in a private garden. Leaving from Kings Courtyard Inn, Mon-Sat, at 9:30 A.M. and 2 P.M.

Confederate Ghost Walk at Magnolia Cemetery. 795-2099. Guests are led by tour guides in 1860s period clothing through the cemetery to watch reenactments of events that took place in the lives of famous Southerners interred there.

Doin' the Charleston Tours. A 90-minute bus tour of the downtown historic district, with a laser disk show on board. Bus leaves from the visitors center.

Festival of Houses and Gardens. 723-1623. Tour of treasured homes and gardens, which are especially beautiful in the spring.

Fort Sumter Tours. 722-2628. Boat departs from Charleston City Marina at 17 Lockwood Blvd. and from Patriots Point Naval and Maritime Museum in Mt. Pleasant. Tour includes 1 $1/4$-hour tour of Charleston Harbor and a one-hour tour of Fort Sumter. Dinner and harbor cruise also available.

Gray Line Water Tours. 722-1112; (800) 344-4483. Narrated tours of the harbor, including the Battery, Forts Sumter and Moultrie, the shipyards, and islands. Galley and bar on board. Departing from the City Marina at 10 A.M., 12:30 P.M., and 3 P.M. each day.

Gullah Tours. 556-7243 or 789-9044. A van tour of black life in Charleston, including stories told in the Gullah dialect. Departing from the Charleston Visitors Center at 10 A.M. and 12, 2, and 4 P.M.

Naval Base Harbor Tour. 722-1691. A two-hour narrated tour of the naval base and part of the harbor. Departing at 10 A.M., 12:30 P.M., and 3 P.M. from Patriots Point.

Palmetto Carriage Tours. Rainbow Market at 40 N. Market St.; 723-8145. One-hour narrated tours, leaving every 15 minutes, covering about 25 blocks of the city's downtown and historic districts.

■ E D I S T O   I S L A N D

Edisto's Golden Age Tour. The historic plantations and churches of the island are the focus of a self-guided tour.

■ G E O R G E T O W N

Ghost Tour. Georgetown Chamber of Commerce; 546-8437. A self-guided tour sponsored by the "Ghost Capital of the World."

Island Queen Boat Tours. 527-3160. Departing from the Landing Marina, Mon-Sat. Ghost Story Cruises at 8 P.M. and two-hour Historic River Cruises at 2 P.M.

Miss Nell's "Real South" Tours. 546-3975. Walking tours of 8, 12, or 24 blocks (depending on visitor) led by Nell Cribb, departing from the front of the Mark Twain bookstore (723 Front St.) at 10:30 A.M. and 2:30 P.M.

Plantation Tours. 527-4106. Capt. Sandy guides visitors up the Waccamaw and Pee Dee rivers on a three-hour tour of the area's plantations every Mon, Tue, Thurs, and Fri at 1 P.M. Also offers a Ghost Story Tour.

Spring Tours. 527-3653. Annual tour of antebellum rice plantations, colonial townhouses, and magnificent gardens, some closed to the public during the rest of the year.

Tram Tours. 546-6827. 55-minute tours of the historic district leaving every hour from 10:30 A.M. to 2:30 P.M. Tickets available at 627 Front St.

■ G R A N D   S T R A N D

Barefoot Princess. North Myrtle Beach; 650-6600. Sightseeing, sunset, and dinner cruises, leaving from Barefoot Landing.

Capt. Dick's Marina. Murrells Inlet; 651-3676. Ocean cruises Mon-Sat 7 P.M. to 9 P.M., going to the pavilion area and back. Explorer cruises Sun-Fri 7:30 P.M.-8:45 P.M. Narrated history of Murrells Inlet legends and ghost stories.

Hurricane Fleet. North Myrtle Beach; 249-3571. Sightseeing, dinner, and dance cruises, leaving from Vereen's Marina.

Southern Star. Myrtle Beach; 650-6600. Sightseeing, sunset, and dinner cruises, departing from the Holiday Inn at Waccamaw Pottery.

■ H I L T O N   H E A D   I S L A N D

Adventure Cruises. 785-4558. Offers dinner, sightseeing, dolphin-watching, and murder-mystery cruises, all departing from Shelter Cove.

Discover Hilton Head. 842-9217. Daily historical tours of the island.

St. Luke's Tour of Homes. The beautiful homes and plantations of Hilton Head Island are showcased in a self-guided tour.

■ M c C O N N E L L S

Brattonsville Christmas Candlelight Tour. 684-2327. The historic homes of Brattonsville are decorated with traditional holiday fruit, greenery, and candles. Interpreters help portray the period.

■ S T A T E   P A R K S

Fall Color Walks. Division of State Parks, 1205 Pendleton St., Columbia 29201; 734-0155. Guided walks along some of the most scenic nature trails in the state park system, celebrating the beautiful transformation to fall.

Spring Wildflower Walks. 734-0155. Guided walks led by experts, showcasing the blooming flora of South Carolina state parks.

■ Y O R K

Christmas in Olde York Tour of Homes. 684-2590. Homes and a historic church are decorated for the holidays with traditional greenery, fruits, and candles.

■ PARKS AND FORESTS

For guides, maps, and brochures of the state's parks and forests, as well as a more complete list, contact South Carolina State Parks, P.O. Box 71, Columbia 29202; 734-0156.

■ C H A R L E S T O N   A R E A

Francis Marion National Forest. North of Charleston off US 17; 765-5222. Site of the battle between forces of the British Col. Banastre Tarleton and Revolutionary Gen. Francis Marion, "the Swamp Fox." Now a wildlife-rich 245,000-acre forest. Camping, hiking, picnicking.

Hampton Plantation State Park. 8 miles north of McClellanville off US 17; 546-9361. The ancestral home of Archibald Rutledge. The plantation house and outbuildings are on the National Register of Historic Places. Call for times.

Old Dorchester State Park. On SC 642 about 6 miles south of Summerville; 873-1740. On a bluff overlooking the Ashley River, ruins of an 18th-century town and the tabby walls of an old fort. Archaeological relics on display.

Old Santee Canal State Park. South of Lake Moultrie off US 52; 899-5200. Contains the southern end of the 1800 Santee Canal, the first dug channel canal in America. Canoe rentals, docks, trails, boardwalks, picnicking, museum, and interpretive center are offered.

Santee Coastal Reserve. Off US 17, just south of the Santee River; 546-8665. 24,000 acres, including an 11-mile stretch of beach. A haven for waterfowl, wading birds, alligators, snakes, raccoons, and deer. Endangered sea turtles come ashore and lay eggs. Includes nature trails, canoe trail, bike trail. Call for times.

■ GRAND STRAND

Myrtle Beach State Park. 312-acres on Business US 17 opposite the airport; 238-5325.
Includes about 100 acres of one of the last maritime forests along the Strand. There are
350 campsites and five fully furnished cabins sleeping up to six. Campgrounds include
water and electrical hookups, and laundry facilities.

Huntington Beach State Park. About 15 miles south of Myrtle Beach on US 17, below
Murrells Inlet. 2,500 acres of salt marsh and tidal creeks with boardwalks to fish or
catch crab. It is across the highway from Brookgreen Gardens. Campgrounds include
water and electrical hookups, and laundry facilities.

■ SEA ISLANDS

Edisto Beach State Park. Edisto Island on SC 174, 50 miles SE of Charleston; 838-2156.
A beachcomber's dream, with shells and sand dollars dotting the nearly three miles of
beach. Facilities include cabins by the marsh and campsites by the ocean.

Hunting Island State Park. Sixteen miles east of Beaufort on US 21; 838-2011. Once the
hunting ground of Indians and settlers, now a state park. Beaches, forest trails, marshes,
and a 140-foot lighthouse. Camping, rental cabins, and pier fishing are available.

Pinckney Island National Wildlife Refuge. US 278 just west of Hilton Head Island.
Over 4,000 acres of salt marsh and small islands. 14 miles of trails for visitors to observe wildlife. Daylight hours.

■ COASTAL PLAIN

Aiken State Park. 16 miles east of Aiken, off US 78; 649-2857. Springs that create four
lakes are among the natural features in this park on the South Edisto River. The park
offers camping, swimming, fishing, boat rentals, and nature trails.

Cape Romain National Wildlife Refuge. Off US 17, 20 miles north of Charleston;
928-3411. 65,000 acres. A stretch of barrier islands and salt marshes make up one of
the nation's most outstanding wildlife refuges. Boat leaves several times a week from
Moore's Landing for a day trip to Bulls Island.

Carolina Sandhills National Wildlife Refuge. On US 1, north of McBee; 335-8401.
A 45,586-acre forest and preserve. Longleaf pines dominate the state forest, and the
preserve hosts one of the largest remaining populations of the red-cockaded woodpecker. Two observation towers, a photography blind, and an interpretive display aid
nature study. Hiking trails, an auto tour route, and picnic shelters are available.

Cathedral Bay Heritage Wildlife Preserve. Off US 301 and SC 64. One of the mysterious
Carolina Bays, filled with black water. Canoeing encouraged.

Cheraw State Park. South of Cheraw on US 1; 537-2215. In the sandhills, the oldest state
park in the state offers a championship 18-hole golf course, camping, fishing, picnicking, lake swimming, rental boats, a bridle trail, and rental cottages.

Colleton State Park. Off I-95 on US 15 north of Walterboro; 538-8206. Set in the live oak woods along the Edisto River. A popular campsite and also headquarters for the Edisto River Canoe and Kayak Trail, the state's official 56-mile black-water river course.

Congaree Swamp National Monument. 20 miles south of Columbia just north of Lake Marion on the Congaree River; 776-4396. More than 90 species of trees in the Congaree's 22,000 acres. A boardwalk, 18 miles of hiking trails, canoeing routes, and guided nature walks are available.

Dreher Island State Park. Exit 91 off I-26, near Chapin, in Lake Murray; 364-4152. Picnicking, camping, fishing, a boat ramp, and nature trails are available.

Francis Beidler Forest. 35 miles northwest of Charleston (Take US 78 to US 178 and follow signs); 462-2150. At 5,800 acres, it is the largest remaining virgin stand of bald cypress and tupelo trees in the world. Walk through this portion of Four Holes Swamp on a 6,500-ft boardwalk. There is no camping, no food facilities. Special programs in season.

Givhans Ferry State Park. 16 miles west of Summerville on SC 61; 873-0692. Visitors enjoy cabins and scenic camping among Spanish-moss-draped oaks and high bluffs overlooking the black waters of the Edisto River.

Hitchcock Woods. Aiken. The largest urban nature preserve in the nation, near downtown. The woods have miles of trails for hikes, strolls, or horseback riding for the public, and on three weekends in March, the Aiken Trials.

Little Pee Dee State Park. Southeast of Dillon off SC 57; 774-8872. The Little Pee Dee River offers some of the state's best bream fishing, with nearby campsites and picnic tables.

Lynches River State Park. 12 miles south of Florence, west of US 52; 389-2785. A relaxing retreat offering river fishing, birding, picnicking, and an Olympic-size swimming pool.

Redcliffe Plantation State Park. Southeast of North Augusta off US 278; 827-1473. The antebellum plantation mansion (with many of its original furnishings still on display) was completed in 1859 by James Henry Hammond. The mansion is often used for weddings and is rented by the State Parks Department for similar social events.

Rivers Bridge State Park. 7 miles southwest of Ehrhardt, off SC 64; 267-3675. Ruins of old Confederate fortifications remain near the riverside picnic area. Swimming, camping, picnicking, fishing, and a nature trail are available. The only park in the state commemorating the Civil War.

Santee State Park. On Lake Marion's western shore just north of the I-95 bridge; 854-2408. A prime fishing haven, the park has 30 cabins (some on land, others on piers over the lake), 150 campsites, boat rentals, a swimming lake, boat ramp, tackle shop, hiking trails, tennis courts, and a restaurant.

Santee National Wildlife Refuge. On the east bank of Lake Marion just south of the I-95 bridge; 478-2214. The refuge has a one-mile, self-guided wildlife trail, and an observation tower from which to view wintering flocks of Canadian geese and 17 other species of migratory waterfowl. Call for times.

Savannah River National Wildlife Refuge. I-95 to US 17 south. A nature drive winds through this 25,608-acre preserve. Once a community of rice plantations, now a sanctuary to migratory birds, especially waterfowl, and innumerable species of wildlife. Daylight hours.

Sumter National Forest. Northwest of Columbia on I-26; 765-5222. 75,000 acres of woodland, wildlife, recreation areas, hiking trails, and more.

Woods Bay State Park. West of Olanta off US 301. South Carolina's first all-nature state park, with no camping or playgrounds. There are picnic tables, canoe rentals, a canoe trail into the swamp, and a 500-foot boardwalk reaching into the wetlands.

■ PIEDMONT

Calhoun Falls State Park. North of Calhoun Falls, off SC 81; 447-8267. A 438-acre park on Richard B. Russell Lake, with fishing, swimming, picnicking, camping, and boat ramps.

Chester State Park. Three miles southwest of Chester, on SC 72; 385-2680. Hilly woodlands with camping and picnic areas, an archery range, nature trails, playground, horse show ring and bridle paths. Rental boats available for the 160-acre fishing lake.

Hickory Knob State Resort Park. Outside of McCormick on US 378; 391-2450. Offers a championship golf course and clubhouse, rental boats, an 80-room lodge, a pool, nature trails and programs, tours to nearby attractions such as Abbeville, boat ramp and docks, a restaurant, convention and conference facilities, campsites, and fully furnished cabins. All on Thurmond Lake, with great bass, crappie, and catfish fishing.

Kings Mountain State Park. 12 miles northwest of York between SC 161 and I-85; 222-3209. Offers campsites, fishing, swimming, nature and hiking rails, and "Living Farm," a frontier homestead.

Lake Hartwell State Park. Off I-85 at Fair Play; 972-3352. A 680-acre park with camping, boat-launching, picnic facilities and more at the southern terminus of the Cherokee Foothills Scenic Highway.

Landsford Canal State Park. Off US 21 between Lancaster and Rock Hill; 789-5800. Includes the best-preserved section of the old canals, as well as a museum and interpretive center. The park also offers a nature trail along the canal. Striped bass and bream regularly draw fishermen.

Paris Mountain State Park. Off US 25 north of Greenville; 244-5565. A protected area since 1890, it offers modern and primitive campsites, lake swimming, fishing ponds, pedal boats, hiking trails, and picnicking.

Rose Hill Plantation State Park. Sardis Road, 8 miles south of Union; 427-5966.
Once the home of William Gist, the "secession governor." Rose garden and 44-acre
lawn surround the mansion, which is open for tours. Call for times.

■ BLUE RIDGE

Caesar's Head State Park. US 276 near North Carolina border; 836-6115. At an elevation
of 3,208 feet, this park is at the top of the Mountain Bridge Recreation and Wilderness
Area, and is popular among birders. One of the park's trails is a moderately strenuous,
2.2-mile hike to an overlook at Raven Cliff Falls.

Devils Fork State Park. North of Salem on county road 25 (off SC 11); 944-2639. One
of the newest and most upscale parks, with 20 villas, lakeside tent and RV camping
areas, boat ramp, swimming area, and picnic shelters, on Lake Jocassee. Reservations
are necessary a year or more in advance for the villas.

Jones Gap State Park. 6 miles east of Caesar's Head on SC 11 and US 276. Within a
pristine Blue Ridge valley known for its diverse plant life, hiking trails, and the Middle
Saluda River. Primitive trailside camping is permitted along the five-mile Jones Gap
Trail. Both the Middle Saluda and Cold Spring Branch are noted for rainbow, brook,
and brown trout.

Keowee-Toxaway State Park. SC 11 at Lake Keowee; 868-2605. The park has one large
lakefront cabin for rent, 10 RV sites, and 14 tent camping sites, as well as hiking and
picnic areas.

Mountain Bridge Wilderness and Recreation Area. Just east of Table Rock, the recreation
area includes Caesar's Head and Jones Gap state parks, two of South Carolina's best
fly-fishing streams, Raven Cliff Falls, and a challenging network of mountain trails.

Oconee State Park. Off SC 28 about 2 miles north on SC 107; 638-5353. One of South
Carolina's first state parks, built in the 1930s by the Civilian Conservation Corps.
19 rental cabins (with fireplace, fully furnished, heated, air-conditioned) are available.
There also is a 20-acre lake, rental fishing boats and canoes, lake swimming, and picnic
areas. A good base camp for trips on the Chattooga River or the 85-mile Foothills Trail.

Table Rock State Park. On SC 11 about 4 miles east of US 178; 878-9813. The oldest
and most popular state park in the Blue Ridge. Built in the 1930s by the Civilian
Conservation Corps. 14 rustic cabins with fireplaces, 100 campsites, a restaurant with
dining patio, a 36-acre lake for swimming, rental canoes, boats, and a 10-mile network
of hiking trails.

■ GOLF COURSES

With over 80 golf courses in Myrtle Beach alone, South Carolina is one of the nation's top golf states. Following are a selection of the state's courses, with especially well-known or top-rated courses starred. Keep in mind that private golf courses are often open to guests of select club-member hotels. For more information, call Myrtle Beach Golf Holiday at (800) 845-4653.

■ COLUMBIA
Northwoods Golf Club. Public. 786-9242.

■ GARDEN CITY
Indigo Creek Golf Club. Public. 650-0381 or (800) 833-6337.

■ GOOSE CREEK
Crowfield Golf and Country Club. Public. 764-4618.

■ HILTON HEAD
Country Club of Hilton Head. Public. 681-4653.
Harbour Town Golf Links. Resort. 842-1892 or (800) 955-8337.
Hilton Head National Golf Club. Public. 842-5900.
Indigo Run Golf Club. Public. 689-2200. *
Island West Golf Club. Public. 757-6660.
Old South Golf Links. Public. 785-5353.
Oyster Reef Golf Club. Public. 681-7717.
Palmetto Dunes Resort. Resort. Multiple courses. 785-1138 or (800) 827-3006.
Palmetto Hall Plantation. Resort. Multiple courses. 689-4100 or (800) 827-3006.
Port Royal Golf Club. Resort. Multiple courses. (800) 925-3508.
Shipyard Golf Club. Resort. 686-8802 or (800) 925-3508.

■ ISLE OF PALMS
Wild Dunes Resort. Resort. Multiple courses. 886-2164 or (800) 845-8880.

■ KIAWAH ISLAND
Kiawah Island Resort. Resort. Multiple courses. 768-2121 or (800) 654-2924.

■ McCORMICK
Hickory Knob State Park Resort. Public. 391-2450.

■ MT. PLEASANT
Dunes West Golf Club. Public. 856-9000.

■ MYRTLE BEACH AND THE GRAND STRAND
Arcadian Shores Golf Club. Resort. 449-5217 or (800) 248-9228.
Bay Tree Golf Plantation. Resort. 249-1487 or (800) 845-6191.*
Beachwood Golf Club. Public. 272-6168 or (800) 526-4889.
Blackmoor Golf Club. Public. 650-5555.
Buck Creek Golf Plantation. Private. 249-5996 or (800) 344-0982.
Dunes Golf and Beach Club. Private. 449-5217.*
Eagle Nest Golf Club. Public. 249-1149 or (800) 543-3113.
Heather Glen Golf Links. Public. 249-9000 or (800) 868-4536. *
The Heritage Club. Public. (800) 552-2660 or 236-9318.*
Indian Wells. Private. (800) TEE OFFS or 651-1505.*
Indigo Creek. Public. (800) TEE OFFS or 650-0381.
The Legends. Public. Multiple courses. 236-9318 or 552-2660.*
Long Bay Club. Public. 399-2222 or (800) 422-7274.
Marsh Harbour. Public. (800) 552-2660 or 236-9318.*
Myrtle Beach National Golf Club. Public. Multiple courses. 448-2308 or (800) 344-5590.
Myrtle West Golf Club. Public. 249-1478 or (800) 842-8390.
Myrtlewood Golf Club. Public. Multiple courses. 449-5143 or (800) 283-3633.
Ocean Harbour Golf Links. Private. 448-8398.*
Oyster Bay Golf Links. Public. (800) 552-2660 or 236-9318.
Pine Lakes International Country Club. Resort. 449-6459 or (800) 446-6817.
River Oaks Golf Plantation. Public. 236-2222 or (800) 762-8813.
Surf Golf and Beach Club. Public. 249-1524 or (800) 765-7873.
Tidewater Golf Club. Public. 249-3829 or (800) 446-5363.*
Wild Wing Plantation. Public. Multiple courses. 347-9464 or (800) 736-9464.

■ PAWLEYS ISLAND
Heritage Club. Public. 626-5121 or (800) 552-2660. *
Litchfield Country Club. Resort. 237-3411.
River Club. Resort. 237-8755.
Willbrook Plantation Golf Club. Resort. 237-4900.

■ SANTEE
Lake Marion Golf Club. Public. 854-2554 or (800) 344-6543.
Santee National Golf Club. Resort. 854-3531 or (800) 448-0152.

■ TOURIST INFORMATION

■ STATEWIDE

Hospitality Association of South Carolina (hotels, motels, and restaurants). Suite 505, 1338 Main St., Columbia 29201; 765-9000.

National Forest Service. 1835 Assembly St., Rm. 333, Columbia 29201; 765-5222.

South Carolina Division of Tourism. 1205 Pendleton St., Box 71, Columbia 29202; tel. 734-0122, fax 734-0133.

South Carolina Wildlife Resources Department Division of Game and Freshwater Fisheries. P.O. Box 167, Columbia 29202; 734-3886.

■ REGIONAL

Charleston Trident Convention and Visitors Bureau. 81 Mary St., P.O. Box 975, Charleston 29402; 853-8000, fax 723-4853.

Charleston Visitor Reception & Transportation Center. 375 Meeting St., P.O. Box 975, Charleston 29402; 853-8000.

Columbia Metropolitan Convention and Visitors Bureau. 1200 Main St., 9th floor, P.O. Box 15, Columbia 29202; 254-0479, (800) 264-4884, fax 799-6529.

Columbia Metropolitan Visitors Center. 1012 Gervais St., Columbia 29201; 254-0479, (800) 264-4884, fax 929-3510.

Hilton Head Island Chamber of Commerce. P.O. Box 5647, Hilton Head Island 29938; 785-3673, fax 785-7110.

Lake Murray Tourism & Recreation Association and Lake Murray Country Visitors Center. 2184 N. Lake Dr. (SC 6), P.O. Box 1783, Irmo 29063; 781-5940, (800) 951-4008.

Low Country and Resort Islands Tourism Commission. P.O. Box 366, Hampton 29924; 943-9180.

Myrtle Beach Area Chamber of Commerce and Info Center. P.O. Box 2115, Myrtle Beach 29578-2115; 626-7444 or (800) 356-3016.

Myrtle Beach Hospitality Association Reservation Service. P.O. Box 1303, Myrtle Beach 29578-1303; 626-7477, (800) 866-9785.

Olde English District Tourism Commission. P.O. Box 1440, 136 Main St., Chester 29706; 385-6800 or (800) 968-5909.

Pawleys Island Chamber Visitors' Center. (800) 777-7705.

Pee Dee Tourism Commission. 908 Parker Dr., P.O. Box 3093, Florence 29502; 669-0950, fax 665-9480.

RECOMMENDED READING

■ FICTION

Allison, Dorothy. *Bastard out of Carolina.* New York: Penguin, 1992. A mesmerizing story of a young girl in Greenville County caught between her stepfather's violence and her love for her mother.

Humphreys, Josephine. *Rich in Love.* New York: Viking, 1987. The story of a girl coming of age in Mt. Pleasant, South Carolina.

Peterkin, Julia. *Scarlet Sister Mary.* Dunwoody, Georgia: Norman S. Berg, 1928. The Pulitzer prize-winning life story of Mary, a Gullah woman on a South Carolina coastal plantation.

Poe, Edgar Allan. *Edgar Allan Poe Reader.* Philadelphia: Running Press, 1993. A collection of Poe's most remembered works, including two works relating to South Carolina, "The Gold-Bug" and "Annabel Lee."

■ HISTORY AND CULTURE

Fraser, Walter J., Jr. *Charleston! Charleston!* Columbia: Univ. of South Carolina Press, 1989. History of the city.

Rogers, George C., Jr. *Charleston in the Age of the Pinckneys.* Columbia: Univ. of South Carolina Press, 1980. A history of a prominent Charleston family through the 18th and 19th centuries.

Rutledge, Archibald. "Plantation Lights and Shadows" in *The Carolina Lowcountry.* New York; Macmillan Co., 1931. Life and culture of the Low Country, with essays by DuBose Heyward, Josephine Pinckney, and others.

Twining, Mary A., and Keith E. Baird. *Sea Island Roots: African Presence in the Carolinas and Georgia.* Trenton, N.J.: Africa World Press, 1991. A collection of essays and personal reminiscences about the life and culture of the Gullah.

Wallace, David Duncan. *The History of South Carolina.* New York: American Historical Society, 1934. A history of South Carolina in four volumes.

Winberry, John J., and Charles F. Kovacik. *South Carolina: A Geography.* Boulder and London: Westview Press, 1987. All the facts and figures about the physical and social geography of the state. Part of a series of state geographies.

■ MEMOIRS AND DIARIES

Daise, Ronald. *Reminiscences of Sea Island Heritage; Legacy of Freedmen on St. Helena Island.* Orangeburg, S.C.: Sandlapper Publishing, 1986. A beautiful collection of historic photographs of and interviews with the Gullah people of St. Helena Island.

Higginson, Thomas Wentworth. *Army Life in a Black Regiment.* Williamstown, MA: Corner House Publishers, 1971. Originally published in 1870, a white Union officer records his experience as the officer in command of the First South Carolina Volunteers, the first all-black military unit of any kind mustered into the Union forces.

Robertson, Ben. *Red Hills and Cotton.* Columbia: Univ. of South Carolina Press, 1960. A wonderful account of the traditions, prides, and humilities of a family in the South Carolina Up Country.

Woodward, C. Vann, and Elisabeth Muhlenfeld. *The Private Mary Chestnut.* New York: Oxford Univ. Press, 1984. The Civil War diaries of Mary Boykin Chestnut, daughter of a South Carolina senator and wife of a military aide to Jefferson Davis. Complete candor and caustic wit provide one of the most famous literary insights into the Civil War.

■ GUIDEBOOKS

Ballantine, Todd. *Tideland Treasure.* Columbia: Univ. of South Carolina Press, 1991. A must-read for any beachcombing visitor to Hilton Head Island or the Carolina coast, this book consists of more than 400 hand-drawn and hand-lettered illustrations detailing the biology and complex coastal ecology of this region.

Edgar, Walter B., editor. *South Carolina: The WPA Guide to the Palmetto State.* Columbia: Univ. of South Carolina Press, 1988 (originally published in 1941). This classic guide to the state was part of the highly acclaimed Federal Writers Project of the 1930s and '40s and remains an indispensable resource for those wanting to know more than they need to know about the state.

I N D E X

■ AUTHOR

Henry Leifermann grew up in South Carolina and attended the University of South Carolina. He has worked as a newpaper reporter for *The State* in Columbia covering the South Carolina legislature; for UPI, *Newsweek,* and the *New York Sunday Times* travel section. He is the author of the highly acclaimed *Crystal Lee,* adapted for the Academy Award-winning film *Norma Rae.*

■ PHOTOGRAPHER

Eric Horan is a freelance photographer based on Hilton Head, South Carolina. He has been recognized in state, national, and international competitions including *Studio Magazine's* 1991 Annual Awards Competition, the Timberpeg Award for photographic excellence, awards sponsored by the Sierra Club and *South Carolina Wildlife Magazine,* and the Natural World Photographic Exhibit at the Carnegie Museum. His work has appeared in *Time, Fortune, Business Week, American Fitness, Cruising World, Tennis,* and the *New York Times* travel section.